RICHARD III

Arden Early Modern Drama Guides

Series Editors: Andrew Hiscock, University of Wales, Bangor, UK and Lisa Hopkins, Sheffield Hallam University, UK

Arden Early Modern Drama Guides offers practical and accessible introductions to the critical and performative contexts of key Elizabethan and Jacobean plays. Each guide introduces the text's critical and performance history but also provides students with an invaluable insight into the landscape of current scholarly research through a keynote essay on the state of the art and newly commissioned essays of fresh research from different critical perspectives.

Further titles in preparation

RICHARD III

A Critical Reader

Edited by
Annaliese Connolly

BLOOMSBURY

LONDON • NEW DELHI • NEW YORK • SYDNEY

Bloomsbury Arden

An imprint of Bloomsbury Publishing Plc

50 Bedford Square	1385 Broadway
London	New York
WC1B 3DP	NY 10018
UK	USA

www.bloomsbury.com

Bloomsbury is a registered trade mark of Bloomsbury Publishing Plc

First published 2013

British Library Cataloguing-in-Publication Data
A catalogue record for this book is available from the British Library.

ISBN: HB: 978-1-4411-6825-2
PB: 978-1-4725-0496-8
ePDF: 978-1-4411-2774-7
e-pub: 978-1-4725-3894-9

Library of Congress Cataloging-in-Publication Data
A catalog record for this book is available from the Library of Congress

Typeset by Fakenham Prepress Solutions, Fakenham, Norfolk NR21 8NN
Printed and bound in India

CONTENTS

SERIES INTRODUCTION

The drama of Shakespeare and his contemporaries has remained at the very heart of English curricula internationally and the pedagogic needs surrounding this body of literature have grown increasingly complex as more sophisticated resources become available to scholars, tutors and students. This series aims to offer a clear picture of the critical and performative contexts of a range of chosen texts. In addition, each volume furnishes readers with invaluable insights into the landscape of current scholarly research as well as including new pieces of research by leading critics.

This series is designed to respond to the clearly identified needs of scholars, tutors and students for volumes which will bridge the gap between accounts of previous critical developments and performance history and an acquaintance with new research initiatives related to the chosen plays. Thus, our ambition is to offer innovative and challenging guides which will provide practical, accessible and thought-provoking analyses of Early Modern Drama. Each volume is organized according to a progressive reading strategy involving introductory discussion, critical review and cutting-edge scholarly debate. It has been an enormous pleasure to work with so many dedicated scholars of Early Modern Drama and we are sure that this series will encourage to you read 400-year-old playtexts with fresh eyes.

Andrew Hiscock and Lisa Hopkins

NOTES ON CONTRIBUTORS

Daniel Cadman is an Associate Lecturer at Sheffield Hallam University where he was awarded a PhD for a study on closet drama which he is currently developing as a monograph. He has published work on William Shakespeare, Fulke Greville and Samuel Daniel and has written for *Renaissance Studies*, *Early Modern Literary Studies*, and *Notes and Queries*. He also writes the section on Shakespeare's problem plays for *The Year's Work in English Studies* and is a contributor to the *Lost Plays Database*.

Annaliese Connolly is Senior Lecturer in English at Sheffield Hallam University. Recent publications include 'Guy of Warwick, Godfrey of Bouillon, and Elizabethan Repertory' in *Early Modern England and Islamic Worlds*, Bernadette Andrea and Linda McJannet (eds), (Palgrave, 2011), the entry for George Peele in *The Encyclopedia of English Renaissance Literature* (Blackwell, 2011) and a chapter on the performance history of Middleton's *Women Beware Women* in *Middleton: Women Beware Women* (Continuum, 2011). Her current project is a monograph on George Peele.

Adele Lee is Lecturer in English Literature at the University of Greenwich, London. Her research interests focus on travel writing and the postmodern appropriation of Shakespeare, and she has published articles in *Shakespeare Bulletin*, *Early Modern Literary Studies* and *Quidditas*, among others. Currently, she is working on a book-length study, for Fairleigh Dickinson University Press, of England's encounter with the Far East in both the early modern and postmodern periods, in addition to co-editing a special feature on Belfast for CITY Journal (Routledge).

Rebecca Lemon is an Associate Professor in the department of English at the University of Southern California. She is the author of *Treason by Words: Literature, Law, and Rebellion in Shakespeare's England* (2006), as well as co-editor of *The Blackwell Companion to the Bible in English Literature* (2009), and associate editor of *The Blackwell Encyclopedia to Renaissance Literature* (2012). The recipient of a Mellon fellowship through the American Council of Learned Societies, a Stanford Humanities Center fellowship and a Francis Bacon Foundation fellowship at the Huntington Library, her essays on Shakespeare, early modern political philosophy and law have appeared in numerous journals and edited collections.

Nina Levine is Associate Professor of English at the University of South Carolina. She is the author of *Women's Matters: Politics, Gender, and Nation in Shakespeare's Early Histories* (1998), editor of the Evans Shakespeare *Richard III* (2012), and co-editor with David Lee Miller of the essay collection *A Touch More Rare: Harry Berger, Jr. and the Arts of Interpretation* (2009). Her publications on Shakespeare's history plays also include essays in *Shakespeare Quarterly*, *Renaissance Drama* and *Shakespeare Studies*.

Peter J. Smith is Reader in Renaissance Literature at Nottingham Trent University. His publications include *Social Shakespeare: Aspects of Renaissance Dramaturgy and Contemporary Society* and *Hamlet: Theory in Practice*. His most recent book is *Between Two Stools: Scatology and its Representations in English Literature, Chaucer to Swift*. His essays and reviews have appeared in many journals including *Critical Survey*, *Renaissance Quarterly*, *Review of English Studies*, *Shakespeare*, *Shakespeare Bulletin* and *Shakespeare Survey*. He reviews regularly for *Times Higher Education* and has been involved since 1992 with *Cahiers Elisabéthains*.

Brian Walsh is an Assistant Professor in the English Department at Yale University. His book *Shakespeare, the Queen's Men, and the Elizabethan Performance of History* was published by Cambridge in 2009.

Kate Wilkinson is an Associate Lecturer at Sheffield Hallam University. She was awarded her PhD in 2010 for a thesis on Shakespeare's history plays in performance. She has published a number of scholarly articles and performance reviews. She has recently published a note on allusions to Shakespeare's *Richard II* in Nathaniel Richards' *Tragedy of Messalina*, and has a chapter on ghosts in the history cycle forthcoming in the collection *Reinventing the Renaissance: Shakespeare and his Contemporaries in Adaptation and Performance* to be published by Palgrave.

David Houston Wood is Associate Professor of English and Honors Program Director at Northern Michigan University. He is the author of *Time, Narrative, and Emotion in Early Modern England* (Ashgate, 2009), and is the co-editor, with Allison P. Hobgood (Willamette University), of two essay collections engaging early modern disability: *Recovering Disability in Early Modern England* (forthcoming, Ohio State University Press, 2013); and *Disabled Shakespeares*, published in the journal *Disability Studies Quarterly* (Fall 2009, free online at www.dsq-sds.org). David is also the author of other essays in journals such as *Shakespeare Yearbook*, *Renaissance Drama*, *Prose Studies* and the Blackwell *Literature Compass*.

TIMELINE

1483	Richard III becomes king of England following the death of his brother king Edward IV.
1485	Richard III is killed at the Battle of Bosworth in Leicestershire, he is succeeded by Henry Tudor (Richmons in Shakespeare's play).
1499	Perkin Warbeck hanged at Tyburn as an impostor.
c. 1513	Sir Thomas More's *History of Richard III* written.
1548	Publication of Edward Hall's *Union of the Two Noble and Illustre Famelies of Lancastre and York* written.
1557	Publication of Sir Thomas More's *History of Richard III* in *The Complete Works of Sir Thomas More*.
1564	Shakespeare born.
1587	The second edition of Raphael Holinshed's *The Chronicles of England, Scotland and Ireland* published.
c. 1592–3	Shakespeare's *Richard III* written.
1594	The anonymous Queen's Men play *The True Tragedy of Richard the Third* is published.
c. 1594	*Richard III* performed by the Lord Chamberlain's Men with Richard Burbage as the play's protagonist.
1597	First quarto of *Richard III* published as *The Tragedy of King Richard III*.
1598	Francis Meres in *Palladis Tamia* cites *Richard III* to argue that Shakespeare is 'the most excellent' for 'Tragedy'.
1623	*Richard III* is listed among the histories in the first Folio as *The Life and Death of Richard III*.
1633	*Richard III* performed at court on the occasion of Queen Henrietta Maria's birthday.
1634	Publication of John Ford's play *Perkin Warbeck*.

1699	Colley Cibber adapts Shakespeare's play. Shakespeare's play is heavily cut and replaced with material of Cibber's own invention. This becomes the definitive performance text of the play until the nineteenth century.
1741	David Garrick makes his debut as Richard III at Drury Lane.
1877	Henry Irving performs as Richard using a performance text which incorporates two-thirds of Shakespeare's text.
1896	Henry Irving restores the character of Margaret to the playtext.
1912	Release of silent film of *Richard III*, starring Frederick Warde.
1924	The Richard III Society founded by Saxon Barton with the aim of restoring the reputation of the king. The society received royal patronage in 1980 from His Royal Highness the Duke of Gloucester.
1942	Production at the London Strand, starring Donald Wolfit, drew parallels between Richard III and Adolf Hitler.
1943	Publication of E. M. W. Tillyard's *The Elizabethan World Picture*.
1944	Laurence Olivier plays Richard III at the Old Vic, directed by John Burrell.
1951	Publication of Josephine Tey's detective novel *The Daughter of Time*.
1953	A. P. Rossiter delivers lecture entitled 'Angel with Horns' which is published posthumously in 1961 as part of a collection: *Angel with Horns and Other Shakespeare Lectures*. Rossiter explores the comic potential of the role.
1955	Release of film directed by and starring Laurence Olivier.
1957	Publication of Bertolt Brecht's play *The Resistable Rise of Arturo Ui*.

1963	Publication of Jan Kott's, *Shakespeare Our Contemporary*.
1963-4	Ian Holm in the cycle production at the RSC, directed by Peter Hall and John Barton.
1979	Publication of David Pownall's play *Richard III Part Two*.
1984	Antony Sher at the RSC, directed by Bill Alexander.
1985	Publication of Jonathan Dollimore and Alan Sinfield's *Political Shakespeare: New Essays in Cultural Materialism*.
1990	Ian McKellen plays Richard III at the Royal National Theatre, directed by Richard Eyre.
1992	Northern Broadsides, founded and directed by Barrie Rutter, take a touring production of the play around the UK.
1995	Release of film starring Ian McKellen and directed by Richard Loncraine.
1996	Release of *Looking for Richard*, directed by and starring Al Pacino.
2001	Kenneth Branagh plays Richard III at the Crucible Theatre, Sheffield directed by Michael Grandage.
2002	Release of *The Street King* (*a.k.a King Rikki*), directed by James Gavin Bedford.
2003	All female cast performs *Richard III* at the Globe Theatre, with Kathryn Hunter in the title role.
2008	Release of *Richard III* directed by Scott Anderson.
2011	Release of *Richard III, An Arab V.I.P.* directed by Shakir Abal and Tim Langford. Edward Hall's all-male Propeller company perform *Richard III* and Sam Mendes directed Kevin Spacey at the Old Vic, London.
2012	Excavation at the site of Greyfriars church in Leicester results in the discovery of a skeleton in the choir of the church where Richard III is thought to have been buried. Results of extensive tests to identify the body will be made public in February 2013.

Introduction

ANNALIESE CONNOLLY

Finding Richard

The process of performing the role of Richard III has been likened to a quest with the aim of finding or deciding what actors believe motivates this most iconic of all of Shakespeare's characters. This undertaking requires an engagement with fundamental questions about human nature and the capacity for evil. In February 2013 as this volume goes to press this interpretative journey to 'find' and perform Richard has been given particular resonance by the tangible results of an archaeological dig which has located and identified the skeleton of King Richard III. The confirmed results of the excavation in a car park on the site of the Greyfriars church in Leicester have been made possible by DNA testing of one of the descendants of Richard's sister Anne of York, a Canadian called Michael Ibsen. The injuries sustained by the body and the fact that the skeleton indicates signs of scoliosis, a form of curvature of the spine, have also provided more circumstantial evidence to support the case that it is Richard III.[1] While Shakespeare's play has Richard utter those final memorable lines 'A horse, a horse, my kingdom for a horse!' and shows him cut down on Bosworth Field, what this discovery helps to clarify is what happened to Richard's body *after* the event. Although some historical sources, including Holinshed's *Chronicle* – which Shakespeare used when writing his play – record that Richard was interred at Greyfriars in Leicester, subsequent stories became popular which suggested that Richard's body was thrown into the river Soar on the journey from the battlefield to Leicester.[2] This discovery in 2013 foregrounds the tension between myth and fact and feeds into Shakespeare's own dramatization of the manipulation of history. While the quest to find and identify the body of the last Plantagenet king is now complete, the investigation of Richard on the page, in the classroom and on the stage will continue to provide new readings of this chameleon king.

King Richard III's iconic status as one of the most notorious kings in English history is due in no small part to Shakespeare's play about him. Alongside Hamlet, Richard III is perhaps one of the most readily identifiable of all Shakespeare's protagonists. Yet even as the play appears to fix his identity as Richard Crouchback, the 'bottled spider' and 'poisonous bunch-backed toad' and confirm his reputation as a 'guilty homicide' and 'bloody tyrant', whose reign of terror is part of a providential cycle of English history, so it simultaneously invites and accommodates a wealth of interpretations which complicates an initial sense of a stable reading of its protagonist and the play's account of history. It is this protean quality which makes the play so fascinating to teach and to watch in performance.

Tragedy and History

Coupled with the play's bustling villain is its hybrid status which also goes some way to explain the multiplicity of responses and readings it invites. The play is labelled a tragedy on the title page of the first quarto, published in 1597, and this title remains in place when the play is included in the first Folio of 1623, but here it is grouped with the history plays that Shakespeare wrote during his extensive career. As an early example of Elizabethan tragedy the play can be usefully compared with Marlowe's *Doctor Faustus* (c. 1588–9) as both Marlowe and Shakespeare adapt the medieval templates of tragedy, such as the *de casibus* tradition, to explore complex post-Reformation issues such as the relationship between free will, determinism and the role of an individual's conscience. Both plays also make use of the soliloquy to contribute to the audience's engagement with the moral and religious debates which inform the plays, and draw upon the classical and medieval conventions of using supernatural elements to externalize the moral and religious dilemmas with which the protagonists grapple. Both plays share an interest in the concepts of repentance and damnation as each protagonist is encouraged to 'despair and die', Richard by the ghosts of his victims before Bosworth field (5.3) and Faustus by his own meditation upon his actions (Scene 18).[3] Both men realize that they are damned but for different reasons neither is able to repent:

> O coward conscience, how dost thou afflict me!
> The lights burn blue. It is now dead midnight.
> Cold fearful drops stand on my trembling flesh.
>
> My conscience hath a thousand several tongues,
> And every tongue brings in a several tale,
> And every tale condemns me for a villain.
> Perjury, perjury, in the high'st degree
> Murder, stern murder, in the direst degree;
> All several sins, all used in each degree,
> Throng to the bar, crying all, Guilty! Guilty!
> I shall despair. There is no creature loves me;
> And if I die, no soul shall pity me.[4]

Faustus similarly articulates his spiritual and psychological torment in the hours before his death:

> Let Faustus live in hell a thousand years,
> A hundred thousand, and at last be sav'd!
> O, no end is limited to damned souls.[5]

Interestingly, the full title of Marlowe's play also indicates the blurring of generic boundaries between tragedy and history as it is described as *The Tragical History of Doctor Faustus*. This appellation suggests that a history will not only be concerned with a period of time and deal with historical figures, but that it will also trace the life and death of its protagonist, and certainly this is what we get in both in Marlowe's *Doctor Faustus* and Shakespeare's *Richard III*.

The interrelated nature of history and tragedy is also revealed when examining one of the sources for *Richard III*: Holinshed's *Chronicles*. This history was also the source for a number of Shakespeare's tragedies, including *Macbeth* and *King Lear*, as it was concerned with charting the pivotal events in the history of England, Ireland and Scotland. *Macbeth* serves as yet another important point of comparison for *Richard III* as Shakespeare in this later tragedy returns to a number of themes and issues he explored in his earlier history plays, including the murderous ambitions of those men who wish to seize the crown. Like *Richard III*, *Macbeth* shares an interest in the role of the supernatural in determining the outcome of events and its effect upon the protagonist. *Richard III* can also be usefully situated among some of the later tragedies such as *Othello* and *Coriolanus*.[6] Shakespeare frequently returned to the figure of the soldier in his tragedies and the figure of Richard, Duke of Gloucester, who was first and foremost a soldier, identifies the recurring theme of the role of the warrior in both war and peacetime and some of the tensions attendant upon making the transition from 'the casque to the cushion'.

When Shakespeare began work on the *Henry VI* plays in the early 1590s the history play had already begun to establish its popularity with theatre audiences. The foremost theatrical company of the 1580s was the Queen's Men and in their repertoire they already had a series of history plays, including *The Troublesome Reign of King John* (1591), *The Famous Victories of Henry the Fifth* (1594) and *The True History of Richard the Third* (1594).[7] The popularity of the history play during the late 1580s and 1590s has been attributed in part to a developing sense of English national identity which emerged in response to the increasing threat from Catholic Spain. The plays looked back to foreign victories against the French and to the emergence of the Tudor dynasty and in each case these narratives served to reinforce the sense of nationalism by underlining England's status as a providential nation.

Shakespeare and the Wars of the Roses

Shakespeare wrote ten history plays in total and in the first Folio they are organized chronologically by reign starting with *King John* who reigned during the thirteenth century through to *Henry VIII* in the sixteenth century. Shakespeare's dramatization of Richard and his reign formed the concluding chapter in a sequence of plays which recounted the events of the reign of Henry VI and the conflict known as the War of the Roses. This prolonged period of civil war was a struggle for the throne of England between the Lancastrian descendants of Edward III, who took the red rose for their emblem, and his Yorkist descendants, who were identified by the white rose. In the dispute over the crown each of the two branches of the royal family argued that they had a superior claim. The Yorkists, for example, claimed that Henry VI's grandfather, Henry IV, had usurped the throne from Richard III, the son of Edward III's eldest son, Edward the Black Prince. While the Lancastrians could claim the throne through Edward III's fourth son, John of Gaunt, the Yorkists felt that theirs was a stronger case since they claimed descent through Edward's third son Lionel, Duke of Clarence and his daughter Philippa. The family tree in Chapter 8 of this volume will assist in tracing the lineage and claims of the two competing houses.

The sequence of plays in which this clash between the houses of York and Lancaster is staged is often referred to as the first tetralogy (meaning a set of four plays) and includes the three *Henry VI* plays and *Richard III*. These plays were written and performed early in Shakespeare's career between 1589 and 1593 and served to establish his reputation as the preeminent writer of history plays. Shakespeare's second tetralogy was written and performed between 1595 and 1599 and dramatized an earlier period of history, starting with the reign and deposition of King Richard II and charts the reign of his successors, Henry IV and his son Henry V. In chronological order, in terms of the events they portray, the first play of the first tetralogy is *1 Henry VI*. The play begins with the death of Henry V and the accession of his young son, Henry VI, who had not yet reached the age of majority, so that England was governed with the help of the nobles. The play is characterized by conflict at home among the different political factions within the nobility and abroad, as England seeks to secure its territories in France. The second play, *2 Henry VI*, focuses upon questions of kingship and engages with the particularly knotty political problem of what to do with a weak and ineffectual king? One of the consequences of Henry VI's inability to govern and be a strong ruler is that it enables ambitious rivals to gather support. This play dramatizes the competition for power between two rival groups: Henry VI's wife, Margaret of Anjou, and the Duke of Suffolk on the one hand and Richard, Duke of York and his four sons on the other. This plot is in developed *3 Henry VI* and depicts a series of battles between Yorkist and Lancastrian forces, including the death of Richard, Duke of York at the Battle of Wakefield and the murder of Henry VI after the Battle of Tewkesbury. At the end of the play the Yorkist forces are triumphant and Edward IV is crowned king. It is these events which are recalled in the first act of *Richard III* and here the conflict is no longer between two rival houses but between brothers, as Richard, Duke of Gloucester resolves to seize the throne upon the death of his brother Edward IV, eliminating his nephews as the legitimate heirs to the throne. Richard is defeated at the battle of Bosworth Field by Henry Tudor, Earl of Richmond, who is crowned Henry VII and initiates the Tudor dynasty. Henry VII's claim to the throne came from his position as a descendant of John of Gaunt by his third marriage to Catherine Swynford. The claim was reinforced by his marriage to Elizabeth, daughter of Edward IV, thus uniting the houses of York and Lancaster.

The Tudor Myth

For many years Shakespeare's two tetralogies were discussed in the context of the 'Tudor Myth'. This concept suggested that Shakespeare's history plays exemplified a providential view of history which presented the civil war between the Houses of York and Lancaster as God's punishment for the deposition of Richard II. The defeat of Richard III and the accession of Henry Tudor signalled the start of a new period of peace and prosperity for England. In this context Richard fulfils the role of God's scourge with his acts of murder and treachery serving as part of a wider narrative of divine retribution. It is perhaps unsurprising that the new Tudor dynasty with a comparatively weak claim to the throne would wish to promote its own persuasive ideology of Richard as the diabolically murderous king. This view was promoted in the subsequent accounts of his reign, in particular Thomas More's *History of King Richard III* (c. 1513). This account furnished the work of subsequent historians, including Edward Hall and his *The Union of the two Noble and Illustre Famelies of Lancastre and York* (1548) and Raphael Holinshed's *Chronicles*.[8] These accounts repeated material developed by More concerning Richard's appearance and habits. Shakespeare may also have had access to details of Richard's reign in other texts, including Richard Reynoldes' grammar school primer *The Foundation of Rhetoric* (1563) which included a short account entitled 'King Richard III, the cruel tyrant'. In *The Mirror for Magistrates* (1559–1610), a series of first-person confessions by prominent figures from English history, Richard narrates his life and his story draws upon the material found in Thomas More's *History* which makes explicit the links between his monstrous birth and his prodigious status as the author of England's woes:

> My birth was not as others wont to bee
> First did my feet come forth as if in half
> The child of discord had been set free
> To cause the wretched world to disagree
> Heau'n at that time told b'inauspitious starres
> Nations far off of England's civil warres.[9]

Richard goes on to make his physical deformity an index to his wicked character, utilizing the image of the painter at his canvas:

> If like a cunning painter on a frame
> My shape unto the world I could descrie
> And with a curious pencell paint the same
> In perfect colours, each spectators eie
> Would by my lookes into my manners prie
> The bodies ill-shapte limbes are oft defin'd
> For signes of evill manners in the mind.[10]

This description by Richard of his appearance betrays his own awareness and manipulation of his physicality. It underlines his body's 'actorly' quality, whereby he can 'paint' and shape his appearance to suit his own purpose. This first-person monologue from *The Mirror for Magistrates* also points up the rich theatrical heritage that Shakespeare drew upon in developing his portrait of Richard. The medieval *de casibus* model of tragedy enacts the rise and fall of illustrious men and women, drawing upon the image of the wheel of fortune to indicate how their lives offer a moral message to all. The medieval morality plays served a similar function, but here the focus was upon the lives of ordinary people. One significant addition to the morality play was the figure of the Vice who provided a template for some of the comic possibilities in dramatizing Richard III. John Jowett points out that the morality plays variously presented the Vice as:

> A grim jester, a conniver with the audience, an equivocator, a disguiser, a weeping feigner of empathy and grief, and a misleader of youth. His language is familiar, jocular and sprinkled with oaths.[11]

Shakespeare deploys an array of performance techniques, including soliloquies, asides and wordplay to allow Richard to enter into a conspiratorial relationship with the audience and allow them in on his plans. It is this connection between Richard and the audience which has complicated responses to Richard and encouraged readers and audiences to query the totalizing narrative of the Tudor Myth.

Reconsidering Richard III and the Tudor Myth

The view of Richard III found in More and subsequent publications like *The Mirror for Magistrates* and popularized by Shakespeare's play underwent a series of challenges during the seventeenth and eighteenth centuries by historians and writers including in Sir William Cornwallis's *Essayes* (1601), George Buck's *History of King Richard III* and Horace Walpole's *Historic Doubts on the Life and Reign of Richard III* (1768).[12] In each case the veracity of More's portrait of Richard is placed under scrutiny, while emphasis is placed upon his role as an effective military strategist and administrator. Another strategy which was also used to query the popular diabolical portrait of Richard popularized by Shakespeare was to shift the focus away from Richard and onto the personality and reign of his successor, Henry VII, thus placing the providential model of kingship cultivated by the Tudors under considerable pressure. An early example of this approach can be found in John Ford's history play *Perkin Warbeck*, written in 1633, which looks back to Shakespeare's history plays and shares their medieval and Elizabethan heritage.[13] The play charts the rise and fall of Perkin Warbeck, a young man who challenges Henry Tudor for the throne by claiming to be Richard, Duke of York, one of the princes in the Tower. Warbeck claims he was spared death and escaped to France but has now returned to claim his birthright.[14] This account of what befell the Yorkist princes is in direct contravention of the received history that Richard had both boys murdered. The play invites its readers and audience to consider the slippery nature of history as truth through a number of techniques, including the play's title and subheading: *The Chronicle History of Perkin Warbeck: A Strange Truth*. This title neatly juxtaposes the textual authority of the chronicle histories with Warbeck's own story which is also given the comparable status of truth. The rival claims of Warbeck and Henry Tudor are also carefully rehearsed, beginning with the legitimacy of Henry's accession to the throne. In the first act of the play Henry Tudor's quasi-divine role as England's 'best physician' in uniting

the warring houses of York and Lancaster and bringing civil war
to an end is carefully spelt out.[15] Henry is also at pains to defend
the necessity of Richard's removal by rehearsing the narrative of
the murder of Edward IV's sons:

> Edward the fourth after a doubtful fortune
> Yielded to nature, leaving to his sons,
> Edward and Richard, the inheritance
> Of a most bloody purchase; these young princes
> Richard the tyrant, their unnatural uncle,
> Forced to a violent grave, so just is Heaven.
> Him hath your Majesty by your own arm,
> Divinely strengthened, pulled from his boar's sty
> And struck the black usurper to a carcass.
> Nor doth the House of York decay in honours,
> Though Lancaster doth repossess his right,
> For Edward's daughter is King Henry's queen;
> A blessed union, and a lasting blessing
> For this poor panting island (I.1.27–40).

The irony of this speech is that in painting Richard as 'the black
usurper', Henry is also aligning himself with Richard, since his
accession also involved the removal of the incumbent monarch.
Initially Warbeck's first speech echoes the details of Henry's
speech as he acknowledges the infamous story of these child
murders at Richard's hands:

>   Europe knows,
> And all the western world what persecution
> Hath raged in malice against us, sole heir
> To the great throne, of old Plantagenets.
> How from our nursery we have been hurried
> Unto the sanctuary, from the sanctuary
> Forced to the prison, from the prison haled
> By cruel hands to the tormentors fury,
> Is registered already in the volume
> Of all men's tongues (II.1.45–54).

Warbeck then offers a startling corrective to this received statement of fact by recounting a daring tale of escape:

> But our misfortunes since
> Have ranged a larger progress through strange lands,
> Protected in our innocence by Heaven.
> Edward the Fifth, our brother, in his tragedy
> Quenched their hot thirst of blood, whose hire to murder
> Paid them their wages, of despair and horror;
> The softness of my childhood smiled upon
> The roughness of their task, and robbed them farther
> Of hearts to dare, or hands to execute.
> Great King they spared my life, the butchers spared it;
> Returned the tyrant, my unnatural uncle,
> A truth of my dispatch. I was conveyed
> With secrecy and speed to Tournai (II.1.45–8).

In this account the murderers are paralysed, it seems, by an attack of conscience which prevents them from fulfilling their task. The very fact that Perkin Warbeck makes this astonishing claim brings Henry's earlier version of events and the basis for his position as king into question. Although Warbeck is eventually executed as an imposter his story raises uncomfortable questions about the abuses of history by those in power. Ford's play, published in 1634, during the reign of Charles I, looks back to the inception of the Tudor Myth in order to explore the crisis of monarchy during the 1630s.[16] *Perkin Warbeck's* Janus-like quality is something it shares with Shakespeare's *Richard III*, as the story of a compelling but dangerous protagonist speaks both to the past of the play's events and composition, whilst simultaneously offer startling resonances with the present, a motif which features in discussion of the play in this volume.

One of the dominant narratives in this collection of essays on *Richard III* is the critical re-evaluation of the Tudor Myth. Its longevity as an interpretative model for Shakespeare's history can be attributed in part to the apparently coherent narrative it constructs as part of the two tetralogies and the idealized and persuasive explanation it offers for a complex period of political and civil unrest. The first three chapters in this volume pay particular attention to the effects of this dominant narrative on the play in performance and in literary criticism, with Peter Smith's chapter on the play's critical history surveying landmark publications which have contributed to the body of work on the play. In the concluding section of this Chapter I would like to add two further examples of texts which like Ford's *Perkin Warbeck* deconstruct many of the certainties offered by Tudor ideology concerning Richard III. The texts, a novel and a play, are both products of a sceptical postmodern culture and register their rejection of monolithic narratives by scrutinizing source materials and by creatively re-imagining the relevance of Richard III for the twentieth century and beyond.

The first of these publications is the detective novel *The Daughter of Time* by Josephine Tey (real name Elizabeth MacKintosh), published in 1951. Tey's novels were influenced both by historical crimes and by historical figures. Her novel *Brat Farrar* (1949), for example, contains a charismatic imposter in the mould of Perkin Warbeck while *The Franchise Affair* (1948) is based on the Elizabeth Canning case of 1754.[17] *The Daughter of Time* follows the investigation of the bed-ridden Inspector Grant into Richard III's reputation as a murderer, with the novel adopting a revisionist position towards the traditional view of the king as exemplified by Shakespeare's play. Tey begins by tackling Richard's physicality and challenges the view that Richard's appearance provides a clear motive for his behaviour by opening the novel with her detective trying to identify a portrait of Richard. The discovery that the portrait is of Richard III invites Grant and the reader to reconsider what they know about this king. Grant's assistant is an American student, Brent Carradine, who studies medieval history and locates accounts of Richard's reign by a number of Tudor historians. As the investigation proceeds Grant discovers that many of the accounts of Richard and his reign which were available to Shakespeare were written by Tudor historians who produced a biased account of the last Plantagenet king. The detective evaluates the evidence and motives of the main political players and concludes that Henry Tudor rather than Richard had stronger motives for eliminating the Yorkist claimants.

The novel provides an important snapshot of the developments in the history of criticism on Shakespeare's play and of the developments in historiography during the last half of the twentieth century. The novel was significant for the way in which it popularized the debate concerning the biographical treatment of Richard and his literary afterlife in Shakespeare's history plays. The detective novel proved to be an apt medium for consideration of Richard's reputation as the alleged murderer of his nephews in the Tower and who else may have been involved or responsible for the crime, since features of the genre include questions of motivation and problems of evidence, interpretation and proof. Writers of detective fiction, particularly during the Golden Age of the genre in the 1930s and 1940s, often used Shakespeare to furnish their work with characters, plots and quotations. Shakespeare was also called upon as an authority on human nature with novels drawing analogies between a Shakespeare play and the crime under investigation so that the detective could solve the crime by making the connection.[18] In the case of *The Daughter of Time*, Tey departs from this position of Shakespearean authority on human nature through Grant's examination of documentary evidence and his rejection of the insisted connection between physical disability and motivation. In discussing possible motives for Richard's decision to seize the throne after the death of his brother Edward IV, Carradine's comments help to establish Tey's revisionist agenda:

That's very interesting, though, what you say about Richard being apparently a good sort up to the time of the crime,' Carradine said, propping one leg of his horn-rims with a long forefinger in his characteristic gesture. 'Makes him more of a person. That Shakespeare version of him, you know, that's just caricature. Not a man at all.[19]

The novel also draws upon Olivier's memorable stage performances as Richard III during the 1940s as a shorthand method of
establishing some of the apparent shortcomings of the traditional
view of Richard made available by successful productions of
Shakespeare's play. As Inspector Grant canvasses opinion among
the staff at the hospital about King Richard, his surgeon remarks:

> I once saw Olivier play him. The most dazzling exhibition
> of sheer evil it was. Always on the verge of toppling over
> into the grotesque, and never doing it.[20]

This assessment of Olivier's performance pinpoints one of the
most important issues which face not only the actor playing the
role of Richard but also its audience or reader: what motivates
Richard? How can we account for his behaviour? As Kate Wilkinson
discusses in the chapter on the play's performance history in this
volume, Olivier's performance as Richard was well known for not
offering a rationale for the behaviour of the protagonist. Olivier's
Richard is inherently evil, but in Tey's novel this position is
subjected to the rigours of a police investigation as Inspector
Grant declares 'I want to know what made him tick. That is a more
profound mystery than anything I have come up against of late'.[21]

The tension between Grant's efforts to recover the truth
about Richard from historical sources leads him to brand them
as 'Tonypandy' after a spurious account of a miners' strike in
a Welsh village of the same name in 1910.[22] Accounts of events
by the villagers claimed that the strike was violently suppressed
by government troops, but in fact as Grant explains 'The only
bloodshed in the whole affair was a bloody nose or two'.[23] Despite
the reality of events, Tonypandy takes on the renowned status of
other examples of government suppression such as the Peterloo
Massacre. Grant makes the analogy between Tonypandy and
biographies of Richard III explicit, particularly Sir Thomas
More's, as he explicates the term: 'It is a completely untrue story
grown to legend while the men who knew it to be untrue looked
on and said nothing'.[24]

While Tey's novel made a considerable impact in terms of encouraging a popular audience to reconsider their history of Richard III, two years later in 1953 A. P. Rossiter gave a lecture on the subject of Shakespeare's *Richard III* which made a significant contribution to the academic debate on Shakespeare's handling of his protagonist. As Peter Smith details in his chapter, Rossiter argued that Shakespeare offered a complex portrait of Richard as a charismatic, comic villain which complicates the audience's relationship with him and unsettles those long held assumptions that he is simply an evil figure who can be purged from the play at its conclusion.

Whereas Tey used the example of Tonypandy to make her point about the unreliable nature of history, the dramatist David Pownall meditated upon this point by juxtaposing Richard III with George Orwell and concepts from his novel *Nineteen Eighty Four* such as 'Doublethink' and the 'Ministry of Truth' in his play *Richard III Part Two* (1979). The play brings these two unlikely figures together as their lives have been developed separately as the concept for two board games, 'Big Brother' and 'Betrayal', in the 'present' of the play which is set in 1984. The motif of life as a board game, subject to the roll of a dice, has a number of interesting connections with Shakespeare's play and the way in which Richard self-consciously performs his role as the villain. The idea that the outcome of the Wars of the Roses can be played as a game also raises interesting questions about the providential model of history and its predetermined outcome. The apparent clash between the fifteenth and twentieth centuries is used to underline the manipulation of the truth by a ruling power and to reflect upon the cyclical nature of power politics. The parts of Orwell and Richard III are doubled by the same actor to reinforce this point and the affinity between these time periods is signalled by the patterning of the three time frames for the play: 1484, 1948 and 1984. Here, Pownall's play engages with ideas popularized in Jan Kott's seminal publication in 1965, *Shakespeare Our Contemporary*, which discussed Shakespeare's history plays as an endless staircase where the struggle for power is played out.

The impact of Kott's work on Richard III on stage and in literary criticism is discussed in Chapters 2 and 3 in this volume. In the opening scene of *Richard III Part Two*, Orwell expresses his unease with history and its manipulation:

> What I am deeply concerned about in 1984 is the wilful destruction of historical truth by over-powerful, self-righteous governments. Real history is a law like gravity. There is no greater power in the human present than the human past. The present is the past. Winston Smith, the hero of my book – called after Winston Churchill who wasn't averse to rewriting history himself, in imitation of Stalin we could say – Winston Smith works in the Ministry of Truth as an expert operator of Doublethink. That's his job. Let me illustrate [...] Stage One – you make up a story for propaganda purposes. Stage Two – you deliberately believe that story yourself. Stage Three – you force yourself to forget that you created it. Stage Four – you accept it as history.[25]

Later in act one, Elizabeth Woodville delivers the following speech which articulates the view of Richard popularized by Shakespeare:

> This is a party political broadcast on behalf of the Tudors. Richard the Third was in his mother's womb for two years and when he was born he had hair down to his waist and a full set of teeth ... At number eleven Downing Street the Chancellor, Sir Thomas More, described him as a symbol of evil rather than flesh and blood while William Shakespeare reports in the Globe today that he actually overheard the leader of the Plantagenet party say 'I am determined to prove a villain and hate the idle pleasure of these days' (160).

The play also echoes the suggestion made by Tey that Richard was not in fact responsible for the murder of his nephews. In the play they are shown to have tuberculosis (like Orwell) and during the course of the play Prince Edward dies of his condition and his brother Richard is not expected to survive. In Pownall's play it is Elizabeth Woodville who is the villain as she regards the marriage of her daughter, Elizabeth, to Henry Tudor as her political endgame and the deaths of her sons are dismissed as merely collateral damage in the process. The novel and play by Tey and Pownall are examples of the popular afterlives of Richard III which engage imaginatively with many of the themes explored in Shakespeare's play.

The Guide

The aim of this collection of essays about Shakespeare's *Richard III* is to provide a guide to the play which will give an overview of its critical heritage on the stage and screen and in literary criticism. The volume also includes a summary of current critical trends in the field, while the four New Directions chapters each offer a case study of one of those areas.

The volume begins with Peter Smith's overview of the critical reception of Richard III, pinpointing important trends in interpretation during the play's 400-year history. One of the themes of the volume which Smith's chapter establishes is that the play offers a wealth of interpretations and approaches. Together with Kate Wilkinson's survey of the play's performance history these two chapters complement one another as they provide a clear sense of the critical and interpretive landscape of the play. Both chapters demonstrate first how powerful and pervasive Shakespeare's portrait of the last Plantagenet became for audiences and readers, so much so that he eclipsed and indeed came to stand in for the historical figure of Richard III. The second point which these two chapters establish is the way in which actors, directors and literary critics have engaged with the play to produce a portrait of the king according to the pressures and preoccupations of their own historical moment. The play can therefore serve as a lens through which to view contemporary attitudes towards some of the issues embodied in the play, including political tyranny, evil and its physical manifestation, the staging of history and kingship. Having established the wide variety of readings and reactions prompted by the play these chapters are succeeded by Nina Levine's chapter on 'The State of the Art' which surveys the current critical environment of the play and identifies some new approaches to the play which provide a challenge to the various historicisms as the dominant critical reading of the play during the last 30 years. Here, Levine considers the rise of disability studies, trauma theory and childhood studies as some of the developing areas in literary criticism on the play as well as a growing number of films and mass media adaptations of the play. Levine's chapter should be used in conjunction with Daniel Cadman's chapter on the Resources for Teaching and Studying the play at the end of the volume as this provides an annotated bibliography and makes useful suggestions for pursuing some of the lines of enquiry identified by Levine. The following four 'New Directions' chapters offer cutting edge analyses of the play. These include examination of the hybrid nature of the play, analysis of the legal and political implications of Richard's reign as king, a disability studies reading of the play and discussion of the recent docudrama *Richard III, An Arab V.I.P.* (2011).

Chapters 4 and 5 by Brian Walsh and Rebecca Lemon form a useful counterpoint to each other as they consider the performative quality of power in the play, focusing in particular on the motif of silence and the layers of onstage and offstage audiences whose responses to Richard's accession and rule provide an opportunity to reassess the inevitability of his rise to power. In 'Audience Engagement and the Genres of *Richard III*' Brian Walsh uses the play's hybrid status as history and tragedy as a springboard for approaching the play as 'a species' of performance. Walsh examines a triptych of scenes which features the Scrivener at its centre (3.3) and culminates in the silent reaction by the citizens at the Guildhall to Richard's claim to the throne in scene seven. These scenes encourage to audience to reflect upon the vision of history offered by the play and the potential for the audience to resist Richard's rise to power. As Walsh points out: 'The felicitous forces of providence are nice to believe in. But the Scrivener's haunting assertions that everyone sees but no one speaks or acts against his evil, along with the memory of Shaw's spectacular failure and the silence of the citizens at Guildhall, all call into question in different ways how inevitable Richard's reign really was. The equivocal message about whether or not the people have power to repel or undermine the political machinations of those in power is posed, and is still lingering as the play ends' (133).

In Rebecca Lemon's essay 'Tyranny and the State of Exception in Shakespeare's *Richard III*', she explores how the play can situated among a number of Shakespeare's plays which indicate his preoccupation with the concept of 'exceptional sovereignty' that is those rulers who have acquired and deploy power by undermining or suspending laws and social codes. In a play which dramatizes civil war, usurpation and summary execution, Lemon argues that the play deliberately keeps our attention on legal procedure and that this is part of Richard's own performance of power as he appears to conform to the rules of law and custom which he simultaneously breaks. Unlike Walsh, who sees the silences within the play as a possibility for subversive reaction to Richard's reign, Lemon argues that Richard's law-breaking produces silence among the people and signals their fear. Their resistance comes however, only when they are able to mimic Richard's own deceptive behaviours. The play resists simply depicting Richard as a pariah, who is removed at the end of the play, by underlining the dangerous precedents that his exceptional rule establishes. Lemon concludes by drawing parallels between Richard and Richmond to make the point that in order for Richmond to eliminate Richard he must become like him and deploy forms of illegal behaviour: 'the play does not contain Richard's threat in his villainous body. Instead Richard's opposition becomes increasingly cunning, and men like Richmond lay claim to an exceptional status, coming from foreign exile to usurp the throne. Richard thus pollutes sovereign power, inviting even the audience to sanction lawless resistance to counter him, thereby ensuring a permanent state of exception for England' (156–7).

In her essay Lemon begins by drawing attention to the ways in which Richard's body is used to both figure and justify his exceptional legal and political powers. David Wood's essay situates Richard's body within the critical discourse which has developed around disability in medieval and early modern texts. In 'Some Tardy Cripple: Timing Disability in *Richard III*' Wood examines Shakespeare's play as a disability narrative drawing on the narratology model 'Narrative prosthesis' developed by Mitchell and Snyder which attempts to provide a universal theory of disability narrative. This model establishes a character who deviates from the norm, setting in motion a narrative which seeks to account for that deviation. One explanation for Richard's behaviour is a medical one which applies the concepts of humoural theory and identifies in Richard an excess of choler to account for his murderous conduct and constitutes his inward monstrosity. Wood goes on to consider the correlation between humoural theory and time in *Richard III*, explaining that choler is associated with heat which in turn is linked to temporal urgency. Richard's manipulation of the rhetoric of disability demonstrates an attempt to exert his own agency and shape his destiny. This can be seen in Act five of the play when Richard seeks to feed his choler with a bowl of wine and create the necessary heat to fight in battle. Wood reads this as an example of Richard maintaining his own inward monstrosity and presents a more complex view of Richard's subjective identity.

In her discussion of recent filmic versions of *Richard III* ' "Put[ting] on Some *Other* Shape": Richard III as an Arab V.I.P.' Adele Lee traces some of the fascinating trends in Shakespeare films, beginning by examining the influence of the Americanization of Richard III in recent films and docudramas, starting with Al Pacino's *Looking for Richard* (1996) and its part in shaping the Richards found in *The Street King* (a.k.a *King Rikki*, 2002), directed by James Gavin Bedford and *King Richard III* (2008), directed by Scott Anderson. Here Lee outlines the influence of gang subculture as displayed in gangster films as well as the American concept of the 'self-made man' in these films in their depiction of Richard. The chapter then turns its attention to the docudrama *Richard III, An Arab V.I.P.*, which follows a pan-Arab theatre company as they rehearse and perform a production of *Richard III* at two different locations, one in Washington, DC and one in the United Arab Emirates. While Wood focuses upon the ways in which disability marks Richard as an outsider, Adele Lee in Chapter 7 considers how recent filmic manifestations of Richard III have marked him as racially Other. Productions of *Richard III* in the early and mid-twentieth century were influenced by the rise of fascist and totalitarian leaders in Germany and Russia, but this film takes the contemporary Middle East as the political and cultural prism through which to view the play. The writer and director of the production, Sulayman Al-Bassam, explained that Richard was based upon Saddam Hussain, the former dictator of Iraq, but the characterization of the protagonist suggests that this Richard, played by Fayez Kazak, is more generally a product of an unstable Arab world, an environment created in part by the interference of the British and Americans. The film gives unusual prominence to the play's female characters, particularly Margaret, who opens the film with a soliloquy of her own and offers a direct challenge to Richard's verbal domination of the play. The women's laments and curses are used by the production to draw direct parallels with the images of grieving women in news footage of the conflict in the Middle East to suggest analogies between the victims of the War on Terror and the victims of the Wars of the Roses.

Each of the essays in this collection pays tribute to the mercurial qualities of Shakespeare's protagonist and the varied responses which the play has prompted. The essays widen our understanding of topics such as disability in the context of early modern humours theory, while examination of its performance history and films about Richard III provide important insights into the way in which Shakespeare's play remains an important lens for mediating present day experiences of political tyranny.

CHAPTER ONE

The Critical Backstory

PETER J. SMITH

The historical status and self-conscious performativity of Shakespeare's *Richard III* underline many of the critical and theatrical responses, both ancient and modern. If the play were composed before 1592 it may well have been destined for Lord Strange's Men. Lord Stanley, Earl of Derby, who appears in *Richard III*, was an ancestor of Ferdinando Lord Strange to whose company Shakespeare may have been attached. That might provide a clue as to why Shakespeare's portrayal of Stanley is so sympathetic – an instance of the inflection of the past to suit the present. If the play were composed during 1592–3, it is more likely to have been written for Pembroke's Men, for whose main actor, Richard Burbage, the role may well have been initially designed. Burbage was the son of James Burbage, who built and ran several early playhouses as well as, to begin with, performing in them. Burbage Junior played some of the greatest roles of the day – Hieronimo in Kyd's *Spanish Tragedy*, as well as Hamlet, King Lear, Othello, Ferdinand in Webster's *Duchess of Malfi* and, according to one of the most salacious rumours of the day, the title role in *Richard III*.

In March 1602, in the days before super-injunctions, William Towse recounted to his associate, John Manningham (who recorded it in his diary), the following scandal of showbiz rivalry and sexual mischief:

Upon a tyme when Burbidge played Rich[ard] 3 there was a Citizen grewe soe farr in liking him, that before shee went from the play shee appointed him to come that night unto hir by the name of Ri[chard] the 3. Shakespeare, overhearing their conclusion, went before, was intertained, and at his game ere Burbidge came. Then message being brought that Rich[ard] the 3[d] was at the dore, Shakespeare caused return to be made that William the Conquerour was before Rich[ard] the 3. Shakespeare's name [being] William.[1]

The story provides us with an insight into the erotic capital of player and playwright which demonstrates the ease with which the charisma of Richard, the creation of both artists (and already sexually successful in the case of Lady Anne), carries beyond the fictional world of the stage. More intriguing though is the manner in which, if the story is to be believed, Shakespeare steps into the breech(es) of an historical figure, appropriating the identity of William the Conqueror who comes (in all senses) before the displaced Richards (Burbage and Plantagenet).

Burbage's association with these heavyweight roles, and that of Richard in particular, is attested by the anonymous *Second Part of the Return from Parnassus* (1598 to 1602) in which, in the company of the character of Will Kempe, he is seen taking the audition of the Cambridge students, Philomusus and Studioso, both of whom appear to be trying to join the Chamberlain's Men. Kempe immodestly remarks that he and Burbage are household names: 'they come North and South to bring [money] to our playhouse, and for honour, who of more report then *Dick Burbage & Will Kempe*? Hee's not counted a Gentleman that knows not *Dick Burbage & Wil Kemp*' (1790–3).[2] Later, Burbage turns to Philomusus and remarks, 'I like your face and the proportion of your body for *Richard* the 3., I pray [you] M. *Philomusus* let me see you act a little of it' (1835–7). The effect of telling his protégé that he is perfectly proportioned to play the humpbacked king is not lost on Philomusus; it is a wonderfully bitchy remark and although Philomusus responds by rattling off 'Now is the winter of our discontent [...]', he subsequently refers to acting as 'the basest trade' and to Burbage and Kempe (following their exit) as

'leaden spouts, / That nought do vent but what they do receiue'
(1848).

Burbage died in 1619. In a poem of the same year the bishop
Richard Corbett remarked how, while on a tour of Bosworth
Field, his guide, 'full of *Ale* and *History*', ran together in his mind
the historical Richard and the theatrical one. It is another instance
of the superimposition of historical fact and dramatic fiction:

> Why he could tell
> The inch where *Richmond* stood, where *Richard* fell:
> Besides what of his knowledge he can say,
> He had Authenticke notice, from the Play;
> Which I might guesse, by mustring up the Ghosts
> And policyes, not incident to Hosts:
> But cheifly by that one perspicuous thing,
> Where he mistooke a Player, for a King.
> For when he would have sayd, King *Richard* dyed,
> And call'd, a horse, a horse; he, *Burbidge* cry'de.[3]

The host's knowledge is supplemented by his familiarity with
Shakespeare's play – the ghosts and policies are not the usual fare
of landlords ('not incident to Hosts'). However, the remarkable
thing is the complete saturation of the historical Richard by
his thespian protagonist so that their very names become inter-
changeable. This is the kind of personal and psychological
empathy required by Method Acting, 400 years ahead of its time.

The English Civil War and the Restoration

King Charles I was a connoisseur of visual and dramatic arts
and, under his patronage, the court masque and theatrical entertainment flourished. On 16 November 1633 *Richard III* was
staged at Court. Eliard Swanston took the title role (he also played,
like Burbage before him, the title role in *Othello*). Unsurprisingly,
given their dependence on royal patronage, not to mention their
understandable opposition to Puritan anti-theatrical prejudice,

most actors in the King's Men took up the Royalist cause during the English Civil War. Swanston was a notable exception.

The theatres were closed by the victorious Parliamentarians in 1642 and Charles was executed on 30 January 1949. Charles's spiritual autobiography appeared soon after as *Eikon Basilike* (the actual, though disputed, author was the king's chaplain, John Gauden). John Milton was called upon to refute this sentimental account and justify the ways of regicides to men. His response, *Eikonoklastes*, attempted to denigrate Charles by demonstrating his tyranny and dishonesty. At one point, Milton (a huge admirer of Shakespeare) draws upon *Richard III* as an example of the despotism Charles was supposed to have personified:

> From Stories [...] both Ancient and Modern which abound, the Poets also, and som English, have bin in this point so mindful of *Decorum*, as to put never more pious words in the mouth of any person, then of a Tyrant. I shall not instance an abstruse Author, wherein the King might be less conversant, but one whom wee well know was the Closet Companion of these his solitudes, *William Shakespeare*; who introduces the person of *Richard* the third, speaking in as high a strain of pietie, and mortification, as is utterd in any passage of this Book; and sometimes to the same sense and purpose with some words in this place, *I intended*, saith he, *not only to oblige my Friends but mine enemies.* The like saith *Richard, Act 2, Scen. 1,*
>
> I doe not know that Englishman alive
> With whom my soule is any jott at odds,
> More then the Infant that is borne to night;
> I thank my God for my humilitie.[4]

The quotation, II.i.68–71, is word-perfect, suggesting Milton's assiduous regard for Shakespeare.[5] The accusation, that dictators are commonly holier-than-thou and frequently display, in a manner of which Machiavelli would wholeheartedly approve, the piety associated with the most devout, demonstrates Milton's awareness of the play's compelling mendacity – remember Richard's hollow protestations that, 'earnest in the service of my God' (3.7.105), he has neglected his friends. As we have seen above, the reshaping of history is one of the text's most pertinent and salient themes; Milton has the dangerous job of applying it to a real-life monarch and reading the factual king in the light of Shakespeare's fictional creation.

Following the opening of the theatres at the Restoration, *Richard III* was revived by the King's Company under Thomas Killigrew in order to demonstrate the tyranny not of Charles but of the autocratic Oliver Cromwell. A new prologue shows the monarch not as an oppressor, in Miltonic terms, but as divinely appointed and splendidly resilient. The political reading of the play has shifted, therefore, through 180 degrees:

> Tyrants (like childrens bubbles in the Air)
> Puft up with pride, still vanish in despair.
> But lawful Monarchs are preserv'd by Heaven,
> And 'tis from thence that their Commissions given.
> Though giddy Fortune, for a time may frown,
> And seem to eclipse the lustre of a Crown.
> Yet a King can with one Majesticke Ray,
> Dispearse those Clouds and make a glorious day.
> This blessed truth we to our joy have found,
> Since our great master happily was Crown'd.[6]

The helio-majestic Restoration has more than a smack of Prince Hal's imitation of the sun 'Who doth permit the base contagious clouds / To smother up his beauty from the world, / That when he please again to be himself, / Being wanted he may be more wondered at / By breaking through the foul and ugly mists / Of vapours that did seem to strangle him' (*I Henry IV*, 1.2.195–200). Charles II, exiled in France, has banished the clouds of the Interregnum and returned as England's Sun King.

The Eighteenth Century

As Corbett's capernoited host demonstrated with his confusion of Burbage and Richard, popular history of Richard Crookback is derived not from the archives or history books but rather from Shakespeare's dramatization of previous sources. Similarly what we know of the performances of the greatest Shakespearean actors of the eighteenth century – David Garrick, John Kemble, Edmund Kean and George Frederick Cooke – derives from their performances in a *Richard III* that is not even Shakespeare's. In July 1700 Colley Cibber's adaptation of Shakespeare's play premiered at the Theatre Royal. In the opinion of the play's editor, it was 'theatrically the most popular of all the Shakespeare adaptations'.[7] The play held sway until Henry Irving challenged its ascendancy with his 1877 production at the Lyceum. But even then he accepted some of the alterations Cibber had made almost 200 years earlier.

On the eve of the battle of Bosworth, Richard attempts to galvanize his troops by insulting their opponents (a kind of debased obverse of Henry's positive encouragement on the eve of Agincourt): 'A sort of vagabonds, rascals and runaways, / A scum of Bretons [...] these bastard Bretons' (5.3.316–7, 333). In spite of its longevity, Cibber's adaptation has been frequently treated as bastardized Shakespeare, an illegitimate appropriation and perversion of the culturally sanctioned and enshrined *Richard III*. As recently as 1920, for instance, George C. D. Odell described the adaptation as 'mangled [and] a thing of shreds and patches' though he excuses the literary vandalism by pointing out that Cibber's raw materials are not of the finest to begin with: 'as Shakespeare's play is not among his best, perhaps no great harm is done'.[8]

From its beginnings, Cibber's version was not to be as he had planned. He wrote the adaptation with Samuel Sandford in mind to play the lead but, as he reminisces in his autobiography (1739), his first choice was contracted elsewhere. Cibber stepped into the role himself and played the part 87 times including in three performances staged for the king. In spite of this huge number of performances he never seems to have inhabited the role himself. Bizarrely, he played it in such a way as he supposed Sandford would have done:

> When first I brought *Richard the Third* (with such Alterations as I thought not improper) to the Stage, *Sandford* was engaged in the Company then acting under King *William*'s Licence in *Lincoln's-Inn-Fields*; otherwise you cannot but suppose my Interest must have offer'd him that Part. What encouraged me, therefore, to attempt it myself at the *Theatre-Royal*, was that I imagined I knew how *Sandford* would have spoken every Line of it: If, therefore, in any Part of it I succeeded, let the Merit be given to him: And how far I succeeded in that Light, those only can be judges who remember him. In order, therefore, to give you a nearer Idea of *Sandford*, you must give me leave (compell'd as I am to be vain) to tell you that the late Sir *John Vanbrugh*, who was an Admirer of *Sandford*, after he had seen me act it assur'd me That he never knew of any one Actor so particularly profit by another as I had done by *Sandford* in *Richard the Third*: *You have*, said he, *his very Look, Gesture, Gait, Speech, and every Motion of him, and have borrow'd them all only to serve you in that Character*. If therefore, Sir *John Vanbrugh*'s Observation was just, they who remember me in *Richard the Third* may have a nearer Conception of *Sandford* than from all the critical Account I can give of him.[9]

The extract is extraordinary in as much as Cibber seems to be performing Sandford performing Richard. There is a peculiar echo of that weird amalgam of playwright and performer that we saw above in respect of Shakespeare and Burbage. The faux-modesty of the phrase, 'compell'd as I am to be vain', might not be as affected as it first appears for elsewhere in his *Apology*, Cibber notes that his fantasy of playing a romantic lead is dashed by his blemished physical appearance. Like his deformed protagonist, Cibber recognizes that he is not shaped for sportive tricks, 'The first Thing that enters into the Head of a young Actor is that of being a Heroe: In this Ambition I was soon snubb'd by the Insufficiency of my Voice; to which might be added an uninform'd meagre Person, (tho' then not ill made) with a dismal pale Complexion.'[10] Then, in what sounds like a direct allusion to Richard's frustrated libido, Cibber continues: 'Under these Disadvantages, I had but a melancholy Prospect of ever playing a Lover' – compare Richard's 'I that am rudely stamped, and want Love's majesty / To strut before a wanton-ambling nymph' (1.1.16–17). An anonymous reviewer in *The Laureat* noted of Cibber, perhaps somewhat unkindly: 'He was in his younger Days so lean, as to be known by the name of *Hatchet Face*'.[11]

However George Steevens, almost a century after its composition, defended Cibber's adaptation in his 1793 edition of Shakespeare's *Works*. In particular Steevens praised its cutting of what were considered to be, in an age of Augustan decorum, the play's tedious redundancies. Steevens's patrician condemnation of these irrelevancies tells us a good deal about the priorities of his own time. Again the play changes its shape, moulded by the various tastes of the historical periods it occupies:

the favour in which this tragedy is now received must [...] in some measure be imputed to Mr. Cibber's reformation of it, which generally considered, is judicious: for what modern audience would patiently listen to the narrative of Clarence's Dream, his subsequent expostulation with the murderers, the prattle of his children, the soliloquy of the Scrivener, the tedious dialogue of the citizens, the ravings of Margaret, the gross terms thrown out by the Duchess of York on Richard, the repeated progress to execution, the superfluous train of spectres, and other undramatick incumbrances which must have prevented the more valuable parts of the play from rising into their present effect and consequence?[12]

The effect of omitting these 'undramatick incumbrances' is, in absolute terms, to shorten the play; Cibber's version is less than half the length of Shakespeare's. In relative terms the culling of Clarence, Edward, Margaret, Hastings and the trimming of Buckingham, serve to foreground the protagonist. In Shakespeare's play, Richard appears in 15 of the play's 25 scenes; in Cibber's, in 15 of the play's 20 scenes. In Cibber's adaptation, he has 40 per cent of the lines rather than, in Shakespeare's, 31 per cent. But the increased prominence of Richard is also effected by Cibber's giving him no fewer than seven soliloquies. The effect of these close-ups on Richard is to make the character more prominent and, in some ways, to turn the role into a star vehicle. It was with this newly prominent Richard that David Garrick would later launch his magnificent theatrical career.

Unsurprisingly for a dramatic text, much of the criticism on the play during the eighteenth and nineteenth centuries was written in response to individual performances (some of the material discussed will converse with Kate Wilkinson's chapter on the play's performance history that follows). Critical accounts of the play as a work of literature seem to come much later. Although John Jowett insists on the importance, from the earliest times, of *Richard III* 'as a reading text', Samuel Johnson had virtually washed his hands of it, insisting on the shortcomings of Shakespeare's play in spite of the contemporary popularity of Cibber's adaptation: 'I know not whether it has not happened to [Shakespeare], as to others, to be praised most when praise is not most deserved.'[13] Johnson dismissed *Richard III* as containing parts that 'are trifling, others shocking, and some improbable' and went on to declare: 'I have nothing to add to the observations of the learned criticks, but that some traces of this antiquated exhibition are still retained in the rustick puppet-plays, in which I have seen the Devil very lustily belaboured by Punch, whom I hold to be the legitimate successor of the old Vice.'

The Nineteenth Century

Writing in 1801 Charles Lamb saw in Shakespeare's original version a level of complexity which Cibber's adaptation could never match: 'Shakspeare [*sic*] has not made Richard so black a monster as is supposed. Wherever he is monstrous, it was to conform to vulgar opinion. But he is generally a Man. [...] *Richard itself* is totally metamorphosed in the wretched *acting play* of that name, which you will see, altered by *Cibber*.'[14] The following year, in a review of Cooke's performance, Lamb reiterated his disgust for Cibber's adaptation: 'We are ready to acknowledge, that this Actor presents us with a very original and forcible portrait (if not of the *man Richard*, whom Shakespeare drew, yet) of the *monster Richard*, as he exists in the *popular idea* [...] in the impertinent and wretched *scenes*, so absurdly foisted in by some, who have thought themselves capable of adding to what *Shakespeare wrote*.'[15] In 1817 Hazlitt was equally damning:

> The manner in which Shakespear's [*sic*] plays have been generally altered or rather mangled by modern mechanists, is a disgrace to the English stage. The patch-work *Richard III* which is acted under the sanction of his name, and which was manufactured by Cibber, is a striking example of this remark. [...] Some of the most important and striking passages in the principal character have been omitted, to make room for idle and misplaced extracts from other plays; the only intention of which seems to have been to make the character of Richard as odious and disgusting as possible. It is apparently for no other purpose than to make Gloucester stab King Henry on the stage, that the fine abrupt introduction of the character in the opening of the play is lost in the tedious whining morality of the uxorious king (taken from another play); – we say *tedious*, because it interrupts the business of the scene, and loses its beauty and effect by having no intelligible connection with the previous character of the mild, well-meaning monarch.[16]

In spite of the mixed reactions to Cibber's adaptation of *Richard III*, it was, as noted above, this version which was used by Garrick to propel himself to stardom on the London stage on 19 October 1741 at Drury Lane. Indeed it was not until 1877 and again in 1896 that Shakespeare's version was resurrected.

Henry Irving's Lyceum productions, nearly two decades apart, were influenced by the extravagant illusionism of the day: his 'pictorial stage, like his acceptance of Shakespeare's text, appealed to a newly respectable and educated middle-class audience'.[17] Irving was the first manager to cover the house lights, and the illuminated proscenium arch offered a striking realism. As with Cibber's version (vestiges of which remained, such as the ghosts appearing on the eve of Bosworth to Richard but not Richmond), the accent was firmly on the protagonist. George Bernard Shaw, in the *Saturday Review* (26 December 1896) remarked in his account of the second production that 'the real objection to Cibber's version is that it is what we call a "one man show" '.[18] This however, seems entirely appropriate to Shaw's caustic opinion of Irving: 'Sir Henry Irving never did and never will make use of a play otherwise than as a vehicle for some fantastic creation of his own.'[19] Of Richard seducing Lady Anne, Shaw gloated, Irving played 'the scene with her [Julia Arthur] as if he were a Houndsditch salesman cheating a factory girl over a pair of second-hand stockings'.

Joseph Knight's reaction to the earlier production was similarly unimpressed. Having lauded Irving for 'bringing for the first time, the "Richard the Third" of Shakespeare upon the stage, under conditions which secure it an immediate triumph', he is less positive about the production itself.[20] Though Irving's perform-mance in the earlier part of the play was praiseworthy, as the production went on, 'Mr Irving falls into the old extravagance. In the last act he lengthened out the syllables of words until they seemed interminable, and his utterance grew inarticulate – he marred the presentation by grimace and by extravagance of gesture, and went far towards destroying the impression he had made.'[21] The focus, with Cibber's soliloquies cut, might have broadened to the company more widely but Irving's central performance seems still to have dominated: 'What remains to be shown is that he will continue to use the power of self-restraint he possesses, and will be content to forego the enthusiasm extravagance begets in the less educated portion of an audience.'[22]

Irving's Richard seems to have shaped the play around its central character, refashioning, as it were, Shakespeare's play within a Cibberian mould. The prominence of the play's protagonist was a driving force behind the performances of John Barrymore in the United States. The *New York Times* critic (8 March 1920) described Barrymore's 'titanic quality' and wrote of Richard as a 'Heaven-challenging giant standing outside and above the pygmy mortals with whose destinies he toys so lightly'.[23]

1900–1945

In a period of colonial initiative, Shakespeare's history cycles became vital as the means to inculcate a proud nationalism. Coleridge had insisted as early as 1813 on a sentimental allegiance to an idea of nationality that runs throughout the history plays. In *Lectures on the Characteristics of Shakespear*, he writes: 'One great object of his historic plays [...] was, to make his countrymen more patriotic; to make Englishmen proud of being Englishmen.'[24] The nineteenth-century's geographical and industrial expansionism looked to the chronicle histories as the defining documents of a sovereign identity. For Thomas Carlyle, writing in 1840, 'There are right beautiful things in those Pieces [history plays], which indeed together form one beautiful thing. [...] A true English heart breathes, calm and strong, through the whole business; not boisterous, protrusive; all the better for that.'[25] He goes on to assert that the Shakespearean vim that so galvanizes the colonial enterprise will long outlive it: the 'Indian Empire will go, at any rate, some day; but this Shakspeare does not go, he lasts forever with us; we cannot give-up our Shakspeare!'[26]

This nationalistic Shakespeare became all the more intense as the horrors of the Great War brought home the vulnerability of

Englishness, fighting for its survival. To add insult to injury, the enemy had long claimed Shakespeare as their own. Writing from the trenches in 1915, Professor Hecht trumpeted the suitability of Shakespeare to the German nation: 'We believe that we Germans are truer heirs to his genius than his own compatriots who have betrayed their cousins-in-blood for the sake of material gain.'[27] Ludwig Fulda maintained, in 1916, that Shakespeare 'happened to be born in England by mistake' and suggested that military conquest ought to compel cultural surrender too: 'Should we succeed in vanquishing England in the field, we should, I think, insert a clause into the peace treaty stipulating the formal surrender of William Shakespeare to Germany.'[28] In 1918, Sir J. A. R. Marriott's majestically entitled *English History in Shakespeare* metaphorically returned fire. The golden age of Elizabeth was to him just as much as an ideal vision as it would prove to Tillyard during World War II (see below). Marriott writes;

> all through these Chronicle Plays, [Shakespeare] harps upon the supreme duty of promoting national unity and social solidarity. It was because the Tudors secured to the country these greatest of blessings that the hearts of patriotic Englishmen went out to them, despite faults and blemishes of character, with reverence, gratitude and affection; and to none of the Tudors, in fuller measure, than to the Virgin Queen whose happiness it was to count among her subjects a Raleigh and a Drake, a Spenser and a Shakespeare.[29]

In the words of Harold Jenkins, Marriott 'found in the history cycle political messages for our age which he thought Shakespeare must have intended for his own. The need for national unity was the dominant theme and lesson.'[30]

Just two decades later, the War to end all Wars was followed by yet another. The desire to uncover and underline the full political dimensions of Shakespeare's history plays may have 'loomed larger for a generation which had witnessed a world war and great social revolutions'.[31] In Chapter 2 of this volume, Kate Wilkinson describes Donald Wolfit's 1942 *Richard III* as a production explicitly linking its protagonist to Hitler. One year later, Tillyard's *The Elizabethan World Picture* (1943) insisted on the ubiquity and validity of an organic world view that smoothed out the local irregularities of historical contingency in the service of the restoration of natural harmony. The wartime contribution of Tillyard cannot be overestimated and though he has, of late, been attacked as a spokesperson for a thinly veiled conservative orthodoxy, he can hardly be blamed for his determination to promote a version of Shakespeare which looks back, from the ruins of the Blitz, to a harmonious Elizabethanism. Such a congenial take on Tudor England, in the opinion of Tillyard's detractors, is another version of Professor Welch's phoney 'Merrie England' from Kingsley Amis's *Lucky Jim* (1954).[32] Notwithstanding the fact that *The Elizabethan World Picture* tells us more about the England of the 1940s than that of the 1590s, 'the general effect of Tillyard's criticism is to reveal in the whole [history] cycle a richness and a complexity not fully appreciated before'.[33]

Tillyard's method in *World Picture* is to cite a poem or prose extract from an Elizabethan work which is arguing for a cosmo-logical, philosophical, moral or even psychological consistency and order (one of his chapters is called 'Order'). The usual suspects appear, Sir Thomas Elyot's *The Book Named The Governor*, the Church Homily *Of Obedience*, Sir John Davies's *Orchestra* and various extracts from Shakespeare. These passages are quoted and then Tillyard, with bludgeoning authority, will conclude that their harmonious world visions were ubiquitously shared as fundamental principles by the entire populace: 'It is what everyone believed in Elizabeth's days'; 'The conception of order described above must have been common to all Elizabethans of even modest intelligence'; 'cosmic order was [...] one of the master-themes of Elizabethan poetry'.[34]

The following year Tillyard's *Shakespeare's History Plays* was first published; it is more of the same. Its chapter titles include 'The Cosmic Background' and 'The Elizabethan World Order'.

Its fundamental assumptions are pretty much identical to those of the earlier study: 'The Elizabethan political order, the Golden Age brought in by the Tudors, is nothing apart from the cosmic order of which it is a part.'[35] What Tillyard is keen to establish is that this assumption of order is finally victorious over the temporary discords and maladies wrought by Vice characters like Richard of Gloucester: 'when Shakespeare deals with the concrete facts of English history he never forgets the principle of order behind all the terrible manifestations of disorder'.

Thus in the case of *Richard III* then, the divinely sanctioned concord of history is temporarily ruptured by Richard, only to be restored by the morally inspired Richmond. It is not difficult to see the scheme writ large in the contention of Churchillian England struggling against Nazi aggression. Like Richmond, Tillyard assures us, the Allies will prevail: 'In spite of the eminence of Richard's character the main business of the play is to complete the national tetralogy and to display the working out of God's plan to restore England to prosperity.'[36] In spite of the short-lived victories of the enemy, the longer view (seeing this play as the concluding movement in the saga of the whole tetralogy) will ensure that what Richmond refers to as 'God's fair ordinance [will] Enrich the time to come with smooth-faced peace' (5.7.31–3). As Tillyard puts it: 'the greatest bond uniting all four plays is the steady political theme: the theme of order and chaos, of proper political degree and civil war, of crime and punishment, of God's mercy finally tempering his justice, of the belief that such had been God's way with England.'[37]

Laurence Olivier opened his *Richard III* in the same year as that of the publication of Tillyard's providential study. Like Wolfit before him, the immediacy of political tyranny was unsurprisingly uppermost in his mind: 'I had got a lot of things on my side, now I come to think of it, from the point of view of timelines. One had Hitler over the way, one was playing it definitely as a paranoic, so that there was a core of something to which the audience would immediately respond.'[38] In his review of the production, Kenneth Tynan noticed that, much like one of the Führer's demagogic rallies, Olivier was at his most dynamic when addressing others:

> He needs other people on the stage with him: to be ignored, stared past, or pushed aside during the lower reaches, and gripped and buttonholed when the wave rises to its crested climax. For this reason Olivier tends to fail in soliloquy – except when, as in the opening speech of *Richard*, it is directed straight at the audience, who then become his temporary foils. [...] Olivier the actor needs reactors: just as electricity, *in vacuo*, is unseen, unfelt, and powerless.[39]

Of course the discomforting symbiosis of Adolf Hitler and Richard of Gloucester would reach its darkly comic consummation in Bertolt Brecht's 1941 rewriting of Shakespeare's villain as the ruthless vegetable salesman in *The Resistible Rise of Arturo Ui*, a thinly veiled parody of Hitler's bullying ascent to power which references scenes like the wooing of Lady Anne or the Bosworth-eve ghosts from Shakespeare's *Richard III*.

During the early 1940s George Wilson Knight was also thinking through the implications of the current state of war for a reading of Shakespeare's history plays. In 1944 he published *The Olive and the Sword* which contained his analysis of *Richard III*. Whereas Tillyard's optimistic Elizabethanism implicitly offered a paradigm to which 1940s London could aspire, amid the rubble of the Blitz, Wilson Knight drew a parallel between the belligerence of the world of the play and that which surrounded him: '*Richard III* presents a reading of tyranny which we, in our time, should be in a peculiarly good position to appreciate'.[40] Wilson Knight's attitude to Shakespeare's evil protagonist is a good deal more ambiguous than Tillyard's. Indeed, there is something of a begrudging esteem for the enemy's stubborn heroism: 'We cannot deny to Richard a certain semi-reluctant admiration. Though wicked, he remains great'.[41] Wilson Knight's conclusion is particularly intriguing given the current embattled state of the nation: 'England is felt as rejecting from her own constitution, as a foul disease, the tyrannous and bloody thing which she has so often since opposed in other nations; and the play ends with some great lines by Richmond on the peace won by his victorious arm.' Yet even here, there is a lingering fascination for Richard's superhuman courage: 'But that is not the whole story: for Richard's address to his army wielded also a burly patriotism of its own; an element of British virility is clearly part of him, and Shakespeare even underlines it by a reminder of Richmond's dependence on a foreign army'.[42] The optimistic faith of Tillyard is here diluted by a sense of villainous intrepidity which serves to illustrate that even in the most apparently clear cut battle between good and evil, Shakespeare's theatre is anything but straightforward.

Tantalizingly, when Tillyard revisited *Richard III* after the war in 1949, he wrote of the protagonist less as a tyrannical scourge than a scapegoat: 'The victim [of a "sacrificial purgation" – the phrase is Tillyard's] may be good or bad. Shakespeare's Richard III is a perfect example of a sacrificial victim carrying the burden of his country's sins; and he is bad'.[43] After the horrors of World War II, with the enormity of the destruction coming into focus, it seems as if Tillyard's wartime optimism has started to fade.

Post-war Criticism

Writing in 1985, Dennis H. Burden acknowledged the authority of Tillyard's criticism: 'The influence of Tillyard's thesis can be seen in the amount of reference to it in later work'.[44] Much of this subsequent analysis was antipathetic to Tillyard, especially in the case of the British Cultural Materialists. As Burden mischievously noted: 'To some perhaps [Tillyard's criticism] came to seem the product of the view from a Cambridge college window looking out on a world at war and nostalgic for a more stable and comprehensible historical process'.

In a 1953 lecture, subsequently published posthumously, A. P. Rossiter argued that Tillyard's work cramped Shakespeare's imagination into a system of beliefs which was not supported by the plays themselves. The 'historic myth' of Tillyard's *Elizabethan*

World Picture 'offered absolutes, certainties'. Shakespeare, argues Rossiter, by contrast, 'always leaves us with relatives, ambiguities, irony, a process thoroughly dialectical'.[45] As we have already noted, Tillyard's championing of a benevolent historical scheme probably has more to do with an attempt to allay the insecurities excited by World War II than the play of *Richard III* and Rossiter does appreciate the comfort of belief in a positive history: 'Men have always looked for [...] a predictability in history: it gives the illusion of a comfortably ordered world'.[46] But Rossiter insists that rather than 'writing *moral history* (which is what Dr Tillyard and Dr Dover Wilson and Professor Duthie have made *out* of him)', Shakespeare was actually writing '*comic history*'. Richard, in Rossiter's scheme, occupies the role 'of the diabolical humorist': 'a good third of the play is a kind of grisly *comedy*; in which we meet the fools to be taken in on Richard's terms, see them with his mind, and rejoice with him in their stultification'.[47] As this suggests, Rossiter is one of the first critics to pay serious attention to the Vice figure as a centre of comic energy and, correspondingly, stresses the importance of the performer:

> An aspect of Richard's appeal, which has, I fancy, passed relatively unexamined, is one that we can be confident that William Shakespeare felt and reflected on. I mean the appeal of the actor. [...] The specific interest here is the *power* that would be in the hands of an actor consummate enough to make (quite literally) "all the world a stage" and to work on humanity by the perfect simulation of every feeling.[48]

Richard, argues Rossiter, 'through his prowess as actor and his embodiment of the comic Vice [...] offers the false as more attractive than the true'.[49] In his seduction of the audience, Richard the performer becomes 'God's agent in a predetermined plan of divine retribution'. In this way he 'functions as an avenging angel. Hence my paradoxical title, "Angel with Horns"'. While Rossiter dissents from a simplistic Tillyardian faith in the order of things, there is an acknowledgement in the governing presence of a divine being, albeit one that moves in counter-intuitive ways.

Perhaps most extreme in the diversity of its aims and achievements from Tillyard's work is *Shakespeare Our Contemporary* by Jan Kott which was first published in Polish in 1964 and then, a year later, in an English translation.[50] In his Preface to the volume, Peter Brook explains Kott's academic *raison d'être* in terms of his membership of a Communist state. If Tillyard pondered the world beyond his Cambridge college window, Kott, says Brook,

> makes one suddenly aware how rare it is for a pedant or a commentator to have any experience of what he is describing. It is a disquieting thought that the major part of the commentaries on Shakespeare's passions and his politics are hatched far from life by sheltered figures behind ivy-covered walls.[51]

For Brook, Kott's access to the Elizabethan sensibility is entirely a result of the political upheavals he had experienced growing up under Russian occupation: 'It is Poland that in our time has come closest to the tumult, the danger, the intensity, the imaginativeness and the daily involvement with the social process that made life so horrible, subtle and ecstatic to an Elizabethan,'[52]

For Kott, the histories are the foundations of the Shakespearean edifice: 'one should start the reading of the plays with the Histories, and in particular, with *Richard II* and *Richard III*.'[53] Shakespeare's English kings personify the bleak and impersonal process of history, a history without conscience or morality, not unlike the one-party state in which Kott was writing. Nothing could be further from Tillyard's benign Christian faith. Kott's is the mid-century of the dictator, Hitler, Mussolini, Franco and Stalin – one of his chapters is entitled '*Hamlet* of the Mid-Century'. These autocratic despots are without character or identity; they merely personify the forces of a historical process which crushes all before it, before they, in their own turn, are run over:

Richard is impersonal like history itself. He is the consciousness and mastermind of the Grand Mechanism. He puts in motion the roller of history, and later is crushed by it. Richard is not even cruel. Psychology does not apply to him. He is just history, one of its ever-repeating chapters. He has no face.[54]

Kott's explanation of the highly patterned speeches of the mourning queens exemplifies his profoundly negative assessment of human relationships. Margaret's strange incantation lists the killed and their killers: 'I had an Edward, till a Richard killed him. / I had a husband, till a Richard killed him ...' (4.4.40-1). For Kott their shared names underline the ruthless logic of their mutually assured destruction:

Even their names are the same. There is always a Richard, an Edward and a Henry. They have the same titles. [...] Feudal history is like a great staircase on which there treads a constant procession of kings. Every step upwards is marked by murder, perfidy, treachery. Every step brings the throne nearer. [...] From the highest step there is only a leap into the abyss. The monarchs change. But all of them – good and bad, brave and cowardly, vile and noble, naïve and cynical – tread on the steps that are always the same.[55]

This profoundly bleak vision reads Shakespeare as a prophet or seer who had seen into the eternal and immutable wickedness of human corruption: the first of the book's three appendices is called 'Shakespeare – Cruel and True' as though truth could only be cruel and cruelty is a *fait accompli*. It was against this nihilistic, and arguably defeatist, criticism that Marxism and materialist approaches reacted.

Contemporary Criticism

The rise of Cultural Materialist criticism was triggered by, in part, the vandalism against higher education under Margaret Thatcher's administration.[56] The abolition of professional tenure, the erosion of academic freedom and the reduction of funding to collegiate universities sharpened the oppositional relationship between the establishment and more Marxist academics. The University of Oxford's refusal to award the prime minister an honorary degree (until that time a mere formality) was the symptom of the enmity between the academy and the government. At the same time, the canonical status of some texts (conspicuously Shakespeare) were, in the light of new theoretical approaches, being re-evaluated and subjected to sociological and ideological interrogation. Their continued promulgation by state apparatuses such as the National Curriculum or state sponsored institutions such as the National Theatre or the Royal Shakespeare Company was also being challenged.

The key text, here, was *Political Shakespeare: New Essays in Cultural Materialism* (1985). In their foreword / manifesto, Jonathan Dollimore and Alan Sinfield threw down the gauntlet and attempted to galvanize a politically progressive programme for Shakespeare studies: 'Cultural Materialism does not, like so much established literary criticism, attempt to mystify its perspective as the natural, obvious or right interpretation of an allegedly given textual fact. On the contrary, it registers its commitment to the transformation of a social order which exploits people on grounds of race, gender and class'.[57] Inevitably, Tillyard's complacent securities would have to go. Rather than read the articulation of *The Elizabethan World Picture* as a comforting statement of a universally held truth, Dollimore argues the opposite – that the regularity of its re-articulation testifies to its being under attack: 'Tillyard's world picture, to the extent that it did still exist, was not shared by all; it was an ideological legitimation of an existing social order, one rendered the more necessary by the apparent instability, actual *and* imagined, of that order'.[58] In the words of

Graham Holderness, 'Tillyard, Wilson Knight and Dover Wilson all found in Shakespeare's history plays a ruling ideology of order because that is precisely what they wanted to find'.[59] As Tillyard's world picture was undermined, so assumptions about patriarchy, racial hierarchies, sexualities and so on came under scrutiny. In the case of *Richard III* for instance, Dollimore challenges the notion of the unity of human subjectivity and demonstrates how social pressures fragment identity. Commenting on Richard's schizo-phrenic attack on the eve of the battle of Bosworth (5.4.161–85), Dollimore writes, 'at that point when power is slipping from him; an attempt to reassert autonomy collapses into paradoxical self-division'.[60]

Like Cultural Materialist criticism, Feminism is explicitly engaged with the transformation of lived experience and the redistribution of socio-political power. At her most materialist, Phyllis Rackin sees female agency as inimical to the contin-uance of patriarchal history itself. The early modern obsession with fidelity and legitimacy, the period's pained anxiety towards cuckoldry (more so perhaps in comedy than tragedy or history) stems from the importance of primogeniture. As Rackin explains, 'women represent a constant threat to the legitimacy of patriarchal succession, but they also represent its ultimate warrant'.[61] *Richard III* culminates in the promise of the marriage of Richmond and Elizabeth, Lancaster and York, which signals the accession of the Tudor dynasty and the arrival (for the play's first audiences) of the present historical epoch. Of course the influence of female figures speaks precisely to a kingdom under the sovereignty of Queen Elizabeth I whose grandmother, Elizabeth of York has, in Rackin's scheme of things, brought internecine masculine history to a close. On the other hand, might the play not be challenging the easy solution of the Tudor myth, questioning the providential view of the accession of the Tudors championed by Sir Thomas More?

Richard III is unusual among the history plays in the promi-nence of its female characters. Richard's opening soliloquy dwells on his determination to turn villain because he cannot prove a lover. Then, as we have already seen, his wooing of Lady Anne demonstrates his rhetorical brilliance (to us) and the fickle stupidity of women (to him). As the scenario is reprised later in his wooing of Elizabeth by proxy (4.4.184–430), he again remarks on the pliability of a mother (the Queen, also named Elizabeth) who can promise him her daughter in spite of the fact that she knows he is responsible for the slaughter of her sons: 'Relenting fool, and shallow, changing woman' (431). Throughout the play, misogyny is not very far from the surface and Jowett argues that it takes two forms: 'hostility to the maternal and aversion to female sexuality'.[62]

With their rigid patriarchal hierarchies and the exclusion of women from the decision-making processes of high politics, the history plays might not seem to offer much of a haven for feminist analysis. Jean E. Howard and Phyllis Rackin read the history plays in the light of the 'ambivalent place of women in early modern England and the instabilities of the gender ideologies that attempted to contain them'.[63] In *Engendering a Nation*, they analyse the portrayal of the female characters in the history plays, showing how the differences in their characterization are symptomatic of the emergent structures of capitalism and the early modern state. For instance, they note that the women of the history plays are mainly foreign or of low birth – Mortimer's wife speaks only in Welsh (*1 Henry IV*) and we are shown Princess Catherine receiving an English language lesson (*Henry V*). In *1 Henry VI* Joan la Pucelle confesses her lowly origins, 'I am by birth a shepherd's daughter' (1.3.51). However, as Howard and Rackin point out: 'In direct antithesis, all of the female characters in *Richard III* are highborn English women who speak in the undifferentiated, formal blank verse that constitutes the standard language of the playscript'.[64] Thus, they argue, the marginal or subversive is here transformed into the central and compliant, in order to meet the demands of a masculine political culture: 'the female characters in *Richard III* are confined to domestic roles and domestic settings'.[65] The containment of potentially dissident women reaches its ascendancy in the marriage of

Richmond to Elizabeth (the Princess on whom Richard had his own designs). This marriage 'satisfies the ideological imperatives of an emergent capitalist economy and an emergent nation state that increasingly employed the mystified image of a patriarchal family to authorize masculine privilege and rationalize monarchial power'.[66] Through the marriage and the unification of the red and white roses, Richmond takes up the role of 'benevolent paterfamilias', not merely of his dynasty but of the nation.[67] It is this secure patriarchy that engenders the Tudor settlement, presided over by Richmond's grand-daughter, Elizabeth. According to this analysis, *Richard III* serves to defuse the subversion articulated by marginal (in this case, female) voices, and thus enforce compliance to the emergent ideological structures of an incipient capitalist economy. Typical of the New Historicists, Howard and Rackin genuflect submissively in front of the absolute patriarchy of the early modern state.

Similarly Stephen Greenblatt's desire to 'speak with the dead' is frustrated by the totalitarianism of social institutions – church, family, gender, education, the court and so on – which overwhelm the early modern subject: 'there were, so far as I could tell, no moments of pure, unfettered subjectivity'.[68] In his reading of Shakespeare's history plays, Greenblatt shows how they flirt with the idea of subversion before containing and cauterizing any revolutionary impulses: 'There is subversion, no end of subversion, only not for us'.[69]

This apparently contradictory reading might be indicative of a logical inconsistency in New Historicist criticism or, more likely, it is the demonstration of the ways in which Shakespeare's work, in general, and *Richard III*, in particular, demands of literary criticism constant re-evaluation. Later in this volume Nina Levine describes the interpenetration of past and present, insisting that *Richard III* 'enacts what may be a universal practice of interpreting the present in relation to a particular time in the past'. As the opening word of the play reminds us, *Richard III* is a history play that refuses to allow us to consign it to some historical past. It is 'Now' (1.1.1), and will remain, too much with us.

CHAPTER TWO

Richard III on Stage

KATE WILKINSON

Richard III is one of the most infamous of English kings. This is due in large part to Shakespeare's presentation of him in his play and the various portrayals of Shakespeare's character on stage over time. Indeed, it is possible to argue that research into the performance history of *Richard III* does not give us a sense of the play in performance but of the character and his many interpretations. *Richard III* has been popular since it was written and has remained so for over four centuries. It became one of the best known and enduring of the Restoration adaptations of Shakespeare's plays. This chapter aims to trace the history of *Richard III* in the English theatre from its first performances, focusing on some of the most significant productions of the past 400 years into the twenty-first century. Because *Richard III* has been performed on so many occasions this chapter will cover a selection of productions, aiming to survey some of the most important developments and innovations in the play's stage history. Thus, this chapter will discuss the earliest performances: Colley Cibber's adaptation of the play and its interpretations in the eighteenth and nineteenth centuries; a number of famous twentieth-century productions, including those of Laurence Olivier, Antony Sher and Ian McKellen; the all-female production at the Globe theatre; and *Richard III* as part of a history cycle.

Although very little is known of the earliest performances of *Richard III*, we can make guesses about it from what we do know of the period. Shakespeare's drama drew on a rich history of medieval and morality plays. The idea of Richard as an evil character lacking a conscience perhaps lies in the theatrical background against which he was written: when Shakespeare wrote his *Richard III* his audience would have been fully aware of the tradition and recognized elements of it within the drama, as indeed Richard recognizes it in himself: 'Thus like the formal Vice, Iniquity, / I moralize two meanings in one word (3.1.82–3)'.

Richard can be seen to have his roots in the medieval figure of the Vice, and in the demonization of the historical Richard which began during the reign of Henry VII (or *Richard III*'s character Richmond). With this knowledge we can begin to speculate as to how the play's first audiences may have responded. Julie Hankey has observed '[b]y the time Shakespeare wrote his play ... Richard was vividly alive in the popular imagination' and that, because of the reference to Richard as the Vice '[e]ven as the audience were laughing they would have seen the devil's horns'.[1] Hankey also makes the point, important to understanding the development of Richard over the play's stage history, that '[h]e is perfectly realised, without being psychologically elaborated'.[2] The drive to 'find' Richard, his character and motivations is something that has been more apparent in the most recent interpretations of the play (indeed, as Hankey's remark implies, there was no early psychological interpretation of the character) – perhaps only really in the last quarter of the play's life.

The first performance of Richard is hard to pin down. As with the majority of Renaissance plays, there are no detailed eyewitness accounts of the performances. *Richard III* was probably first performed in 1593 by Pembroke's Men at The Theatre with Richard Burbage in the lead role. Burbage was a leading actor of the day and became famous in roles such as Hamlet, Othello and King Lear. The popularity of *Richard III* is evident in the publication of six quarto editions before the First Folio in 1623. Frequent reprinting of the text suggests the continued popularity of the play until the English Civil War and the closure of the theatres which lasted through the war and the ensuing Protectorate until the Restoration when *Richard III* was revived, albeit infrequently, for the court of King Charles II.

One of the most significant developments in the history of *Richard III* occurred in December of 1699 when the actor-manager Colley Cibber took to the stage of the Theatre Royal Drury Lane to perform *The Tragical History of Richard III*, his own adaptation of Shakespeare's play. Although Cibber himself was not so very successful in this play, its influence was to be felt for the next 200 years. Cibber adapted Shakespeare's text so that it might be more appealing to the sensibilities of his audience.[3] This meant making some quite drastic changes to the play: of Shakespeare's 3,800 lines, Cibber retained only 800. To these he added lines from other Shakespearean history plays and 1,000 lines of his own. The result was to simplify the text, focusing entirely on Richard and removing the ambiguities of the character and his motivations. The very radical nature of the editing can be seen in the list of now absent characters: Edward IV, Clarence, Hastings, Margaret and the two murderers were all cut, as was most of Act 1 Scene 1, Act 2 Scene 1, and Scenes 2, 4, 5 and 6 of Act 3.[4] Nevertheless, there were some additions made too: the play no longer began with the 'Now is the winter of our discontent' (1.1.1) soliloquy but with Richard's murder of Henry VI from *Henry VI, Part Three*, and seven new soliloquies were added for Richard.[5] The overall effect of Cibber's alterations was to turn *Richard III* into a 'star vehicle' for a leading actor, a consequence of there being, as Lull states, 'nothing left to balance Richard's overwhelming dominance'.[6] Indeed, from having 31 per cent of the lines in Shakespeare's text, Cibber's Richard now took 40 per cent. This dominance of Richard which allowed actors to showcase themselves is perhaps one of the main reasons for the longevity of Cibber's adaptation: the play became one of the must-play roles for up and coming actors in the eighteenth and nineteenth centuries and, indeed, into the twentieth century as we shall see.

From the first performance of the text in 1699 Cibber was to play the role himself 84 times over the next 40 years but he was never particularly successful in the role and has received some harsh criticism over the years. Hankey has written that Cibber turned the play into a 'rant' arguing that 'Cibber's adaptation ... was written with nothing more in mind but to give Colley Cibber in the lead a chance to strut and rant almost without interpretation'.[7] Indeed, Hankey observes that a result of the simplification of the text and character was to create 'a piece of theatrical sensationalism, a way of displaying and relishing plain nastiness'.[8] Hankey's assertions are supported by firsthand accounts of Cibber's performances. Hankey quotes the anonymous critic of the *Laureat* stating that Cibber ' "screamed through 4 acts ... without Dignity or Decency" and in the fifth [he] degenerated into a panic-stricken version of his own fop, Sir Novelty Fashion in *Love's Last Shift*, screaming "A Harse! A Harse, my kingdom for a Harse!" '.[9] Aaron Hill in the *Prompter* also drew attention to Cibber's reputation as a comic, stating that Cibber was '*born to be laugh'd at*' but that his Richard consisted of 'the distracted heavings of a disjointed caterpillar'.[10] That Cibber's audience liked him as a comedian was the reason given by Thomas Davies for their continued acceptance of him in *Richard III*: Davies stated that Cibber was 'endured in this ... and other tragic parts on account of his general merit in comedy ... the public grew out of patience and fairly hissed him off the stage'.[11] Davies' view was further supported by the *Laureat*, the writer suggesting that: 'When he was kill'd by *Richmond*, one might plainly perceive that the good People were not better pleas'd that so *execrable* a *Tyrant* was destroy'd, than that so *execrable* an *Actor* was silent'.[12]

These reviews may suggest that the persistence of Cibber's adaptation was by no means guaranteed. Rather it was Cibber's adaptation in the hands of another actor-manager, David Garrick, which would ensure its continued usage on the stage into the twentieth century. Garrick made his London debut in the role of Richard in 1741, and he would play the role a further 213 times in the years between 1747 and 1776 when he was in charge at the Drury Lane Theatre, London. His performance as Richard made Garrick 'an instant star'[13] and as Garrick's popularity rose so did that of his dramatic vehicle. The theatres of the Restoration period were small, and even when Garrick extended his theatre's auditorium it remained intimate: actors performed at the front of the apron stage close to the audience who were able to see them clearly. This was important for Garrick who was famous for his use and control of facial expression as an acting tool. Garrick was a physical performer and his 'style was pantomimically extremely detailed'.[14] This physically expressive detail was so much a part of the performance that anecdotes of the time suggest that full accounts of the play could be given by audience members simply by imitating Garrick's movements without any recital of the text.[15] This also suggests a cynicism on Garrick's part as he was accused 'of employing "claptraps" ... tricks of voice and gesture as a signal for a round of applause'.[16]

The history of *Richard III* on stage is intimately tied up with the role of Richard and his interpretation by the lead actor, and Garrick was perhaps one of the first, in spite of Cibber's simple text, to find and imbue his Richard with psychological motivation: 'Garrick ... asked himself why Richard was a villain' and played him both as 'warrior and hero' and also as 'deliberating, subtle, calm'.[17] Hankey argues that through this calmer Richard, Garrick created a character who was more 'understandable'.[18] The idea of evil as understandable fed into other performances of the Romantic era, most notably those of Edmund Kean whose performances, according to Paul Prescott, 'captured the spirit of the age'[19] which included the notion that 'evil is somehow made splendid by the aspiring genius of the wrongdoer'.[20] Kean also performed his Richards at the Drury Lane Theatre, which was facing bankruptcy at the time he was starting out. In contrast to Cibber, who said that *The Tragical History of Richard III* 'did not raise me £5 on the third day', Kean's performances in the play in 1814 saved the theatre by bringing in £500 a performance.[21]

Oxberry's 1822 edition of the play with extensive notes of Kean's performance gives us a very clear impression of what Kean's Richard looked like, noting that he wore:

[a] ruffle for neck white pocket [handkerchief] [...] First dress – wig scarlet doublet, trunks, cloak, hat with [...]

feathers, white hose, russet boots, shoes – order of St
George, garter – [...] sword and chain, also black [...] for
second dress.

This is a somewhat rambling list but it helps to create the image,
even 200 years after the performance. In the preface to the 1959
facsimile edition, Alan Downer writes that this is the 'fullest and
most detailed account in existence of Edmund Kean's moves,
business and rhetorical delivery and gesture'.[22]

The theatre reviewer William Hazlitt also gives us a good sense
of Kean's performance and understanding of Richard. Kean was
one of Hazlitt's favourite actors of Shakespeare but although he
praised Kean hyperbolically, he also acknowledged his failings.
Hazlitt stressed the originality of Kean's performance stating
that 'Mr. Kean's manner of acting this part has one particular
advantage; it is entirely his own, without any traces of imitation
of any other actor' and he goes on to state that 'we cannot
imagine any character ... more perfectly articulated in every part'.
However, this is not unqualified praise as Hazlitt went on to say
that 'we sometimes thought he failed, even from an exuberance
of talent'. Hazlitt argued that Kean 'gives an animation, vigour,
and relief to the part' although he thought Kean 'deficient in
dignity; and particularly in the scenes of state business, there
was not a sufficient air of artificial authority'. In spite of Hazlitt's
tributes to Kean's performance of Richard, he only discussed
Richard and did not cover any other character or performer in
the productions. Even when writing about the seduction of Anne,
the actress playing the lady did not get a mention while Hazlitt
praised Kean's 'smooth and smiling villainy'.[23]

The last of the great Richards before the twentieth century was
Henry Irving who performed the part in 1877 and 1896. These
performances are in part notable because, in the first instance,
Irving made a step away from Cibber and towards Shakespeare's
original text. In some ways this marks a general turning point in
the history of the play back to Shakespeare's text (although, as
we shall see, there was an important exception to this in Olivier's

1944 production). In 1877 Irving used two-thirds of Shakespeare's text, the remaining third was cut and the performance ended on the 'A horse! A horse!' (5.4.7) speech. This conclusion highlights how, even though it was mostly Shakespeare's text that was used, the play remained a star vehicle about the lead actor and the use of cutting in order to keep the focus on Richard's character followed the example set by Cibber in his adaptation. There was a slight change to this in Irving's 1896 production as some attention fell on Margaret which may have been because her character was restored to Act 4 Scene 4. Scholars have noted that Irving's two Richards two decades apart represented two different interpretations of the part. Prescott writes that in 1877 Irving played a Richard 'embittered at the hand that Nature had dealt him' whereas in 1896 he performed Richard as an 'arch and polished dissembler, the grimmest of jesters, the most subtle and the most merciless of assassins and conspirators'.[24] Hankey argues that Irving played Richard with a 'lightness of touch' but also draws attention to Shaw's discussion of the 'pathetically sublime ending'.[25] Hankey goes on to state that 'While both these Richards were praised by some, there were others who took offence at one or the other of them', noting that Joseph Knight 'objected to the affectation of Irving's acting' as 'Shaw had objected to the sentiment'.[26]

Beyond his return to Shakespeare and his performance as Richard, Irving is also noted for his use of scenery and creating unification between the 'text, scenery and character interpretation'.[27] Prescott quotes Madeline Bingham at length describing the set design that Irving used. Bingham states that the 'whole production was in the best realistic style, from the picturesque streets of old London and the gloom of the Tower to the scene in the Council Chamber (most substantially constructed with broad, massive stairs and a lofty gallery)'.[28] As with the best of theatre writing, Bingham creates an impression of what the stage looked like to the audience and the impressiveness of the sizable set pieces. The set for the night before the battle of Bosworth was also noteworthy as a tent 'occupied the whole stage, complete with a luxurious couch, armour lying about, a coal fire ... a view of the battlefield'.[29] This provides quite a contrast to the productions of the later part of the twentieth century that would follow.

Although there were a number of performances between Irving's production in the 1890s and Laurence Olivier's, it was the 1940s that were a watershed for *Richard III* in production. With war ravaging Europe, London under attack from the skies, and the German forces led by a man hell-bent on power at any cost, it was not hard for English audiences to try to imagine the evil of Richard or his motivations. Indeed, as theatre reviewer Harold Hobson wrote, audiences 'found the spectacle of unexplained evil no longer incredible or shocking'.[30] There were two significant Richards in this decade, the first of which is noteworthy because of the way it influenced the second which would cast such a shadow as a definitive production it would shape the way that practitioners and audiences approached Richard for the rest of the century at least. Donald Wolfit performed 'a boisterous, overplayed' Richard in 1942.[31] Wolfit was explicit about the links he saw between Richard's character and that of Hitler: 'There was the same wading through a stream of blood to his ultimate end'[32] and this appealed to the audience because 'the havoc wreaked by this Richard made sense in the context of a country consumed by war'.[33] Two years after Wolfit, Laurence Olivier played Richard in one of the definitive productions of its history at the New Theatre, London. Olivier was influenced by the way that Wolfit had responded to the current situations and characters. Olivier's production[34] can be seen as a turning point for the play in production: it marked the end of the Cibber era, '[combining] the influences of the entire Cibber tradition'[35] but in the success of this production, its extensive international touring, and the later film, Olivier also seemed to have exhausted this tradition and it was the last Cibber-style production of note.

The physical look of Olivier's Richard has become iconic – the black page-boy haircut and prosthetic nose, the slight limp and hunched back – as has the voice. Olivier used a high pitched, nasal tone, which he said he based on Henry Irving. The theatre reviewer Kenneth Tynan noted that 'Olivier's face is not especially mobile: he acts chiefly with his voice',[36] a comment that underlines the importance of this tool, which was 'slick, taunting, and curiously casual; nearly impersonal'.[37] Tynan also wrote about the physical performance, stating that '[i]n movements he is gawkily impulsive, with a lurching limp' but that 'only the arms, wonderfully free and relaxed, are beautiful'.[38] Tynan also explored the psychology of Olivier's Richard in his account of the performance, describing Richard's 'good humour'[39] but also observing the evil of the interpretation, stating that '[o]nly afterwards are we struck with the afterthought that we have just laughed at a very foul piece of casual dissembling: and we are rather ashamed'.[40] Thus, in this piece Tynan details how Olivier's Richard drew his audience in through humour and then implicated them in his evil acts.

Olivier's production, while marking a departure from the 'ordinary'[41] Richards of the previous years, was also very much in the tradition of Garrick in that it was a showcase for Olivier's talents at the expense of the other characters: however, critics noted that Sybil Thorndike's Margaret, in the single scene which the character was given,[42] 'pour[ed] the acid so generously that we were sorry to miss a second draught'[43] and Ralph Richardson performed Buckingham with 'a kind of humane splendour', but the rest of the cast was 'little more than a chorus'.[44] Tynan observed that, when the production was revived in 1949 it was 'with a vastly inferior supporting company', but he does not actually mention the company of 1944.[45] Considering Olivier's Richard has been so influential and cast such a shadow over productions of the play, there is surprisingly little written about the stage production. In 1955 Olivier turned his stage production into a film (this time directed by as well as starring himself) and it is this production, perhaps because it endures on celluloid, video tape and DVD, that most critics tend to write about.

The six years of the Second World War was a definitive moment of the twentieth century in Britain and the continued fascination with this period may to some extent explain the continued interest in *Richard III* in England – it has certainly given a great deal of imagery, iconography and context for practitioners to draw on. This chapter has, so far, focused on standalone productions of *Richard III* where the play is seen in isolation. However, some of the most significant productions of the twentieth century have involved the play in a cycle where *Richard III* is performed in its tetralogical context as the conclusion of a number of plays about the history of England. The full eight-play cycle runs from *Richard II* through the *Henry IV* plays and *Henry V* to the three parts of *Henry VI* and ends with *Richard III*. In some cases, it is only the last four plays, or tetralogy, that are covered, in others these plays have started the cycle and the *Richard II–Henry V* tetralogy has been added at a later date.[46] In many productions the three parts of *Henry VI* have been adapted into two parts and the full play of *Richard III* has been performed as the final play of a trilogy. The presentation of *Richard III* as a part of a cycle of plays can have a profound effect on how the play, its characters and the various themes of the play are performed and received.

When *Richard III* is seen as part of a long narrative which is presented over a number of plays, how the audience see the play changes: characters that seem problematic (for example, Queen Margaret who was easily cut from earlier productions including Olivier's) begin to make sense, the thematic thrust of fighting for and seizing power has a much longer background that shows a great number of characters, not just Richard, caught up in a power struggle. The characters of the play also have a longer development as many are featured in the *Henry VI* plays before *Richard III*. The design of the production is also not individual to *Richard III*. One of the most significant cycle productions of Shakespeare's plays was staged by the Royal Shakespeare Company in Stratford-on-Avon during 1963–4. Directed by Peter Hall and John Barton, the production has achieved 'the enduring status of myth'[47] and was about radical change (of theatrical norms and audiences, and of the text), which challenged institutional 'sanctions'.[48] According to Stuart Hampton-Reeves and Carol

Chillington Rutter, Hall 'discovered "political Shakespeare"…
a Shakespeare who articulated "the pressure of now"'[49] and who
was heavily influenced by the philosophy of Jan Kott the Polish
theatre critic who saw direct connections between Shakespeare
and modern European dramatists such as Brecht and Beckett.[50]
Hall and Barton's *Richard III* was in production as Kott's book
Shakespeare Our Contemporary (in which he read Shakespeare's
histories and tragedies in light of contemporary politics in Europe
in particular) was published.

Scott Colley writes that Hall found Kott's ideas 'revolutionary:
Richard of Gloucester thus becomes part of the retribution that is
visited upon England after a long period of civil disorder.'[51] The
production design reflected the modern ideas and recent history:
'a cruel, harsh world of decorated steel, cold and dangerous'.[52]
Although Hall states that '[t]he armoury of Warwick Castle was
our inspiration',[53] the set did not reflect the medieval period
but was instead 'steel walls and floors and fearsome military
technology' which, for Robert Shaughnessy, 'resonated with
echoes not only of Hitler's bunker and the gas chambers, but also
of a totalitarian near-future'.[54]

Ian Holm performed his Richard with a club foot and a humped
back but, he was also noted by Colley as being 'a type who had
not been seen before'.[55] Holm's Richard was naturally different to
others because he played the role as part of and therefore subject
to a larger narrative. In contrast to other standalone productions, this Richard was not the entire focus of the production
because *Richard III* also concluded the stories of other characters,
such as Margaret, which had been told over the previous plays.
The length of the production run also gave Holm great scope
to develop the power and authority of his performance. Holm
emphasized both the leadership ability of his character and his
madness, although he also 'maintained his innocent facade, even
during direct address to the audience' and in perhaps a menacing
manner he whispered rather than shouted.[56] Nevertheless, some
reviewers of the production invoked Olivier's Richard 'in order
to take a stick to Holm's',[57] arguing that 'Shakespeare's text has

a splendid swooping force that demands such performances as those of Olivier'.[58]

Thus Olivier's interpretation continued to dominate responses to Richard through the twentieth century. Indeed, it would be the 1980s before a performance challenged his for the title of definitive. In 1984 the RSC staged one of its most impressive seasons, including a Henry V performed by Kenneth Branagh and *Richard III* starring Antony Sher. Directed by Bill Alexander, Stanley Wells wrote that this was a 'big, bold production ... distinguished by its respect for the text, its confident but sensitive response to verbal style, and its willingness to draw on the traditions of spectacular theatre'.[59] Sher recorded his performance in a diary which was later published as *The Year of the King* which gives great insight into his process of researching, developing, and becoming Richard III. In this account, Sher describes how the ghost of Olivier's Richard haunted him throughout his journey into the character. He observes how in his sketches of himself as Richard 'What I find ... [is] the lips I have drawn are not my own, but Olivier's'[60] and, in rehearsal, on discovering that an idea to use ropes has already been done by Olivier 'I drop the idea like a hot brick and will never bring it up again'.[61] Indeed, in the Introduction to a later edition Sher observes how on re-reading the book 'I was surprised by my obsession with Olivier's Richard III'.[62]

Sher conducted a great deal of research into the character of Richard, both in terms of his physical and psychological disability, involving visits to the physically and mentally handicapped and drawing on his own experience as a 'cripple' in the previous year.[63] At various times Sher considered Richard's disability as polio, kyphosis and scoliosis and the different types of disability would in turn affect how Sher's Richard moved and how his body was twisted and crippled.[64] Thus, Sher's Richard was physically disabled with a hump and, most memorably, a pair of crutches which seemed to look like an extra pair of withered legs. Yet, although this helped to underline the disability, it was undermined by the 'interpretation which was both dazzlingly

Although reviewers wrote of the production's setting in specific terms, initially the performance was rather non-specific, indeed it was only as the play reached the point of Richard's ascendancy to king that the imagery became strikingly fascist: Richard greeted his people with a Hitler-style salute while standing in front of Nazi-style flags (bright red but with a boar on a white circle instead of a swastika); he changed his regular suits and uniforms to that of a Mosleyite blackshirt; and he was later seen in front of a nude portrait of himself which was 'an exact reminder of the self-mythologising quality of fascism'.[82] For many reviewers this was a step too far: Robert Hewison explained that 'up to this point McKellen has been developing an entirely convincing portrait of an entirely possible English fascist … but when the interpretation becomes a matter of historical comparison, the imaginative possibilities are lost'.[83] Indeed, Hewison stated that McKellen's performance moved from 'character to caricature'.[84]

McKellen provided a rather different Richard from those that had been seen before: the disability all but vanished, being only a frozen withered arm with a hand constantly clenched in a fist. There was no hump or limp but in its own way this minor affliction had a tendency to become something of a distraction as audiences watched 'how he will use his one good hand to dress, seduce or, most sinister of all, handle a Bible'.[85] Rather than a cripple from birth, and in line with other interpretations of Richard, this Richard was a warrior: he first appeared as 'a First World War officer in a full uniform, cap and greatcoat'[86] looking as though he was 'a survivor of the Somme'.[87]

McKellen's notion of national theatre as theatre that is available and accessible to the whole nation was taken up by a new theatre company in 1992 which used *Richard III* as its launch pad. Barrie Rutter founded Northern Broadsides with the audacious mission to '[interpret] the classics in a manner which makes what is often regarded as "difficult" work extremely accessible'.[88] The company, which is based in Halifax, West Yorkshire but tours to many unlikely venues which have been transformed into theatre spaces, is perhaps most famous for its use of regional accents when performing Renaissance drama. Rutter launched Northern Broadside with *Richard III* precisely because 'Richard gave Rutter the one role in the canon that "naturally" talked Northern';[89] indeed, Carol Chillington Rutter has written that 'Rutter's original Northern Richard was undoubtedly a gimmick, a way one "upstart" actor saw of legitimating his plebeian access to "royal" Shakespeare'.[90] If this is so, the gimmick paid off as Northern Broadsides were invited to perform their *Richard III* at the Tower of London for the celebrations of Shakespeare's birthday in 1994.

Northern Broadsides' *Richard III* was a high speed affair; the company prides itself on its simple approach to plays both in terms of performance and design seen, for example, in *Richard III*'s use of borrowed rugby pads for the hump, old fur coats, porters' trolleys, and boiler suits.[91] What made this a significant production though was the regional voices speaking the verse. Peter Holland observed that 'the text whistled by, concentrating on the thrill of the unfolding narrative ... the lines had an easiness and immediacy, almost a contemporaneity, in the way they seemed to fit the actors' tongues so naturally'.[92] Such an approach, although mocked by some critics, has a political end point in that 'audiences in the north of England, for whom the production had been conceived, were not required to see Shakespeare as an expression of Home Counties middle-class culture which patronised them'.[93] It is ironic then that such a regional production should transfer to London and the heartland of the 'patrons', but it speaks volumes that this production was only reviewed by the national press, thus giving it a record in the annals of performance history, when it had its residency at the Riverside Studios, London.

The history and understanding of *Richard III* as a star vehicle that perhaps defines both the actor's and the play's career has meant that when a star takes the role of Richard the combination can be electrifying. In 2001 Kenneth Branagh, after years making films, made his return to the stage as Richard III at the Crucible Theatre, Sheffield directed by Michael Grandage. Branagh had developed a career that, if not actually modelled on, at least seemed to parallel that of Laurence Olivier: he took starring roles in Shakespeare plays and later turned his stage performances into films. As Olivier had before him, Branagh had made films of his *Henry V* and *Hamlet*, and his choice of *Richard III* as a theatrical comeback prompted speculation that this too would become a film as Olivier's had (as yet Branagh has not done so, but it should be remembered that Olivier's *Richard III* was not immortalized on celluloid until 11 years after his first stage performance as Richard). It was also striking that Branagh chose Sheffield as the place for his return – not London or Stratford-on-Avon. One attraction to this regional theatre may have been the presence of Michael Grandage – a very successful artistic director with a reputation for staging classy productions of Renaissance drama which had put the Crucible and Sheffield Theatres on the map.[94]

However, reviewers of Grandage's *Richard III* found the *mise en scène* dull. Michael Dobson described the design as 'penny plain' using 'monochromatic more-or-less modern dress'.[95] This impression was seconded by Benedict Nightingale in *The Times* who called the production 'spare'.[96] Nevertheless in spite of the negative language, Michael Billington in the *Guardian* described 'astonishing images [created] through diagonal lighting or fierce overhead wattage' and talked of the set constructed of 'massy background pillars' and '[cleared] space for the central action' which took place on the Crucible's large thrust stage.[97] The reviewer for the *Evening Standard*, Carole Woddis also noted these pillars, describing them as 'looming stone' and also referred to the 'slanting light and martial percussion'.[98]

As in the past, Richard garnered the most attention. Branagh played an interesting Crouchback who was markedly different to other more recent portrayals. The production opened with a stunning *coup de théâtre*, as Dobson described:

> Branagh began delivering [the opening soliloquy] a good way towards the rear of the stage, on his back, with his feet towards the audience, while two white-coated

assistants methodically detached his wrists and ankles from
the extraordinary contraption that was his bed – something
like a medieval rack, in which, we gathered, this Richard
had to sleep every single night.[99]

This device was also referred to as 'a Heath-Robinson contraption,
part-stretcher, part-trolley, part-rack'[100] and was 'a startling
spectacle that looks, at first blush, like a kinky advertisement for
Calvin Klein male underwear'[101] because at this point Richard
was dressed only in his underpants. Indeed, Dobson went on to
describe Richard's process of dressing which accompanied his
delivery of the speech, stating that he had to 'bind himself into the
stiff straitjacket-like waistcoat which alone could brace his spine
sufficiently to keep him upright'.[102] This process, from beginning
on the rack with assistants or physiotherapists, to dressing in
his straitjacket and 'leather and steel' calliper underlined this
Richard's deformity as disability and the importance of Richard's
physical body to this production. Dobson saw disability, being
'in continual physical pain', as Richard's motivating factor.[103]
This is supported by Woddis who stated that '[d]eformity has
really driven this Richard mad'.[104] Nevertheless, Branagh played
a Richard who, in spite of physical disability, was very physically
expressive, indeed, Woddis wrote that Branagh was 'one of the
most physical I can remember',[105] and Benedict Nightingale wrote
that 'when he's desperate for Queen Elizabeth to let him marry
her daughter, his most effective ploy is to play the polio victim,
writhing painfully on the ground'.[106]

Nightingale saw Branagh's Richard as an actor, something that
a number of reviewers picked up on. Nightingale interpreted the
writhing he noted as part of the playing, while Michael Billington
wrote that the opening scene was Richard '[assembling] himself
for public display, and what we see is Richard the consummate
actor'.[107] Paul Taylor in the *Independent* stated that Branagh gave
'a very funny performance as a Richard who plays up to the
audience like a nippy music hall comedian'.[108] Many reviewers
saw this Richard as a funny character although Dobson stated

that he was 'no gleefully cocky Mr Punch' and that this 'was a Richard who was less of a satanic practical joker than any I have seen before'.[109]

Unlike previous productions, other characters did get a mention in the reviews of Grandage's production: Billington noted Claire Price as Lady Anne and Phyllis Logan as Queen Elizabeth who 'effectively [showed] their initial revulsion at Richard turning to sexual fascination',[110] and Dobson drew attention to Barbara Jefford as a Queen Margaret who 'Richard was clearly in awe of' and a Buckingham who was 'the cast's professional Machiavel'.[111] Indeed, many reviewers noted that Branagh's Richard was not particularly evil: Dobson, in what is a new twist on the exploration of Richard's evil, went so far as to say that 'it was almost as if we were watching an essentially moral person who was experimenting with evil'.[112]

The production ended as it had begun with a *coup de théâtre*. Richard slept in his rack-bed on the night before Bosworth and was wheeled frighteningly around the stage by the ghosts. At the battle the monochrome was forsaken by Richard who wore a blood red 'prosthetic musculature ... as if he were wearing someone else's powerful and half-dissected torso, complete with a line of exposed vertebrae down its back'[113] although Woddis wrote more romantically of this as 'a dashing red doublet with a prickly golden spine'.[114] This provided a flash of colour in an otherwise dark production in which the minor characters faded into each other while Branagh took the spot light.

One of the most striking productions in the performance history of *Richard III* was staged at Shakespeare's Globe Theatre in London in the summer of 2003.[115] The productions that summer were united under the thematic title of 'Regime Change' and were a season that attempted to respond to the war in Iraq which began that spring.[116] *Richard III* was staged in a repertoire that also included *Richard II* and Christopher Marlowe's *Edward II*. All three of these productions were performed by single-gender casts as part of the original practices approach that the Globe uses for some of its productions. While *Richard II* and

Edward II used the all-male casts that Shakespeare would have been familiar with, *Richard III* was an experiment – one of the first and very few times that an all-female cast has been used at the theatre and the first known production of *Richard III* which featured a woman, Kathryn Hunter, in the title role.

Before the production run began, Claire Allfree raised the issue of what all-female casting might do to the play, suggesting that 'with experimentation comes anxiety about what it all means ... there is the potential for argument about tradition vs modernity and merit vs gimmick [*sic*]'.[117] In response, the director of the production Barry Kyle asserted that an all-female cast would 'rehabilitate the notion that the female voice is also a voice of history, just one that's rarely heard'. However, in using an all-female cast to play men, this notion of the female voice of history was lost because the women were seen by the audience as men, not women: the feminine voice of history remained confined in the play to the female characters. Kyle and Hunter both believed that the all-female casting was not a major issue: Kyle stated that 'as practitioners, we see it in broader terms' and Hunter said that 'for me, it's a play about a person slowly learning that it's impossible to operate without a conscience'.[118]

The all-female casting dominated the way that reviewers responded to the production and it is now remembered for and discussed in terms of this novel approach. Lois Potter points out that *Richard III* is 'perhaps the most macho of the history plays' and it was the performance of masculinity that was at the heart of Hunter's reading of Richard. Hunter's Richard was, according to Elizabeth Klett, 'perhaps the most disabled Crookback since Antony Sher'[119] and this disability was presented as equal to the issue of Hunter's gender in creating a convincing performance of masculinity. In her review of the production Kate Bassett wrote that 'Gloucester hobbles out to eye the groundlings with a mesmerizing, assertive gait. The right hip thrusts forward with the foot permanently on its toes'[120] and Klett wrote that this physical impairment together with Hunter's very slight stature combined to create 'the impression of Richard as extremely deformed, even grotesque'.[121] Hunter suggested that a sense of failure motivated Richard, which she presented in an over-performance of sexuality: Richard would stroke his codpiece when he spoke of women as though to underline the fact that he was a man and a sexually alive one at that. That this was constantly in juxtaposition with the female gender of the performer, and that in stroking the codpiece the audience was constantly reminded of the dual gender of the actor/character underlined the inevitable failure of Richard's sexual and masculine ambitions.

Lois Potter has also asserted that whatever political message there may have been behind the production 'was lost in the general bewilderment at the effect of this casting on the female roles'. Potter discusses how the female actors were perceived by reviewers to be better at playing the male than the female roles in the production. Elizabeth Klett has also noted this odd presentation of femininity in her analysis of the all-female cast, stating that the use of make-up for female characters in *Richard III* 'reinforced the sense of femininity as drag'.[122] Alongside Hunter's performance Linda Bassett was praised for her portrayal of Queen Margaret as 'a sort of Miss Havisham with added venom'[123] and Amanda Harris as 'a superb, rabblerousing Buckingham'.[124] Aside from these performances, there was little praise from the reviewers for the rest of the cast: Meredith MacNeill's Lady Anne was criticized for being 'too stiff' while 'others in this ensemble are bland'[125] and many reviewers commented that at times the production was reminiscent of a 'school play at some posh girls' school'.[126]

Another single-gender company staged one of the first *Richard IIIs* of the second decade of the twenty-first century although not one review compared that production to what one might see at a boys' school. At the end of *Richard III*, Richmond declares that 'England hath long been mad' (5.5.23) and in 2011 Edward Hall's all-male Propeller company staged a production that was fully informed by Richmond's ideas of the madness of the nation: this *Richard III* was a diseased nightmare of the grotesque and increasingly extreme. Reviewers variously, and revealingly, referred to the set as both a hospital and an abattoir.[127] It was a dark set constructed from scaffolding, with lighting used to create bright patches in otherwise shadowy areas, gradually turning from bright white to red as the play reached its bloody climax. The cumulative effect of set and lighting design was to create a sense of fear in an anonymous threatening space which was compounded by an omnipresent chorus of masked men who filled the stage as the audience entered. They stood, crouched, sat, all cradling weapons of torture – saws, clubs, hand-drills – all watching the audience members. They all wore long, beige mackintoshes and full white face-masks covering their ears and with only holes for eyes and mouth. The anonymity of the men, the instruments they held, coupled with the set, created a powerful atmosphere of menace before the play began. The sinister sense this presence created was compounded by the way they sang throughout the production – folk songs, 'Down Among the Dead Men', '*Dies Irae*', and a lullaby for the princes.

Unlike many standalone *Richard*s which, as this chapter has shown, focus on the character of Richard at the expense of all others, this production was a more truly ensemble piece: the chorus and the other characters were as memorable as Richard Clothier's king. In part this was because of the extremity of the violence portrayed. Indeed, as Peter Smith wrote, 'this *Richard III* is not for the faint of heart'.[128] Smith noted that the violence was 'frequently outrageous' and went on to detail the atrocities:

> As the opposing factions are brought together, they toast their rapprochement with test tubes of each other's blood. Clarence is despatched not in a butt of malmsey but by having his eyes drilled out. Hastings is dismembered with a chainsaw. Buckingham is eviscerated and his ghost subsequently appears, clutching his sausage-string entrails.[129]

Smith's listing of the violent episodes has the effect of mirroring the unrelenting horror that Hall's production staged which was usually either performed or observed by the masked chorus, and the horror is evident in the fact that many reviewers also chose to simply list how each character was murdered. Body bags were a feature of the production: Rivers was bundled into a bag before being clubbed to death; Clarence's body was dumped on stage in a body bag in front of Edward and was the event which caused Edward's final attack; and at Richard's coronation he and Anne walked over a small pile of these bags, perhaps suggesting the murders instigated by Richard but their stumbling, struggling motions rendered the moment as ridiculous as the acts of violence themselves.

Indeed, Richard was not presented as having a deep sense of motivation as explanation for the violence perpetrated by him and in his name.[130] Rather, in a move which seems to bring us full circle and return to the earliest, Vice-like performances, Smith stated that 'Richard is a complete maniac ... The violence is enjoyed in and of itself rather than aiding him to the crown'.[131] Clothier was a physically attractive Richard – 'unusually tall',[132] 'a severe–yet–suave figure sporting short peroxide-blond hair'[133] – so his descants on deformity did not ring true: rather than physical disability, this production was about the nightmare of a nation. Indeed, Peter Kirwan noted the enhanced 'terrifying' presence of Ratcliffe who was 'an administrator responsible for making sure everything happened to time, he was frequently found in the abattoir surrounded by the chorus, holding up his watch until the ticking stopped, at which point he nodded for the killings to commence'.[134] What was particularly striking about this is that Ratcliffe remained after Richard had died, suggesting, as Kirwan says, 'it was administrators, not monarchs, who perpetuated the system'[135] and thus that this kind of nightmare would continue after the ascension of Richmond to the throne.

In contrast to the Globe's production in which the women playing women were criticized for their presentation, the men playing the women in Propeller's production were praised for being the 'emotional core'.[136] Indeed, the gender of the performers lent weight to the portrayal of the women: 'the female impersonation carried a plausible sense of warrior-like resolve

– because women in that cut-throat world had to be as tough as the men-folk'[137] and this was true as the heads of the two princes (performed by puppets) were presented to Elizabeth pickled in a jar.[138]

Sam Mendes' production of *Richard III* at the Old Vic, London, performed only months after Propeller's tour, was something of a relief after the gore of Edward Hall's production. Both Mendes and the star of the production, Kevin Spacey, suggested the play was relevant because of 2011's Arab Spring and the allusions that can be made between Richard and modern tyrants but, as the reviewer for the *New York Times* pointed out, the production seemed to speak more pertinently to the *News of the World* phone-hacking scandal which was featuring very prominently in the British press during the production run. That the production was concerned with alluding to the media – Richard was first seen in an armchair with Pathé news on the television in the background, and the scene appealing to the public was presented with Spacey offstage but featured on a huge cinema screen – compounded the sense that Mendes was offering a comment on issues 'closer to home'.[139] The use of television screens details how the production was staged in a non-specific modern day time frame against a largely white set which consisted of exposed floorboards and, 'eerily',[140] doors around the sides and rear: as each character met his end Margaret would mark a door with a black cross.

Spacey as Richard was the big draw and selling point of the production. His was an over-blown Richard both physically and vocally: he was bent up with a hump, had a long bald spot on his head, and was quite horribly deformed with an in-turned leg which was supported by a metal calliper and caused dependence on a walking stick. The restriction on his height because he was bent over and that he had to look up to other characters suggested something of the child about him. This played into his manipulations: Michael Billington wrote that Spacey's Richard displayed 'a power-lust born of intense self-hatred'.[141] This was evident in the seduction of Lady Anne which was not something that he enjoyed; indeed the statement 'was ever woman in this humour wooed?' (1.2.230) was to point out the fickleness of the woman rather than celebrate his own ability. This Richard was a misogynist and this moment was about humiliating and degrading Anne.

Spacey's performance received much of the attention in reviews of the production, however, unusually for the productions discussed in this performance history, the female performers also received a lot of positive attention. Haydn Gwynne was particularly singled out for her 'red-eyed'[142] performance which 'perfectly [caught] the moral revulsion of Queen Elizabeth at being enlisted by Richard'[143] and Gemma Jones was also praised for her performance of Margaret. Indeed, in spite of his praise for Spacey, Billington wrote that 'it is the women who emerge most strongly'.[144]

Although receiving critical acclaim, Mendes' production did seem heavily influenced by other productions of *Richard III*. For example, despite his physical disabilities, Spacey's Richard moved very quickly across the stage, most notably in the opening scene when he moved from his position sprawling in the armchair to the front of the stage at 'I, that am not shaped' (1.1.14). This directly echoed Sher's performance in 1984. Further, the calliper suggested Branagh, and the large portrait of Richard at the coronation brought McKellen to mind. It is revealing that many reviewers referred to Olivier in their reviews of Spacey. The headline in the *Daily Mail* read 'Showmanship supreme but, alas, Spacey is hardly Olivier' thereby bringing the comparison to the reader's mind before they began the review, and Michael Billington wrote: 'Spacey doesn't radically overthrow the Olivier concept of Richard the Satanic joker ... What he offers is his own subtle variations on it'.[145] These kinds of comparisons may have been more apparent because Olivier was director of the National Theatre when its home was at the Old Vic, however, the reviewers did not allude to this comparison, only the similarities between the performances of Richard.

What these comparisons of a current performance with a

performance nearly 70 years old do is to show the theatrical tradition that exists in the popular consciousness of what Richard is and how he should be performed. In *The Year of the King*, Antony Sher reflects on his experience of *Richard III* and states: 'I now believe that a significant part of Shakespeare's genius, and one of the reasons why his work has lasted four hundred years, is that he constantly yields himself to re-interpretation'.[146] This stage history of *Richard III* demonstrates the many, many ways that *Richard III* has been imagined on English stages over the play's 400-year history and the many, many ways that actors have interpreted and reinterpreted the role of Richard. From a Vice-like figure with no interior, to psychological studies, disability studies, and as a manner by which to make sense of the world in which the practitioners and audiences live, *Richard III* is a play that through the presentation of evil invites audiences to engage with the bottled spider at its heart.

Reviews of Productions Cited

McKellen

Michael Billington, 'Enter Richard the Blackshirt', *Guardian*, 27 July 1990.

Robert Hewison, 'Parallel Portraits produce a Dark Double Vision', *The Sunday Times*, 29 July 1990.

Peter Lewis, 'McKellen and his Foot Soldiers', *The Sunday Times*, 22 July 1990

Benedict Nightingale, 'A Very Modern Nightmare', *The Times*, 26 July 1990.

Branagh

Michael Billington, *Guardian*, 20 March 2002.

Benedict Nightingale, *The Times*, 19 March 2002.

Paul Taylor, *Independent*, 20 March 2002.

Carole Woddis, *Evening Standard*, 20 March 2002.

Globe

Claire Allfree, 'Enter His Majesty the Queen', *Independent*, 8 May 2003.

Kate Bassett, *Independent on Sunday*, 15 June 2003.

Michael Coveney, *Daily Mail*, 13 June 2003.

Lyn Gardner, *Guardian*, 13 June 2003.

Propeller

Michael Coveney, 'Two Plays Propelled by Fierce Energy', *Independent*, 7 February 2011.

Dominic Cavendish, '*Richard III/The Comedy of Errors*', *The Telegraph*, 31 January 2011.

Peter Kirwan, '*Richard III* (Propeller) @ The Belgrade, Coventry', Bardathon blog, 10 February 2011. http://blogs.warwick.ac.uk/pkirwan/entry/richard_iii_propeller/ [accessed 20 October 2011].

Peter J. Smith, 'A Self, Reflected', *Times Higher Education*, (7 July 2011), 50.

Spacey

Michael Billington, '*Richard III* – review', *Guardian*, 29 June 2011.

Ben Brantley, 'Old Stories, Spun Anew', *New York Times*, 11 July 2011.

Quentin Letts, '*Richard III*: Showmanship Supreme but, Alas, Spacey is Hardly Olivier', *Daily Mail*, 30 June 2011.

Paul Taylor, 'Mendes, Spacey and a flick of Söze – this is not the usual *Richard III*' *Independent*, 30 June 2011.

CHAPTER THREE

The State of the Art

Nina Levine

If there are any doubts about *Richard III*'s enduring popularity, recent scholarship should put them to rest. Three impressive scholarly editions have ushered the play into the twenty-first century: the *New Cambridge Shakespeare* (1999), edited by Janis Lull, the *Oxford Shakespeare* (2000), edited by John Jowett, and the *Arden Shakespeare 3* (2009), edited by James Siemon. An equally impressive collection of books and essays charts new critical directions. The historicist approaches of the 1980s and 1990s remain influential, not surprising, perhaps, given *Richard III*'s own notorious historicizing. Critics continue to explore the play in relation to the period's historical and political cultures even as the notion of 'period' is itself undergoing something of a shift, with scholars tracing continuities as well as divisions between medieval and early modern. But as much as recent criticism of the play is fascinated by the cultural landscape of an earlier time, it is also thoroughly modern, or post-modern, in its use of contemporary critical theory, as scholars draw from performance and media studies, queer theory, and disability studies, opening up the play within our own cultural and political moment.

What's abundantly clear from recent work on *Richard III* is that Shakespeare remains our contemporary. The play's relevance for modern times is an abiding refrain, not just in performances and playbills but in criticism as well. Richard's strategic terror anticipates modern totalitarianism, Jan Kott observed in the early 1960s, and the crook-backed tyrant has a long political history, recently surveyed by M. G. Aune (2008), standing in for Robert Cecil in Shakespeare's time and Nazis, petty dictators, corrupt

CEOs and disgraced presidents in our own. The play possesses 'a startling modernity', Marjorie Garber remarks in *Shakespeare and Modern Culture* (2008), in its interrogation of the power of fiction-making, for one, but also in Richard's tech-savvy intimacy with audiences.[1] Another mark of *Richard III*'s contemporaneity is its increasingly global reach, signalled by numerous international conferences and essay collections, with two excellent recent collections devoted exclusively to the play and its mediations: *William Shakespeare* Richard III: *Nouvelles Perspectives Critiques* (2000), edited by Francis Guinle and Jacques Ramel, and *Shakespeare on Screen: Richard III* (2005), edited by Sarah Hatchuel and Nathalie Vienne-Guerrin (2005).

To survey the 'state of the art' is, of course, to be selective. The World Shakespeare Bibliography Online lists over 750 items for 'Richard III' for the period between 2000 and 2011, and part of my task has been to identify key areas of critical focus within this dauntingly expansive scholarly field. Although I began sifting the material with certain themes already in mind, based on previous critical work, I was soon struck by the many new areas of interest shaping the 'state of the art'– mourning and trauma theory, for example, disability studies, and childhood studies. The topics that follow are often overlapping, and while some items intersect with several categories, others resist categorization altogether. Rather than a fixed image of recent scholarship, what follows is intended as a fluid mapping of the field that positions current work on the play not as a series of discrete essays and monographs but as part of an ongoing and often collaborative conversation.

Mourning, Memory and Trauma

Richard III is a play haunted by the dead, by the victims of civil war and cold-blooded murder who return to the living in ghostly dreams, lamentations and memories. It is also a play that is itself in the business of memorializing a traumatic chapter in the nation's past. Recent scholarship on mourning and memory in the play extends from the rigorously historical, focused on shifting relations between the living and the dead in post-Reformation England, to the psychoanalytical, bringing recent trauma theory to bear on our understanding of Richard's violence and even on the traumatic changes imposed by the Protestant reformation itself.

Stephen Greenblatt takes up the play's ghostly visitations in *Hamlet in Purgatory* (2001), in a chapter entitled 'Staging Ghosts'. Ghosts did not simply disappear with the Reformation, Greenblatt contends; instead they reappeared on stage, materializing psychic disturbances, historical nightmares and, above all, the realm of theatrical imagination. *Richard III* stages its ghosts in a series of 'spectral dreams', beginning with Clarence's nightmare and concluding with the ghostly visitations to the sleeping Richard and Richmond on the eve of the battle of Bosworth Field. Greenblatt's interest lies with terror and its power to shape the imagination of its victims, even in their sleep. Yet inasmuch as the play exposes the mechanisms of terror, in the end it defeats its own subversive power. On the eve of battle, the ghosts function as 'the memory of the murdered', not only in the mind of the tyrannical king but also in the kingdom's 'collective consciousness' and in blessing the rebel Richmond, the ghosts become 'agents of a restored health and wholeness to the damaged community'.[2] Following Greenblatt, Stephen Marche explores Richard's relation to tragedy, theatre and the determinations of history in 'Mocking Dead Bones: Historical Memory and the Theater of the Dead in *Richard III*' (2003).

As recent feminist work reminds us, it is not only ghosts who memorialize the dead in *Richard III*. Scenes of female lamentation figure importantly in two book-length studies on death and mourning in the period: Patricia Phillippy's *Women, Death, and Literature in Post-Reformation England* (2002) and Katharine Goodland's *Female Mourning in Medieval and Renaissance English Drama* (2005). Both studies situate the play in relation to the Reformation's exhortations against 'wailing the dead', decried as excessive, feminizing, and a threat to civil and religious authority, and both elaborate a dichotomy of public grieving within the play that complicates the gender dynamics of Protestant mourning practices. Phillippy argues, for example, that the women's lamentations, in challenging Richard's Machiavellian statecraft, also challenge Protestant ideals of moderate mourning – an ideal that Richard himself undermines by theatricalizing sanctioned mourning practices with his seemingly decorous tears. Although the play's close might appear to subsume female lamentation within the providential frame of Tudor propaganda, Phillippy suggests that the 'specter' of their mourning remains to trouble the political and spiritual teleologies of post-Reformation England. For Goodland, the play's representation of women's mourning is itself a form of grieving, to the extent that it registers 'a sense of loss for the medieval structure of communal mourning and remembrance that was dismantled by the Reformation'.[3] In this account, lamentation's efficacy resides not so much in its prophetic power, or in its call for divine justice, but rather in its powerful articulation of the 'collective consciousness of the kingdom', which thereby aids in its healing. Alison Thorne, in an essay on female complaint in *Richard III, King John, and Henry VIII* (2010), likewise emphasizes the role of collective memorializing in national healing.

Studies of historical trauma also look to *Richard III's* staging of memory and mourning. Steven Mullaney, in 'Affective Technologies: Toward an Emotional Logic of the Elizabethan Stage' (2007), considers the theatre's response to the traumatic aftermath of the Reformation's attacks on collective memory by generating a new 'affective technology'. He then illustrates the workings of this technology with a brilliant reading of Richard's battlefield nightmare. Misinterpreting the ghostly parade as his own conscience, Richard imagines himself to be the moral being he is not, an error that suggests at once a Protestant demystication of the sacred as the theatrical and the tyrant's mistaken recognition of his own conscience. But if Richard's sudden discovery of affect is based on a fiction, Mullaney argues, it is nonetheless real in its affective power, for him as well as for the audience who pities him. Patricia Cahill also turns to the ghostly visitations on the eve of Bosworth in the epilogue to her book, *Unto the Breach: Martial Formations, Historical Trauma, and the Early Modern Stage* (2008). What the spectral processions affirm, in Cahill's reading, is not a reassuring moral universe, as Greenblatt asserts, but an 'unalterable, endlessly repeating past', a realm of unassimilated trauma to which all, including the play's spectators, are vulnerable.[4] In ' "Shame and Eternal Shame": The Dynamics of Historical Trauma in Shakespeare's First Tetralogy' (2008), Laurie Ellinghausen draws on recent trauma theory to explore England's relation to its past in Shakespeare's first tetralogy, emphasizing the latency of traumatic experience that will only be grasped when it emerges years later, presumably in the peaceful present of the play's performance.

Questions of memory and trauma are central to Philip Schwyzer's essay, 'Lees and Moonshine: Remembering Richard III, 1485–1635' (2010). In contrast to recent work on memorializing within the play, Schwyzer sets out to explore the broader 'culture of memory' out of which *Richard III* emerged, and subsequently influenced, by charting the transmission of memories over a 150 year period, from the battle of Bosworth Field to the death of Tom Parr, reputed to be the last surviving witness to Richard's reign. Part of the story here is archival, and Schwyzer collects an impressive array of citations, starting with the personal memories of those alive during Richard's reign. Collective memories tend to operate in 20–30-year cycles, Schwyzer contends, an observation supported by the appearance of More's monumental *History of Richard III* nearly 30 years after Bosworth, following what was largely a period of silence about Richard's reign. Schwyzer next turns to the second cycle, a period of active or 'communicative' memories transmitted over several generations in the latter half of the sixteenth century, before concluding with the third cycle in the years following Shakespeare's play. Timing is everything in this account, and *Richard III*, poised at the moment when active memories of the reign were disappearing, aligns two different cycles of memory – one that looks back to Richard's reign and the other to the upheavals of the Reformation. The play's memorializing is hardly nostalgic; rather it enacts what may be a universal practice of interpreting the present in relation to a particular time in the past, as Walter Benjamin put it, 'seiz[ing] hold of a memory as it flashes up in a moment of danger'.[5]

Linguistic Performances: Curses, Promises and Silence

Wes Folkerth's *The Sound of Shakespeare* (2002) opens with an account of Henry Irving's delivery of *Richard III*'s opening soliloquy in the first sound recording of Shakespeare, produced in 1888 and now accessible on YouTube. Just as Irving's voice speaks to us from a distant past, Folkerth argues, so too do Shakespeare's playtexts record 'past acoustic events', giving voice to 'sound-scapes' from another time and place.[6] Folkerth's concern is with the ethical registers of these soundscapes or acoustic communities, and Richard's soliloquy is again instructive in that it describes the altered political landscape in terms of sound – 'stern alarums' give way to 'delightful measures' and 'the lascivious pleasing of a lute' – even as it marks the speaker's exclusion from the new soundscape. The play's actual soundscape, of course, is not exactly pleasing, except maybe to Richard's ears. Harsh and discordant, it is filled with lamentation, cursing, false accusations and the resonant silence of those who must 'not be aknowen what they know', as Thomas More famously described the citizens' much-debated response to Richard's sham election.

It's not surprising, then, that a number of recent studies have looked to the play's striking dramatization of speech acts. Kate Brown and Howard Kushner (2001) explore the 'efficacy of the curse, and its capacity to go astray of intention', in a wide-ranging essay on the poetics of cursing that links the play's maledictions to comedy routines and the eruptive cursing that can accompany Tourette syndrome.[7] Malediction offers a fantasy of performative speech – a speaking self crying out for justice – and yet to the extent that its effects lie in the future, malediction remains subject to unpredictability, as is strikingly the case with Lady Anne whose curses misfire, falling back on her. Gina Bloom explores sound's unstable materiality in *Voice in Motion: Shaping Gender, Shaping Sound in Early Modern England* (2007), delineating the divergent effects of the breath's volatility for male and female speakers. If male control is threatened by vocal instability, Bloom argues, for women, this volatility can be a source of agency, as illustrated by the movement between lament and curse in *Richard III*. To the grieving Elizabeth, who fears her words are 'dull', the vengeful Margaret counsels: 'Thy woes will make them sharp and pierce like mine' (4.4.124–5) – instruction that the Duchess of York will put to use in the next scene when she curses her son as he marches off to battle. Building on Bloom's work, Rebecca Totaro (2010) turns to humoral physiology and Aristotelian meteorology in order to explore the internal conditions that give rise to Margaret's cursing. David Schalkwyk, in 'Text and Performance, Reiterated: A Reproof Valiant or Lie Direct?' (2010), mediates recent debates about text and performance by way of Stanley Cavell's notion of 'passionate utterances'. As hybrid speech acts, Anne's curses are 'passionate utterances' mobilizing the play of illocutionary and perlocutionary speech that is also, Schalkwyk observes, a play of text and performance. Mark Robson's essay, 'Shakespeare's Words of the Future: Promising Richard III' (2005), draws on speech act theory to explore the properties of promises in the play in relation to recent critical debates about anachronism. Richard both exploits and then falls victim to the 'futural logic' of promises, as exemplified by his exchange with Buckingham in 3.1 and then with Elizabeth in 4.4. In this reading, a promise, to the extent that it depends on a temporal gap between the uttering of the promise and its fulfilment, imagines a future that is at once inevitable and unpredictable – a logic that for Robson also suggests the impossibility of choosing between critical practices of historicism and presentism.

James Siemon considers the soundscape of silence in 'Sounding Silences: Stubbs, More, and Shakespeare's Richard Plays' (2001). Concerned with silence's modalities, this essay examines a series of 'speaking silences', extending from Camden's account of

Stubbs' punishment to More's description of Richard's bid for 'election', parliamentary records, and Shakespeare's presentation of the citizens' 'wilfull silence' in response to Buckingham's appeal in *Richard III*. What these texts document is that in moments requiring assent, silence does not always signify submission. It may instead be a strong statement of disapproval and even resistance, as the citizens suggest in act 2, scene 3, when they talk freely among themselves, giving voice to their fears and opinions. The politics of assent and silence is also the subject of Ramie Targoff's essay, ' "Dirty" Amens: Devotion, Applause, and Consent in *Richard III*' (2002), which explores post-Reformation understandings of devotional consent. In Jewish and Catholic ritual, 'amen' operates as a fairly straightforward form of performative speech in which saying is doing; by saying 'amen', or 'so it be', worshippers at once affirm and appropriate the prayers of the rabbi or priest. Protestants, however, began to tie the phrase's performative efficacy to congregants' thoughts and intentions, and to discredit hollow affirmations as 'dirty' amens. Linking the play's obvious example of a 'dirty' amen – in Buckingham's call for the citizens' consent to Richard election in act 3 – to Richmond's call for affirmation in his final speech ('What traitor hears me, and says not amen?') – Targoff points to the interplay of theatrical and devotional affirmation at the play's close as audiences mixed applause with their amens, approving the play together with the Tudor reign.

In 'Conscience and Complicity in *Richard III*' (2009) Harry Berger Jr, reconsiders Richard's scene before the citizens in act 3 in relation to what he sees as the play's pervasive pattern of linguistic manipulation by which characters at once invoke and evade the call of conscience – a pattern that extends from Brackenbury, who tries not to read the commission for Clarence's murder so that he 'will be guiltless of the meaning' (1.4.86), to Clarence, who acknowledges his crimes only to shift the blame to Edward IV, to the murderers who must wrestle with their conscience, and to the self-absolving Scrivener. Although commoners have a harder time justifying their murderous deeds than the nobles, all find their rationale within what Berger, borrowing from Nicholas Brooke, calls 'the gigantic Christian machine'. Conscience is a 'force to be reckoned with' within this community, but it is also, Berger observes, 'a force the Christians *can* reckon with', fending off attacks of conscience by shifting the burden to others.[8] Aligned with providential Tudor history, the 'Christian machine' reallocates some of the work of conscience to the machinery itself – to the ghosts, Margaret, and even to Richmond at the play's end. But when the play is over, and the actor playing Richard rises from the dead to receive the audience's applause, Richard perhaps goes beyond the deterministic frame of Tudor history to live, Berger suggests, as 'a darkling entertainer'.[9]

Histories and Historicisms

Interest in *Richard III*'s relation to history, a centrepiece of twentieth-century criticism on the play, shows no sign of abating. Following E. M. W. Tillyard's study of Shakespeare's histories in the mid-1940s, much has been said about the play's historical and political contexts. Yet this does not mean that there is now consensus on the subject – either about the politics of the play and its sources or about how we read historical materials. If anything, the debates have become more complex and more attuned to operations of history and historiography. As is often remarked, the play itself displays a striking consciousness of its own place in history, in Richmond's closing prophecy of Tudor prosperity, to be sure, but also in the haunting exchange between Prince Edward and Richard in act 3 when the young prince, still innocent of his fate, defends history as a kind of eternal 'truth' that 'should live from age to age' (3.1.76). Even as the play might seem to endorse the prince's idealizing view of historical truth, it also suggests that history's 'truths' bear the shape and pressure of the times, as Phyllis Rackin persuasively argues in *Stages of History: Shakespeare's English Chronicles* (1990). It's not surprising, then, that the past decade has seen renewed attention to the historical record and the pressures at work in history's construction, with scholars looking closely at a range of historical materials and at the ways the play itself performs history on the Elizabethan stage.

A number of studies continue to explore the play's sources in terms of the broad historical and literary traditions first outlined by Tillyard. Marie-Hélène Besnault and Michel Bitot provide an overview of the play's historical legacy in an essay in *The Cambridge Companion to Shakespeare's History Plays* (2002), highlighting sources for Shakespeare's monstrous king that extend from chronicles to medieval cycles and moralities to biblical references. Dominique Goy-Blanquet, in *Shakespeare's Early History Plays: From Chronicle to Stage* (2003), offers a useful companion for those sifting Shakespeare's sources, with two chapters that summarize accounts of Richard's reign, from Polydore Vergil to More to Edward Hall and including *The True Tragedie*. Catherine Grace Canino mines new source material in *Shakespeare and the Nobility: The Negotiation of Lineage* (2007), examining the play and its chronicle sources in relation to sixteenth-century aristocratic genealogies, the compilations of family histories that were becoming increasingly popular in the period. As a member of the troubled Stafford family, Shakespeare's Duke of Buckingham is shaped by these genealogies, she suggests, in accounts transmitted by the chronicles themselves (Hall's chronicle, for example, was published a year after the Staffords were restored to the peerage and so may reflect the shift in status) and perhaps, and more immediately, by rumours in the mid-1590s of Sir Edward Stafford's nefarious espionage. Richard Wilson explores the play's Stanley connections in an essay that appears in *Shakespeare's Histories and Counter-Histories* (2006); the blatant Richard III–Robert Cecil parallels, he argues, promote the political and religious interests of the Stanleys, including Lord Strange, Shakespeare's patron at the time. Lisa Hopkins, in an essay in this same collection, sees the play as consistent with the Stanleys' on-going propaganda campaign to bolster their place in English history.

If the new historicism and cultural materialism of the 1980s and 1990s revised the critical narrative of Shakespeare's history plays by refuting assumptions of a unified and univocal Elizabethan world picture, more recent work has extended this approach by subjecting the historical record to even closer scrutiny. James Siemon, in 'Reconstructing the Past: History, Historicism, Histories' (2000), makes the case for understanding Shakespeare's historical sources as polyphonic rather than univocal, observing the gaps and dissonances embedded in the material's discursive registers. In 'Making History Memorable: More, Shakespeare, and Richard III' (2005), Andreas Höfele considers the interplay of literature and history in More and Shakespeare, exploring ways in which history is produced through language. Paul Strohm, in *Politique: Languages of Statecraft between Chaucer and Shakespeare* (2005), makes use of the chronicles to chart the continuity of sacred and secular from the late medieval to early modern periods, a position at odds with Greenblatt's contention that the sacramental experience is simply converted to the theatrical in post-Reformation England. In a chapter entitled 'Royal Christology: York's Paper Crown', Strohm persuasively follows the symbolic mobility of the crown image from the Davies or *English Chronicle* to Shakespeare's *3 Henry VI*. For those wishing to delve further into *Richard III's* sources, this analysis brilliantly models the rewards of careful attention to fifteenth-century literary and historical texts.

Studies of *Richard III* continue to reflect on the vexed question of how to understand individual plays in relation to the totality of Shakespeare's English histories. Do we see the plays as tetralogies, designed to be part of a grand narrative of Tudor nationalism, or as discrete and even fragmentary dramas, as is now commonly assumed? Nicholas Grene makes the case for a third possibility in *Shakespeare's Serial History Plays* (2002), regarding the plays as serial dramas motivated more by commercial theatre than state politics. Building on the successes of Marlowe's two-part *Tamburlaine,* he contends, Shakespeare serialized the sprawling material of the Tudor chronicles into a sequence of interlocking plays; and as a serial play, *Richard III's* closing celebration of providential destiny seems more open-ended than unequivocally final. Graham Holderness begins *Shakespeare: The Histories* (2000) by reviewing the tetralogy debates, but rather than choosing sides, his aim is to explore the plays in relation to the period's competing historiographies. With chapters that begin with *Hamlet* and end with *Richard II*, this study proceeds non-linearly and so conspicuously resists the chronologies of both chronicle history and the Folio's editors.

Brian Walsh, in *Shakespeare, The Queen's Men, and the Elizabethan Performance of History* (2009), explores the play's contribution to Elizabethan historical culture. His concern is less with historical events themselves than with the ways in which the theatre *performs* these past events. The Elizabethan history play, he contends, evinces 'a historical consciousness in which the conceptual status of the past is defined by its embeddedness in the present tense of cultural production'.[10] His approach brings recent work in performance studies together with theatre history to focus on popular history plays in the repertory of the Queen's Men, including *The Famous Victories of Henry V* and *The True Tragedy of Richard III* along with many of Shakespeare's histories. In the chapter entitled '*Richard III* and *Theatrum Historiae*', Walsh makes a case for performance itself as a mode of history. He begins by suggesting that the play invites scepticism about conventional historical modes of transmission, exemplified by More's written compilation of oral histories. In place of both oral and written history, Walsh argues, *Richard III* performs or materializes historical operations through its dense network of citations to events previously staged in *3 Henry VI*. In this account, *3 Henry VI* is not simply a past play; rather it begins to take on characteristics of the past itself, in the sense that it documents, or enacts, events that will then return as part of *Richard III's* historical memory, memories recounted by the living and the dead and, one assumes, by many in the play's audience. Walsh also considers the much discussed theatricality of the play's leading character and actor as contributing to the play's historical consciousness.

History also comes into play in several essays concerned with questions of reading, interpretation and theatricality. James Siemon, in ' "The power of hope?" An Early Modern Reader of *Richard III* (2003), gives us a glimpse of one of the play's early readers by drawing on a heavily annotated First Folio edition of the play, dating from the 1630s. In comments that mix plot summary and commonplaces, this early reader records fairly conventional attitudes towards social and political stability, matters of conscience, family relations and possibilities for hope. Elizabeth Williamson (2009) re-examines Richard's prayerbook scene before the citizens in 3.7 in light of post-Reformation anxieties about devotional texts whose very physicality risked objectifying acts of piety. Using a prayerbook as a prop, Richard's performance reiterates anti-Catholic satire by showing devotion to be a role one might play and yet, at the same time, Richard manages to deflect judgment from the dangers of theatrical performance itself. In 'Time and Talk in *Richard III* I.iv' (2005), Jeremy Lopez explores the temporal modalities of historical drama as exemplified in Clarence's murder scene. Marked by dilation – on the part of Clarence himself, recounting his dreams and then later stalling for time, and on the part of the talkative murderers – the scene makes the audience wait for the murder. Eliding 'stage time' and 'historical time', this historical tragedy stretches out stage time 'to accommodate the ominous ironies characteristic of tragedy'.[11]

Children and Childhood

Recent interest in the history of childhood has turned new attention to *Richard III*'s representations of children. The play places children at the centre of dynastic conflicts, as the promise of future succession and as innocent victims of civil war, figured by the deaths of Rutland and Prince Edward in *3 Henry VI* and echoed by the mothers who cry out for justice in *Richard III*. The play also contains an unusually large number of children's parts: Clarence's two children, the two princes, and a page – the latter the 'boy' that Richard, with characteristic irony, sends to summon Tyrrel for the murder of the princes (4.2.41). Heather Dubrow (2000) explores the play's royal children, all of whom lose their fathers, within the context of early modern surrogacy and the widespread fears that complicated the loss of parents with the prospect of a threatening guardian or stepparent. Richard, of course, is the guardian from hell and, as Ann Blake argues in 'Shakespeare and the Medieval Theatre of Cruelty' (2008), his crimes against children echo the familiar stories of Abraham and Isaac and Herod's slaughter of the innocents featured in medieval mystery cycles.

Debates about childhood's invention and its cultural history frame a number of essays. Robert Reeder (2001) considers young York and Edward in terms of conflicting attitudes towards precocious children in the period: are they wise beyond their years or puppets manipulated by adults or, as Reeder contends, does their strange attraction reside in the tension between these attitudes? In light of modern assumptions about childhood's lack of agency, Lucy Munro (2005) explores the political agency of Shakespeare's royal children in three twentieth-century films (Benson, Olivier, Loncraine). The play itself sentimentalizes the royal children with Tyrrel's report, with its strangely lyrical monumentalizing of the 'gentle babes', enshrined in each other's 'alabaster innocent arms', images reported by the murderers, who wept like children themselves at the sight of their 'ruthless butchery'. In tension with this sentimental rhetoric, however, is Shakespeare's presentation of the princes as precocious adolescents. Catherine Belsey (2007) reconsiders conventional views of the royal children as vulnerable innocents, serving only as a 'screen' on which Richard's tyranny is projected. In an age where childhood was largely unremarked, she argues, the play's representation of children is complex, ironic and ambiguous, as registered, for example, in the differences between the two princes, one cautious, the other provocatively mischievous. Joseph Campana (2007) also questions sentimental readings of the princes. Their innocent beauty in death plays up Richard's depravity, as we might expect, but it also commodifies the future along the lines of Lee Edelman's argument about children and futurity. Children in this account take on the hopes, desires and agency of others, mothers and murderers alike.

Deformity and Disability

Richard's deformities have been a persistent topic in late twentieth-century studies of the play, as critics have debated the origins, psychology,and power of Gloucester's twisted form. His body owes its shape in part to the operations of Tudor history that saw fit to mark its enemy as a malformed villain. As Marjorie Garber argues (1987), Richard's body thus encodes an historical practice that necessarily deforms and *un*forms the past. Linda Charnes (1993) extends this argument to link Richard's project to Shakespeare's: both commit themselves to constructing other versions of Richard of Gloucester separate from Tudor historiography, and it's Richard's bold attempt to remake his deformed body into the perfect body of the king that audiences find so fascinating. As Ian Frederick Moulton (1996) contends, Richard's monstrosity also bears the shape of an aggressive masculinity that refuses the boundaries of patriarchal structures and succession, glancing at Elizabeth's own uncertain succession. Robert Weimann (2000), discussing the theatrics of disfigurement, views Richard's 'unfinished' status and lack of proportion as exemplary of a doubleness in the period's hybrid staging practices. Richard's 'difference' from others is at once characterological, motivating his isolation and his compensatory ambitions, and theatrical as registered in the 'dramaturgy of his theatrical transaction'.[12] Like the medieval Vice, *Richard III* 'unfolds an ambidextrous design from within the text of the representation itself', as Gloucester's self-presentational displays turn disfigurement into agency.[13]

Building on this substantial body of scholarship, recent studies have usefully explored the play's descants on deformity within a variety of contexts. Michael Torrey (2000) considers deformity alongside early modern physiognomy to argue that Richard's paradoxical success reflects the period's increasingly complex, and increasingly ambivalent, understanding of disfigurement, as registered in writings of Francis Bacon and Montaigne, among others. Mark Thornton Burnett, in a chapter entitled ' "Monsters" and "Molas": Body Politics in *Richard III*' (2002), observes

Richard's ambivalent significations in relation to early modern monstrosity; as a figure for the body politic, Richard's 'unfinished state' offers an analogue to the succession crisis looming at the end of Elizabeth I's reign. Andreas Höfele, in *Stage, Stake, and Scaffold: Humans and Animals in Shakespeare's Theatre* (2011), uses *Basilikon Doron*, with its anxieties about public display, to link the 'visual regime of absolutist kingship' to the spectacle of the scaffold and the bear at the stake.[14] James Siemon, in his essay 'Halting Modernity: Richard III's Preposterous Body and History' (2008), draws on Bourdieu's notion of *habitus* to explore the capacity of Richard's body to figure in ways that are at once historically specific – in relation to the 1593 Dutch Church libel, for example, and libels against Robert and Cecil Burghley – and trans-historical, speaking to us across time.

Recent work in disability studies has also brought new attention to Richard's body. David Mitchell and Sharon Snyder, in *Narrative Prosthesis: Disability and the Dependencies of Discourse* (2000), dedicate a chapter to tracing the historic variations in criticism and performance of Richard's disabilities, from More to Bacon and Montaigne to twentieth-century film. Viewed within the contested space of Renaissance disability, Shakespeare's Richard is 'liberated' to fashion his disability 'as a full-blown narrative device that accrues force for his own machinations'.[15] Building on Irina Metzler's work on medieval disability, Abigail Elizabeth Comber (2010) considers the historical constraints of Richard's 'disability'. Insofar as the term 'disability' is a construction of modern medical discourse, categorizing bodies as 'normal' or 'abnormal', she argues, medieval moral constructions, to the extent that they linked physical impairment with sin, also created disabling conditions. In 'Enabling Richard: The Rhetoric of Disability in *Richard III*' (2009), Katherine Schaap Williams resists readings that understand Shakespeare's character in terms of pre-modern notions of disability and thereby equate physical deformity with moral evil. Instead, she explores Richard as a 'dismodern subject', as Lennard Davis uses the term, so as to emphasize the instability of both able-bodied and disabled selves. In this account, Richard's deformities provide him with 'a technology of performance' that he utilizes to consolidate his power. See also Robert McRuer's essay, cited below under 'Screen Richards'.

Political and Moral Philosophies

Philosopher Agnes Heller's *The Time Is Out of Joint: Shakespeare as Philosopher of Moral History* (2002) devotes a chapter to the play's dramatization of the mechanism of tyranny. Not unlike modern totalitarian tyrants, Heller contends, Richard is a rational and rationalistic tyrant. A figure of 'radical evil', he *chooses* himself as evil, an existential choice he reconfirms before his death in lines that anticipate 'a perfect Nietzschean hero beyond good and evil': 'Slave, I have set my life upon a cast, / And I will stand the hazard of the die' (5.7.9–10).[16] Tzachi Zamir's *Double Vision: Moral Philosophy and Shakespearean Drama* (2007) also explores intersections of philosophy and literature. In a chapter on *Richard III*, he too focuses on Richard's willful choice of villainy, although contrary to Heller, Zamir sees this choice not as 'radical evil' but as a love replacement, compensating for his alien and alienating ugliness. Jacques Lezra, in '*Phares,* or Divisible Sovereignty' (2006), turns to the play's closing speech to elucidate Derrida's observations about 'divisible sovereignty'. Focusing on Richmond's obscure phrase – 'All this divided York and Lancaster, / Divided in their dire division' – he positions Richmond's notion of sovereignty in relation to Richard's. While politically strategic, Richmond's apocalyptic tone in this passage also echoes patristic glosses on division in the Book of Daniel, a text Jesuit Robert Parsons draws on in his treatises.

In a comparative essay exploring conscience in Shakespeare and Nietzsche, Sandra Bonetto (2006) begins with George Bernard Shaw's observation that Richard III expresses 'the whole of Nietzsche' with his lines: 'Conscience is but a word that cowards use / Devised at first to keep the strong in awe'.[17] Anticipating Nietzsche's notion of 'bad conscience', she argues, conscience

operates in *Richard III* not as 'the voice of God in man', but as a
human construction, an instrument of control and punishment,
including self-punishment.[18] Richard Strier, in *The Unrepentant
Renaissance: From Petrarch to Shakespeare to Milton* (2011), also
cites Nietzsche in his discussion of the cheerfully unrepentant
Richard; although villainy is eventually punished, and villains do
have bouts of conscience, the play exposes the limits of a moral
framework. Ken Jackson, in ' "All the World to Nothing": Badiou,
Žižek and Pauline Subjectivity in *Richard III*' (2005), accounts for
Richard's Nietzschean aspects in terms of the Pauline distinction
between love and grace, which, he argues, furnished Shakespeare
with a grammar for understanding the 'split subject.' Joel Elliot
Slotkin, in 'Honeyed Toads: Sinister Aesthetics in Shakespeare's
Richard III' (2007), locates a source for Richard's problematic
appeal in the play's tensions between ethics and aesthetics. In
representing evil, he argues, the play combines 'malevolent theatricality' with a narcissistic 'erotics of deformity'.[19]

Screen Richards

In the mid-1990s, a constellation of *Richard III* films – Richard
Loncraine's and Ian McKellen's screen adaptation *Richard III*
(1995), Al Pacino's docudrama *Looking for Richard* (1996), and
Frederick Warde's silent film *Richard III* (1912), rediscovered
in 1996 in an Oregon basement – coincided with an explosion of
critical interest in Shakespeare and film technology. Numerous
essay collections on film Shakespeare soon followed: *Shakespeare,
the Movie* (1997), edited by Lynda Boose and Richard Burt, *The
Cambridge Companion to Shakespeare on Film* (2000), edited by
Russell Jackson, *Shakespeare, Film, Fin de Siècle* (2000), edited
by Mark Thornton Burnett and Ramona Wray, *Shakespeare, the
Movie, II* (2003), edited by Burt and Boose, and a volume devoted
exclusively to *Richard III* films, *Shakespeare on Screen: Richard III*
(2005), edited by Sarah Hatchuel and Nathalie Vienne-Guerrin.

Approaching the Shakespeare film as a *film*, rather than
simply a recording of a performance, James Loehlin takes up

Loncraine's *Richard III* in an essay, '"Top of the World, Ma'": *Richard III* and cinematic convention' (1997). Concerned with cinematic rather than theatrical conventions, Loehlin explores the film's playful and sometimes parodic riffs on the popular genres of British heritage film and American gangster movie. Barbara Hodgdon explores Shakespeare remediation in her influential essay, 'Replicating Richard: Body Doubles, Body Politics' (1998), by situating the Pacino and Loncraine/McKellen films within media culture of the 1980s and 1990s. Hodgdon's specific interest here is with how the actor's body gets coded by the doubling and redoublings of what she calls a 'collaborative body project', which brings Shakespeare's textual body together with actor, character and spectator.[20] Pacino's performance at once reprises and re-presents his cinematic past within the frame of high culture, whereas McKellen's initiates a cross-over from British stage acting to 'cinematic commodity', and so mischievously glimpses his own previous performances, in Richard Eyre's stage *Richard III* (1990), most obviously, but also in *Bent* (1990). *The Cambridge Companion to Shakespeare on Film* follows with two essays: H. R. Coursen's 'Filming Shakespeare's history: Three Films of *Richard III*' (2002), which reviews Olivier's 1955 film together with Loncraine/McKellen's and Pacino's, and Barbara Freedman's 'Critical Junctures in Shakespeare Screen History: The Case of *Richard III*' (2000), which explores the various effects of shifting media technologies on Shakespeare films and actors, from Warde's silent film to John Barrymore's soliloquy in Warner Brothers' 1929 *Show of Shows* to the films of Olivier and Loncraine/McKellen. In *Framing Shakespeare on Film* (2000), Kathy M. Howlett devotes a chapter of her monograph to the Loncraine film and its striking conjunction of fascist spectacle and film technology which, she argues, is analogous to the Tudor mythologizing of Richard's history. *Shakespeare, the Movie, II* includes an expanded version of Loehlin's earlier essay along with Thomas Cartelli's 'Shakespeare and the street: Pacino's *Looking for Richard*, Bedford's *Street King*, and the common understanding' (2003). Interested in a Shakespeare that is American in language and location, Cartelli follows Pacino into the vernacular space of city streets to consider the effects of Method acting on the language-feeling divide. Anthony R. Guneratne, in a chapter in *Shakespeare, Film Studies, and the Visual Cultures of Modernity* (2008), explores the place of Warde's silent film in American film history.

The question of the actor's body, together with Richard's much maligned form, figures into several studies concerned with the erotic politics of the Loncraine/McKellen film. Stephen M. Buhler, in 'Camp *Richard III* and the Burdens of (Stage/Film) History' (2000), explores the film's camp sensibilities and cinematic excesses, concentrating on McKellen's presentation of Richard as a sexual outsider, an alienation that helps humanize his wickedness; rather than simply reinforcing associations between fascism and homosexuality, the film examines the dynamics of closeted sexuality. Michael Friedman, in 'Horror, Homosexuality, and Homiciphilia in McKellen's *Richard III* and Jarman's *Edward II*' (2009), views the film as yet another version of 1930's horror movies associating monstrosity with homosexuality. In contrast to Derek Jarman's queer *Edward II*, the Loncraine/McKellen film, not unlike McKellen's own brand of gay politics, Friedman contends, accommodates heterosexual audiences, killing off its homosexual monster-tyrant and allowing the 'straight couple' to regain the throne. Robert McRuer, in 'Fuck the Disabled: The Prequel' (2011), complicates the liberal stance of disability studies, which locates Richard's 'problem' not in his body but in society. Instead, McRuer proposes that we bring queer theory to disability studies by way of McKellen's *Richard III* and Greg Walloch's 'Fuck the Disabled'. Both position heterosexuality as 'a laughable ruse', he argues, and show the promises of embracing the antisocial along with the pleasures of 'anti-futural plots'.[21]

Richard III films have also prompted explorations of death and cinema. In 'Cinema and the Kingdom of Death: Loncraine's *Richard III*' (2002), Peter Donaldson considers film as necropolis, drawing on Maxim Gorky's characterization of the 1896 Lumière programme as a 'Kingdom of Shadows', a 'soundless spectre'.[22]

Fascinated by early twentieth-century media technology (silent film, photography, amplified sound, wireless telegraphy), Loncraine's film explores media's use by totalitarian regimes in an allegory that extends to the present moment, in which 'media systems are integrated, protean, and ubiquitous, and in which political leadership is difficult to distinguish from media celebrity'.[23] Sarah Hatchuel, ' "But did'st thou see them dead?": performing death in screen adaptations of *Richard III*' (2005), explores the paradox of cinematic death, based as it is on a 'living corpse'. Whereas cinema often works to create a convincing picture of death, twentieth-century films of *Richard III* (Benson, Keane, Olivier, Loncraine, Pacino) have all exposed death's illusion, turning Richard's death into 'a deliberate moment of play-acting'.[24]

Proceedings of an international conference at the University of Rouen, *Shakespeare on Screen: Richard III* (2005), presents 13 essays, a DVD film by Gérard Dallez, entitled *Looking for Anne*, and a remarkably comprehensive annotated filmo-bibliography on screen adaptations and criticism by José Ramón Diaz Fernández. The essays cover a range of film and television adaptations. Ariane Hudelet and Sébastien Lefait, in essays on *Looking for Richard*, discuss the film's soundscape and its hybridized form, respectively. Essays by Mariangela Tempera and Mark Thornton Burnett explore a range of filmic references, and Kevin de Ornellas examines boar images. Michèle Willems turns attention to Jane Howell's expressionistic BBC version (1983), Dominique Goy-Blanquet reviews text and performance from Olivier's film to Pacino's, and Michael Hattaway considers the *mise-en-scène* in terms of Englishness in this same group of films. Russell Jackson examines Olivier's film within the contexts of British film industry and the coronation film, Anthony Davies reconsiders Olivier's and Loncraine/McKellen's adaptations, and Nathalie Vienne-Guerrin, building on her previous work on the play's 'evil tongues', explores cinematic representations of speech acts as visual image. Lucy Munro's essay on children and Sarah Hatchuel's on death (both previously cited) are also part of this strong collection.

Interested in mass media adaptations of the play, Saskia Kossak's *'Frame My Face to All Occasions': Shakespeare's* Richard III *on Screen'* (2005) surveys a range of twentieth-century cinema and television productions, beginning with silent Richards. Among the virtues of this study is its inclusion of less familiar titles within the list of classic productions – for example, the French silent film adaptation, *Les Enfants d'Edouard* (1910, 1914), now lost, and Raoul Ruiz's French *Richard III* (1986), which played at Cannes but was never commercially released. She also takes up television and video – Peter Hall and John Barton's *Wars of the Roses* (1965), Michael Bogdanov and Michael Pennington's *Wars of the Roses* (1989/90), and Jane Howell's *Richard III* for the BBC Shakespeare series – along with various appropriations in horror and gangster films, including the British comedy series *The Black Adder* (1983) and a number of independent 'small screen' productions in Germany, Austria and Poland, most notably *Schalacten!* (1999) and a televised version of Stefan Pucher's multi-media *Richard III* (2003).

CHAPTER FOUR

New Directions: Audience Engagement and The Genres of *Richard III*

BRIAN WALSH

The genre of Shakespeare's *Richard III* is at first glance obvious and at second glance a matter of considerable complexity. It is obviously a history play because of its subject matter and source material, and by authority of the 1623 First Folio, where it is classified in the catalogue as one of the 'Histories'. Conventions of scholarship, especially from the mid-twentieth century onward, have reinforced this designation. But as has been often noted, its structure is tragic. It was called a 'tragedy' in the stationer's entry for its earliest published form in 1597, as well as on the title page of that edition, and was referred to as such by Francis Meres in 1598. It is titled a tragedy within the First Folio itself.[1] In this chapter, I will note the implications of fixing the play to one or another of these genres, or of finding an alternative label for it, as well as of understanding it as straddling multiple descriptive categories. But my main concern will be to understand *Richard III* as most crucially belonging to the genre of the Elizabethan popular stage play, and to consider how keeping this deceptively simple fact in mind best helps us to gauge its impact and to follow its possible meanings.

I

It is not difficult to supply credentials for *Richard III*'s admission to the 'history play' category, at least as the genre has been conceived since Heminges and Condell formalized it in the Folio.[2] While it has a number of poetic and dramatic antecedents, its

ultimate sources are to be found in the great chronicles printed
in the sixteenth century, Hall's *Union* (1548) and Holinshed's
Chronicles (1577, 1587). Each of these works took the bulk of
their material on Richard's reign from Thomas More's history,
and supplemented it by drawing also on Polydore Vergil's *Anglicae
historiae* (1534) and other accounts. As early as the 1620s some
began to push back against the accuracy of these sources, and
a vigorous revisionist tradition that seeks to clear Richard of
the sinister charges put to him in them, and subsequently in
Shakespeare's play, continues today.[3] But it cannot be doubted
that in its time *Richard III* was taken to be based on a credible
historical foundation, and that it would have been regarded as
representing a segment of the 'real' English past. Aside from its
sources, the content and arc of the play relate it to other history
plays of the period from Shakespeare and his contemporaries.
Richard III explores contested kingship in medieval England,
the basic conflict that drives nearly all early modern history
plays. Understood as a history play, *Richard III* validates many
clichés about the importance of studying the past, for it provides
an easy to apprehend instance of the immoral man whose rise
and fall ought to dissuade others from similar pursuits. Insofar
as Richard's downfall is represented in the play as part of God's
providence, to understand the play as history means to understand history more broadly as providential.

Even my description of how the play might fit in the history
category, though, invoking as it does terms like 'rise' and 'fall',
points to how snugly *Richard III* fits into the tragic genre. The
play's structure follows the *de casibus* tradition popularized in
English by Chaucer and others, and which dominates the historical
poetry collection *Mirror for Magistrates*, one of Shakespeare's
influences for this and other history plays that likewise slip easily
into the tragic mode. Richard is an over-reaching tyrant who
commits bloody crimes against his own family in the best traditions of ancient tragedy. The play's world is bleak and for much
of it there is an emphasis on decay rather than growth and repro-
duction, featuring as it does murdered children and perverse

courtships. Its intensely providential structure can also work to de-historicize it for some audiences or readers, thus abstracting it into the realm of moral art. The more providential a represented world is, the more artificial it might appear to any who are sceptical about how neatly and completely God's hand shapes human affairs. The exemplary end of the arch-villain Richard and the host of unseemly and malevolent figures who die throughout the play make *Richard III* a convenient vehicle for the kind of moral instruction to which tragedy, like history, was ideally suited in the minds of many early modern thinkers, while the deaths of the innocent princes provide essential pathos and perhaps some measure of the fear and pity that lead to catharsis.

In his advertisement for the versatility of the travelling players in *Hamlet*, Polonius mentions 'history' as a type of play, but also immediately begins linking the type to other kinds of dramatic performances, including 'tragical-historical'.[4] If we are to take any of what Polonius says seriously, Shakespeare here offers a simple sounding solution to the problem of what to call *Richard III*, if not how to define such a biform genre. 'Tragical-historical' could be applied to any number of works in the Shakespeare canon. Indeed, Lawrence Danson, in his useful book on Shakespeare's genres, notes that a play like *Macbeth* could as easily be a history play as *Richard III* could be a tragedy. But he sensibly argues:

> We need not decide whether Meres, who conflates tragedy and history, or Heminges and Condell, who distinguish between them, is correct. The point is that the divisions are provisional descriptions of practices which might be described in other terms as well.[5]

In other words what is most worth discussing is not the particular case that might be made for one or another designation for *Richard III*. Rather, it is the considerable interpenetration of generic characteristics it embodies. While Meres's catalogue might 'conflate' genres, choosing tragedy as an umbrella term that can include the 'tragical-historical', Polonius' term gets at something different: explicit mixture. The deliberate mingling of genres was routinely castigated in early modern literary discourses, but the fulminations of Philip Sidney or the Italian neo-classicists did not dissuade most playwrights, as Polonius makes clear. The early seventeenth century in particular saw the rise of a decidedly mongrel form, the 'tragicomedy', which came into vogue and dominated the later end of Shakespeare's career. That category might seem far from our concerns here, but David Scott Kastan has attempted to move the discussion of *Richard III*'s genre in this direction with the somewhat startling claim that *Richard III* is a 'romance', the name that modern critics sometimes use to describe Shakespeare's later experiments in tragicomedy. Kastan concedes that this play is still 'far from the dramatic experience' of those late Shakespeare works we file under that label, such as *Pericles*, *The Winter's Tale*, or *The Tempest*. Yet he makes a compelling case for *Richard III* as a play that 'introduce[s] us to the romance vision', especially insofar as in its ending picture of the emerging Tudor line we have a

> world whose moral dimension and purpose have become clear. England has been redeemed from the evil of its past, paying for its fall from the order of grace and discovering that like so many falls in a providential universe this promises to be fortunate.[6]

Richard III as history play, as tragedy, as 'tragical-historical', even as romance. Each designation makes sense, and each potentially helps us understand the play's implications in somewhat different ways, especially if we are interested in how Shakespeare might have been using *Richard III* to explore the *idea* of tragedy, or of history, or even of the tragicomic or romance vision of life. But in many instances, I think we would find that the interpretative differences these generic distinctions confer are rather slight. The play is so obviously a mixed bag of generic conventions and contours that to press arguments much further for any one fixed generic definition of the play can yield limited returns.

Danson writes that 'Shakespeare's plays are so many explorations and experiments in the endlessly revisionary process of genre-formation'.[7] In this view, literary genres are always in flux and always on the verge of collapsing the boundaries that ostensibly separate them. They are useful organizing tools, but they are better thought of as starting rather than ending points when trying to make sense of something, for they are imperfect ways to fully assess a play's impact or range of significations.

One way forward in thinking about the question of how genre matters to *Richard III* is to broaden the sense in which we are using the term, from kind of play among other kinds of plays to the bigger sense of kind of artistic form among other kinds of artistic forms. In the case of *Richard III*, that form is live dramatic performance, a distinct means of representation from, say, what can be expressed in a painting or a printed book. Although the play has had a long, rich life as a text to be read, its proper milieu is the stage, and it was conceived to do work in that venue, under the conditions and conventions of the popular early modern theatre. In the remainder of this essay I want to examine how thinking of *Richard III* primarily in that sense, as a species of performance, can help us to see important things about how it works, in particular how it works to entice playgoers into thinking of themselves as a community, and about how communities might enable, or possibly resist, tyranny.

II

'Who is so gross / That cannot see this palpable device? / Yet who so bold but says he sees it not?' (3.6.10–12). So says the unnamed 'Scrivener,' alone on stage, after he has prepared an indictment against Lord Hastings, the working up of which *preceded* the crime Hastings supposedly committed. The doomed man's fall was rigged, and not even in an artful way. It is, indeed, a 'palpable device'. The Scrivener's scene is short, consisting of just 14 lines. It is wedged between two intense conversations between Richard and Buckingham. In the first, Richard instructs Buckingham on how to champion his claim for the throne to the London citizens gathered at Guildhall, and in the second Buckingham reports back on the chilly reception Richard's case received there. I will concentrate my consideration of *Richard III* as a species of theatre mainly on the triptych these three scenes form: the way they interrelate, and the ways they interact with the play at large.

The Scrivener's speech works on a simple level as a dramatic device that allows for a time-lapse effect between Richard and Buckingham's comings and goings. But its content is obviously of great importance in adding to the ambience of the world the play sets forth. The Scrivener castigates not just the corrupt figures who manufactured Hastings's fall, but those, himself included, who say nothing in the face of obvious injustice: 'Bad is the world, and all will come to nought / When such ill dealing must be seen in thought' (3.6.13–14). The moral neutrality that enables Richard's rise to power is one of Shakespeare's key points in *Richard III*. Brackenbury is the best example of a character who deliberately seeks an amoral remove from actions like the murder of Clarence (see 1.4.91–6) and the obviously sinister imprisoning and hiding away of the princes (see 4.1.26–7), but he has plenty of company. This is most certainly a rotten state all around.[8] The Scrivener's speech is depressing because in it he seems to confirm that despite the perspicacity of Richard's evil, the English are gripped by an inertia that is absolute and paralyzing. It is remarkable then, that the ensuing scene describes the *failure* of Richard and Buckingham's scheme to win the acclaim of the London citizens. I want to turn back now to the question of how the Scrivener's appearance and brief speech might work specifically in a performance context to help audiences reflect on the consequences of fealty before tyranny and on the possibility of resistance that the London citizens offer.

The Quarto text of *Richard III* indicates that the Scrivener carries a prop: 'Enter a Scrivener with a paper in his hand.' The previous scene had featured another prop, albeit a considerably more sensational one: '*Enter Catesby with Hast[ing's] head*'.[9] In the course of the Scrivener's speech we learn that the paper retroactively authorized the decapitation. The juxtaposition of the objects – first the grotesque and then the mundane – brought on stage by characters entering in successive scenes is chilling in the understated connection that is revealed to be between them. Just as the indictment works retroactively, the 'paper' the Scrivener carries works retroactively on audiences. As he speaks and reveals the reality of the conspiracy against Hastings, the props together forge a link between complicity in dubious legal dealings, the banality of following of orders, and the horrifying materiality of politically-motivated murder.

The Scrivener's scene brings the matter of Hastings back to the forefront just as it might begin to slip away from audience consciousness. After the head is brought on in the previous scene, and after Richard and Buckingham justify Hastings's execution to the cowed Lord Mayor, the conversation shifts. The Mayor exits, and Richard begins to discuss how Buckingham must go to Guildhall to discredit Edward's legitimacy and, by extension, that of his children. Richard then dispatches Lovell and Ratcliffe to find two other surrogates who will preach in support of Richard's claim, the infamous Doctor Shaw and Friar Penker. They exit, and alone on stage Richard resolves to

> Take some privy order
> To draw the brats of Clarence out of sight
> And to give order that no manner person
> Have any time recourse unto the princes.
> (3.5.106–9)

He then exits. Audiences might assume that when the Scrivener immediately enters carrying his paper, it has something to do with one or another of the schemes Richard has just now set in motion – perhaps the 'privy order' for Clarence's children, or the text of Shaw's speech – rather than a reference back to the Hastings matter which has already resolved in his death. In terms of dramatic structure, this reinforces the point the play makes throughout, and that it makes most explicitly on the eve of the Bosworth Field battle, that the past never really goes away, but can always reemerge to haunt the present. Audiences are reminded that memory is a painful, messy but necessary starting point for assessing and perhaps redressing the flow of current events.

The scene further highlights the public forms that Richard's machinations take. As the Scrivener says, the indictment is to 'be today read o'er in Paul's' (3.6.3). Richard organizes a series of public utterances and speeches to promote his cause. The announcement of the Hastings indictment at Paul's Cross is one; Buckingham's words at Guildhall another. Along with the references to Shaw and Penker, we see how Richard and his allies are deploying a full arsenal of public formats to circulate their propaganda. The three scenes I am focusing on here point us to mixed results for Richard, though. We don't see the indictment actually read or hear further about it, so it is safe to assume it goes without a hitch. But while Shakespeare also does not pursue the outcome of Shaw's or Penker's sermons, the failure of Shaw's in particular was reported in detail by More. That Shakespeare would reference the Shaw affair so casually without elaboration suggests his confidence that audiences could identify Richard's orders immediately with Shaw's botched attempt to legitimate Richard's desire for the throne. This reminder that Richard's road to the throne would not be without some hindrance is juxtaposed, then, with the pessimism of the Scrivener's words and the grim reality of which his prop reminds us.

The outcome of the Guildhall speech, as we learn when Richard and Buckingham return to discuss it after the Scrivener exits, bookends the Scrivener's scene with another hint that Richard's rise to power will encounter a rub:

Buckingham: I bid them that did love their country's good
             Cry, 'God save Richard, England's royal King!'
Richard: And did they so?
Buckingham: No, so God help me, they spake not a word

> But like dumb statues or breathing stones
> Stared each on other and looked deadly pale.
> (3.7.21–6)

The men discuss a political problem. Richard seeks to rally, but fails to inspire, popular support for his kingship. It is also a problem that can be understood in theatrical terms: that of a bad audience. Silence in the face of a virtuoso performance such as Buckingham describes is any acting company's worst nightmare, as an Elizabethan audience would have known. What is practically-speaking a bad audience to the men on stage, though, is morally-speaking a good audience from the perspective of the actual audience in the theatre. With historical perspective, audiences of *Richard III* can admire the citizens they hear described for their refusal to give assent to Buckingham's promotion of Richard. They see, in other words, some political bite associated with being a 'bad' audience.

This exchange between Richard and Buckingham probably works best as comedy, inspiring not just admiration but perhaps also laughter at Richard's expense, especially at Richard's vexed cry of 'What tongueless blocks were they! Would they not speak?' (3.7.42). Critics have often noted Richard's resemblance to the Vice figure of older English drama; Richard, of course, makes this association himself (3.1.82).[10] It is easy to imagine Richard's indignant complaint as one moment of contact. Richard Burbage's performance of the king as a historical character taps into memories of performance conventions of the abstraction of evil here, where his anger and exasperation at foiled cunning could produce an uproarious laugh line. If so, the Elizabethan audience to *Richard III* shows it is a good audience in the sense of being receptive to the play's depiction of a momentarily flummoxed Richard. It is an exchange that works as comedy also because audiences might connect it to the frustrations of a bad actor who cannot get a good response from the playgoers, the kind of player whom they can ridicule and dismiss from the stage. But regardless of whether audiences find Richard's reaction funny or not, it forces them to imagine the position of the auditors at Guildhall who heard Buckingham's speech, and perhaps to realize what power a crowd can have to withhold support from acts of demagoguery.

Plays within plays present spectators with images of themselves; such instances, as in *Midsummer Night's Dream*, *Love's Labours Lost*, or *Hamlet*, show to playgoers on-stage auditors to a performance, and can thus can make audiences more aware of themselves as audiences. The dynamic we see at work in *Richard III* is not so explicit. The mention of Shaw's sermon, of reading an indictment at Paul's Cross, and the planning of and then reflection on Buckingham's Guildhall speech do deliberately make the audience mindful of public orations, but in none of the instances cited here do we directly see the various audiences themselves represented. Yet the discourse on these events aimed at audiences in *Richard III* can have a similar effect to the play-within-a-play trope. The play refers to charismatic figures who, in Buckingham's words, 'play the orator', (3.5.95) or 'counterfeit the deep tragedian' (3.5.5) as they attempt to work on a crowd and shape their perceptions of the world. While the Scrivener declares, baldly, that people are capable of seeing through the manipulations of corrupt authorities but choose the easier course of ignoring the truth, the Shaw sermon and the flat response to Buckingham at Guildhall remind audiences that they have power to withhold support, and that sometimes, especially in historically significant moments, they have wielded their power in that way. In some Shakespeare plays, such as *2 Henry VI*, *Julius Caesar* and *Coriolanus*, crowd dynamics are represented cynically. Assemblies, especially urban ones, are irrational mobs, easily swayed by skillful orators. *Richard III*, at least in Buckingham's report on the Guildhall event, offers a contrasting portrait of the restrained crowd, coolly exercising its power to refrain from abetting a tyrannical usurper.

I've been considering this triptych of scenes – 3.5, 3.6 and 3.7 – in order to illustrate what I think is a useful point about *Richard III* in terms of its genre as theatrical performance. The things

I have been discussing could, in general terms, come across in *reading* the play text, or, for that matter, in reading a prose account of, say, Shaw's sermon as it appears in More, or the Guildhall business as it appears in Hall and Holinshed. As the latter reports, after Buckingham's speech 'all was husht and mute, and not one word answered therevnto'. The point comes across plainly. Holinshed goes on to quote Buckingham's assessment of this as 'maruellous obstinate silence'.[11] But to *experience* this account in the playhouse as part of an assembly of people is fundamentally different than to read it alone in a study. Theatre, of course, is distinctive as an art form that takes place in real time. It is an *event*, marked by its 'liveness', and *Richard III* harnesses the dynamics of its form's eventness to create a powerful effect on audiences: reminding them that they are an assembly of people called upon to witness and judge what they are watching and hearing. In the case of *Richard III*, this amounts largely to matters of state.[12]

Countless plays from throughout Shakespeare's era include moments in which actors address the audience, normally positing them as a collective. As one critic has recently argued, even those addresses that seem to dissect audiences into discrete parts nonetheless demonstrate how such theatrical 'self-reflexivity' is ultimately 'a tool for unifying the spectators'.[13] I am not discussing here moments of direct address to playgoers, but moments that are still self-reflexive for they induce contemplation about what it means to be an audience, whether as an assembly at Paul's Cross to hear the phony indictment of Hastings read aloud, or the London citizens at Guildhall listening to Buckingham spinning his case for Richard's legitimacy. The early modern theatre audience is, of course, notoriously easy to oversimplify, as well as notoriously difficult to define in terms of taste, levels of historical and cultural knowledge, expectations and social composition. I am admittedly using the term audience here in a non-discriminating way, in its most ordinary, encompassing meaning of everyone attending a performance of *Richard III* on a given day. This is not to assume a strictly monolithic response to the play, or to deny the power of the debates over the variegated composition of an early modern theatre audience that we find in the work of Alfred Harbage, Ann Jennalie Cook, Andrew Gurr and others.[14] We cannot ignore the reality that those attending plays could have very different *individual* experiences from those around them. But I do agree with Jeremy Lopez's assessment of early modern playgoers, that 'we can to a large extent generalize a playgoing public even while acknowledging that it was in no way homogenous', and I believe that doing so is responsive to the inevitable group dynamic that emerges among those gathered together at a playhouse during a performance.[15] Audiences in Elizabethan playhouses were, by virtue of the prevailing conditions there, intensely aware of each other, and thus of being part of a massed group, at the same time as they were aware of the happenings on stage.[16]

And what is the consequence of this gathering of people when they are aware of themselves existing in bulk? Tiffany Stern has claimed that audiences could wield life or death power over the fate of a play, citing evidence that suggests 'the spectators' 'judgment', solicited at the end of the first performance, would shape what was to be altered or cut from the play – and, more than that, would determine whether or not the play would 'survive' to be performed again.[17] Stern posits a power that comes about through being a collective. In this case, the extent of that power is rather limited. But beyond affording an opportunity to judge *Richard III* on its aesthetic merits or entertainment value, the play presents audiences with an opportunity to imagine themselves in relation to high stakes issues of how to respond to oppressive rule. Whether the power to 'damn' a play, or even the opportunity to sit in collective judgment of a monarch as he is represented on stage, could empower audiences to assume mass political power outside the playhouse is an open question.[18] But the theatrical experience that *Richard III* provides alerts audiences to the fact that monarchial power does not always – or, perhaps, does not ever – exist aloof from the collective judgment of the people. Shakespeare's Richard chases after popular support. He does not catch hold of it. His eventual rise to power seems more a product of his ability to coerce key individuals among the nobility and the episcopacy, as well as the Mayor of London. The vocal resistance to Richard offered by the many strong-willed female characters of the play represents a startlingly frank rejection of his claims and manoeuvres, but it is limited to a few aristocratic women who are related by blood or marriage to Richard, and so are hardly typical or suggestive of a wider pushback.[19] The kind of resistance evidenced by the citizens at Guildhall who refuse to acclaim him could be seen, even if somewhat obliquely, as more significant insofar as it signals a more diffuse unease and a reluctance to sign on to his agenda. His power base from then on is assured to be hollow, and his hold on the crown untenable once a more desirable candidate came forward to challenge him.

In two important moments of public address towards the end of *Richard III*, the early printed texts of the play contain an odd feature, one that lends itself to the 'literary dramatist' reading of Shakespeare recently put forth by Lukas Erne.[20] These occur when Richmond and Richard each deliver pre-battle speeches to their armies. Ahead of Richmond's we read '*His oration to his soldiers*', and ahead of Richard's we read '*His oration to his army*' (5.3.236 s.d., 313 s.d.). These directions follow the way Holinshed titles the corresponding speeches, an unusual instance of Shakespeare apparently importing some extra dramatic apparatus from his sources into the playtext.[21] While the lines appear to be aimed primarily at readers of the play, they are, I would argue, also deeply implicated in the theatrical event the text captures and disseminates. For what Shakespeare – or whoever prepared the texts for publication and supplied these directions – is doing here is recreating for the reader the theatrical moment, asking readers to imagine the lines that follow as they might be delivered to a gathered audience. The printed stage directions call attention to these moments as something special, as orations. Orations are events. The text underlines this fact, thereby imparting the condition of stage playing by reminding readers that the words of these speeches are pitched to crowds. The crowd consists of soldiers within the world the play depicts, few if any of whom would actually be represented on the stage, space and cast limitations being what they were. But the 'oration' note also points implicitly to the *other* crowd, the actual crowd that would be listening, those assembled in the playhouse where *Richard III* was performed. Both of the 'orations' seek to persuade and mobilize auditors to fight for the respective speakers. Once again, theatre audiences can imagine themselves as those who could be inspired by Richmond and his call to join the good fight against 'God's enemy', or repelled by Richard and his attempts to motivate through derision and shame: 'Shall these [Richmond's forces] enjoy our lands? Lie with our wives? / Ravish our daughters?' (5.3.252, 336–7).

Ramie Targoff has incisively examined the dynamics of audience response to some of these key moments in *Richard III*, with special attention to ecclesiastical resonances, noting that it is 'a play keenly attuned to the questions of consent that surround both devotional and political practice in the public sphere'.[22] Relevant to my interests here, she notes the silence, at least according to the play texts we have, that greets Richmond's closing speech, in which there is no scripted show of affirmation. In the final two lines of the play, Richmond proclaims 'Now civil wounds are stopped; peace lives again. / That she may long live here, God say amen' (5.5.41–2). He calls for an 'amen' to seal his legitimacy as the new English king. Given how habituated audiences were to responding in church ceremonies on cue with a cry of 'Amen', Targoff argues that Shakespeare closes the play on this note to ensure 'Henry [Richmond]'s request will be confirmed, if not from the players on the stage, then at least from the crowd in the pit'. Indeed, she writes, such collective affirmation in the playhouse was 'precisely what the theatre could offer'.[23] If audiences at the playhouse where *Richard III* was staged cried out 'Amen' to round out the play, they exerted their collective will to approve the course of English history, the defeat of the tyrant and the ascension of the Tudors. That is an easy enough choice given the depiction of Richard in the play and in English history at large, and it is certainly orthodox

Elizabethan politics.[24] But what the theatrical experience of the play as a whole can also do is prod audiences to reflect on more unsettling questions of how Richard became king in the first place. The felicitous forces of providence are nice to believe in. But the Scrivener's haunting assertions that everyone sees but no one speaks or acts out against his evil, along with the memory of Shaw's spectacular failure and the silence of the citizens at Guildhall, all call into question in different ways how inevitable Richard's reign really was. The equivocal message about whether or not the people have power to repel or undermine the political machinations of those in power is posed, and is still lingering as the play ends.

Whether *Richard III* is a tragedy, a history, or some hybrid form with an unwieldy name is not a trivial matter. Tracing how Shakespeare experiments with, bends, and remakes generic conventions is a revealing means to assess his understanding of literary traditions as well as perhaps his daring in remaking them. But in my view it is in examining his work's status as popular professional stage performances, as part of this bigger (and novel in his lifetime) category of cultural production, that allows us to appreciate most clearly the distinctive way he employs form to create affect and impart meaning. In the case of *Richard III*, the affects and meanings revolve around what it looks and feels like to witness evil ascending. It is not surprising that when in the twentieth century Bertolt Brecht wrote a play that drew heavily on *Richard III* in order to critique the emergence of Hitler it was titled *Der aufhaltsame Aufstieg des Arturo Ui*, or *The Resistible Rise of Arturo Ui*. Shakespeare does not point us so clearly to a moral, least of all in his titles, but there is circulating throughout *Richard III* the sense that for all Richard Gloucester's strange charisma and occasional tactical brilliance, his rise is indeed *resistible*. That he was briefly successful in attaining power and terrorizing his country is most often understood as a matter of providence; this is the 'angel with horns' reading of the play, wherein we understand that God is using Richard in order to accomplish some housecleaning before installing the exalted Tudor line to care for His favoured nation.[25] If such is the case, if his evil was a necessary precursor to Tudor glory, resistance to Richard would always already be a futile gesture. But I have a hard time regarding *Richard III* as a play that encourages passivity by implying that faith in the hand of God is the appropriate response to tyranny and corruption. Shakespeare may not have written Brechtian *Lehrstücke* but *Richard III* surely is meant to prompt thought about the social foundations of political power more than it is geared to assure its audiences that its providential surface is the whole story. It is the *performance* elements of *Richard III* that, I think, best help us see around the play's providential façade to some of its other connotations.[26] Approaching *Richard III* as part of its supra-genre, theatrical performance, can help us follow more acutely not just *what* it signifies but *how* the play provokes reflection in the live audience it was written to address.

CHAPTER FIVE

New Directions: Tyranny and the State of Exception in Shakespeare's *Richard III*

REBECCA LEMON

'The "state of emergency" in which we live is not the exception but the rule'.[1]
(Walter Benjamin)

Richard III boasts an exceptional body: 'rudely stamped', 'cheated of feature', 'deformed' and 'unfinished' (1.1.16, 19, 20).[2] And this body justifies, he claims, his exceptional villainy. In his opening soliloquy he chronicles how he is exiled from love-making with a 'wanton ambling nymph' (17). He is, he tells his audience, 'not shaped for sportive tricks, / Nor made to court an amorous looking-glass' (14-5), he 'want[s] love's majesty' (16), and is 'curtailed of ... fair proportion' (18). He thus rejects the role of lover and accepts what he views as his fated position: 'I am determined to prove a villain' (30). This role, he reasons, is an inevitable outcome of his body.

Shakespeare's Richard might announce that his body destines him for evil. Yet the status of Richard's historical body remains an open question, given the oft-noted efforts of Tudor propaganda to shape Richard as a consummate villain, regardless of the actual condition of his physical frame.[3] Furthermore, Shakespeare's play at the very least depicts Richard's body as much more interpretively rich than Richard's simplistic link of deformity and villainy allows. He successfully plays a broad range of parts over the course of the drama: battlefield warrior, holy man, lover, beleaguered loyalist and national ruler, each part seeming to defy the disability he argues defines him. If the

Renaissance was a period when, as many of the play's critics
have pointed out, the body allegedly announced one's moral
character – Francis Bacon's comments on the link between
deformity and villainy in his *Essays* speak to this point – Richard
is by contrast not limited but emboldened by his body.[4] He
spins tales out of it. He is thus doubly exceptional, both because
of his unusual body, and because of his malleable, and largely
political, uses of the 'deformed' frame that he argues limits
rather than enables his movements. Despite his own claims, his
own body signals to critics unruly masculinity, erotic attraction
and animal propensities.[5] It also figures political and historical
insights, about the distortions of history, the monstrosity of the
wars of the Roses, and the fears of England's political future,
as Marjorie Garber, Linda Charnes and Mark Thorton Burnett
have argued in turn.[6]

   In exploring Richard's exceptionalism, this essay contributes
to the conversation on the wide valencies of Richard's body. It
does so by arguing that Shakespeare's Richard does not only *figure*
or *represent* deformity (as critics have long argued when exploring
Richard's reputation in relation to the Tudor myth of history).
Richard rather *embraces* the political opportunities of de-formity.
Specifically, Richard's exceptional body – whether we call it a
'deformed' body as Richard does, or a particularly malleable body
– figures and indeed justifies his exercise of exceptional political
and legal rights. Richard, allegedly inspired by his own body,
embraces de-formity in all its lawless possibilities.[7] He begins the
play as an outsider – as if he were in exile from court and his own
country. But his outsider claims, which seem to gesture toward his
lack of political authority, prove the source of his supreme power
in the play. He suspends laws, in the name of his own and later
national security. He operates in a state of emergency, defying
custom and acting as the decisionist (if not legitimate) sovereign.
He determines political action even before taking the throne. He
is, thus, what Giorgio Agamben would call the exception, or the
anomie: he is the charismatic figure who manages to undermine
the law and the juridico–political order, ultimately seizing control

of the state even as he continues to label himself an outsider and a political exception.

If Freud illuminates Richard's psychological exceptionalism – Richard, he claims, is an exaggerated version of a psychic wound we all feel – this essay draws specific attention to the *political* and *legal* effects of Richard's exceptional status: Richard is and is not a usurper; he is and is not a legitimate king; he is and is not concerned with security and national stability. Richard both is a tyrant, and defies definitions of the tyrant by mingling 'necessity' and pleasure, legitimacy and charisma. If tyranny theory condemns the ruler who suspends law to suit himself, and if constitutional and state theories permit suspension of the law in times of crisis, Richard blurs such distinctions by embracing war as pleasure, and lawlessness as security, from the play's opening lines. In Richard, Shakespeare not only stages an exceptional figure; in doing so he also collapses tyrant and absolute sovereign into a character that exposes, and encourages the audience to critique, the structural dangers of exceptional rule for the law-bound state.

In approaching *Richard III* as a study in exceptional sovereignty, this essay will answer one of the play's lingering questions: why does Shakespeare so frequently draw our attention to legal procedure in such a lawless play? In a play that stages commissioned murders, several of its key scenes nevertheless hinge on conversations about law: examples include the warrant for Clarence, the confession from Hastings, the indictment from the Scrivener, and the legal status of sanctuary. At times these conversations seem unnecessarily extended, and even out of place. Why harp on the proper legal procedure, we might ask, when two murderers visit one's prison cell? Why secure a belated indictment for one courtier after failing to do so with four others? This essay addresses the peculiar status of the law in the play. In doing so it reveals what is important about rehearsing legal form, even when Richard so clearly relishes physical, social and legal de-formity. Certainly, Richard violates all sorts of forms and boundaries – this is precisely why he is so exceptional. Yet he strains to follow certain legal forms. Shakespeare's portrait of this lawless king thus draws attention to the relationship between the exceptional sovereign and the law, revealing how even tyrannical kings attempt to secure their rule through the very laws they violate. In repeatedly rehearsing the law in strained detail, the play highlights the problematic suspension of, and reliance on, law in the context of a decisionist state.

Richard is perhaps Shakespeare's most extreme form of the exceptional monarch, but he anticipates the other lawless rulers marking the playwright's tragic histories. From *Richard II* to *Macbeth* to *King Lear*, Shakespeare pressingly questions the status of the sovereign as exceptional. To the extent that a monarch can drink with any tinker (as Hal claims to do in *Henry IV*) Shakespeare applauds him. But the sovereign who claims exceptional power – be it godly, demonic, villainous or even patriotic – leads the country to national tragedy. Even exaggerated human ambition might lead, as plays such as *Coriolanus* and *Julius Caesar* reveal, to claims of extra-legal status and resulting bloodshed. In *Richard III* Shakespeare begins this long process of critiquing sovereign exceptionalism, and he does so by exploring the effects of Richard's resolute embrace of deformity in securing sovereignty.

Forms

Richard accomplishes a kind of sorcery with his body. He condemns and thralls Edward's court through references to his twisted frame. Addressing rival courtiers he cries that his arm is 'a blasted sapling withered up!' (3.4.68). Who, he demands, has 'prevailed / Upon my body with their hellish charms?' (3.4.60-1). Richard points to his allegedly deformed body to indict the court. The play's audience understands his gestures as mere trickery, but incredibly the onstage audience seems to fall for his lies. Indeed, as Michael Torrey has persuasively written, 'complicating any simple correlation between Shakespeare's play and physiognomy is the fact that Richard is a successful deceiver.' If his body should announce his villainy (at least according to some of the prejudicial theories of deformity in the early modern period), then why is the court drawn in by him? 'Despite,' as Torrey argues, 'the obvious signs of his wickedness, he repeatedly ensnares his victims . . . In the course of the play, his body alternately does and does not seem to give him away.'[8] Even as Richard insists he is 'deformed' (20), then, his physical condition effectively offers him not limitation but, as Katherine Schaap Williams helps illuminate, freedom: physical, political and even epistemological freedom.[9] Through his body he is able to play out a range of roles, disarm his opposition and evade normative demands.

Richard's distorted physical form runs in tandem with – and arguably fuels, at least according to Richard himself – his distortion of other forms, be they moral, political and legal. Marriage, succession, inheritance, and criminal trial: these legal forms are all frustrated by Richard who undermines them for his own purposes. Indeed, he makes a mockery of legal procedure, even as other characters repeatedly strain to uphold it. As a result, Richard's exceptionalism seems less a function of his body (despite his own opening justification) and more a feature of his pleasure in suspending laws, codes and conduct upon which other characters and indeed court culture rely. This section offers an exploration of his encounters with Anne, Clarence and Hastings in order to reveal how Richard transgresses legal forms before characters that, despite all evidence to the contrary, seem oddly confident in the law's effective presence.

The first example of Richard's violation of law occurs in his exchange with Anne. Critics have pointed to the wooing scene with Anne as evidence of Richard's charisma. But what has gone less remarked is how, in staging Richard's use of charismatic force to lawless ends, the scene establishes his exceptional sovereignty early on: he makes decisions in the first scene that he carries out in the second and third, exercising power of life and death over other characters. The scene with Anne initiates the chain of encounters in the play that demonstrate Richard's position of superior power outside the law. Here sanctified marriage becomes a mere vehicle for Richard. His ironic invocations of 'love' (1.2.192), family and marriage display an earthy realism in contrast to the heavy formality of Anne who follows an 'honourable load,' her husband's 'hearse' (1.2.1–2). Anne attempts to invoke the law: 'Be it lawful that I invocate thy ghost / To hear the lamentations of poor Anne' (8–9). But she demonstrates only the power to curse. Where she might charge Richard, she instead swears at him; where she might indict him juridically, she does so instead emotionally and morally. He is the 'devil' a 'minister of hell' (2.1.45, 46).

Richard proves himself such a 'devil' by running roughshod over the law. First, he flouts natural and biblical law: he plots to 'become her husband and her father', an incestuous solution to the problem of having murdered both men. Second, he mocks courtly form. Rather than deploying formulaic tropes on rosy beauty, Richard tells Anne he murders 'all the world' (126) to lodge in her bosom. This is a strange boast: Richard threatens to make himself the last man on earth in order to have her. But he marries 'not all so much for love,' he quips, 'as for another secret close intent' (1.1.158). Richard transgresses not only familial and marital codes but also rhetorical ones. His language, in its mix of romance with work-a-day colloquialism, sends up the bonds of marriage as a mere fantasy: he 'bustles' (152), he plots to secure a 'wench' (155) and he brings his 'horse to market' (160). His argumentative spontaneity and quickness contrast with Anne's static form of mourning. Indeed, his verbal ingenuity entertains and implicates us. When Anne offers 'obsequious … lament[s]' (1.2.3) and considers if it is 'lawful' to invoke her father-in-law's name, Richard views the marriage proposal as a joke: 'Was ever woman in this humour wooed?' (230). Richard deforms the mourning ritual with irreverent disdain, and he debases the marriage ritual by mocking their union. His second attempt at marriage follows the same lawless pattern when he begs the Queen to 'be the attorney of my love' (4.4.413) to her daughter Elizabeth. Here, the pretence of love disappears entirely. Forms of wooing cede to emergency measures, suspending custom: 'Urge the necessity and state of times' (416).[10]

If the wooing scenes demonstrate Richard's manipulation of rhetorical and cultural forms for his benefit, while also revealing his energetic embrace of murder, the scene of Clarence's death takes Richard's lawlessness a step further. Shakespeare draws specific and indeed extended attention to Richard's manipulation of law, and the inadequacy of legal procedure. Richard, of course, has given Clarence's hired murderers a warrant; they try to console themselves with it: '1 Murderer: "What we will do, we do upon command." 2 Murderer: "And he that hath commanded is our king"' (1.4.192–3).[11] Theodor Meron analyses this exchange thus: 'In a legal sense, the murderers thus enunciate a defence that, in modern terminology, is the justification of superior orders, reliance on the king's orders'.[12] This faith in legal procedure is, of course, misguided. Not only do the murderers trespass theological laws, but also the 'king' who govern them is not the nation's legitimate sovereign. Richard, not Edward, gave these orders: he pays the men and he supplies the warrant. Richard thus takes the law in hand, exercising sovereign power over life and death even when he is not the country's king. Furthermore, in his position as usurping sovereign, he exposes how legal forms might be simultaneously invoked and trespassed by authority.

While the murderers debate the warrant, Clarence engages even more vigorously with legal questions. He asks for the details of the legal proceedings against him:

> What is my offence?
> Where is the evidence that doth accuse me?
> What lawful quest have given their verdict up
> Unto the frowning judge? Or who pronounced
> The bitter sentence of poor Clarence' death?
> Before I be convict by course of law,
> To threaten me with death is most unlawful.
> (1.4.181–6)

Clarence asks potent questions: has a jury met and condemned him, he asks? What is the nature of this legal case, given the lack of jury, judge and evidence? But, as legitimate as such questions might be, they jar with his situation. Clarence faces hired assassins who suspend conscience for reward. He calls upon forms of law and justice in the face of what we know to be the brutality of Richard. To plead the law only exposes its deformity at the hands of the tyrant. Indeed, Clarence's questions reveal the vast chasm within the play between law and Richard's England. What good is a warrant, when it can be forged, or offered by a false authority? What good is the law when faced with hired assassins? These questions lead in one direction: toward a state of emergency, in which the executive sovereign has claimed power beyond the law. As William Carroll puts it, the play 'enacts a radical division between public manifestations of hieratic form and ritual, and the private appetites which undermine and devour them'.[13]

This scene's staging of legal deformity is all the more curious because Shakespeare deviates from his sources. Meron's cogent analysis of the play posits that this deviation helps support the Tudor myth: 'Shakespeare's decision to disregard the chroniclers concerning both the measure of Edward's blame and those forms of law that were in fact followed was deliberate. He must have sensed that the more depraved and evil Richard appeared, the greater the dramatic scope to demonize him in a superb morality tale, and to serve the legitimating purposes of the Tudor court'.[14] While agreeing with this emphasis on Richard's villainy, I think that Shakespeare's deviation from his sources has another payoff. By charting Richard's lawnessness in such detail, the scene illuminates the contrast between legal and sovereign power. Shakespeare condenses the guilt for Clarence's death in the figure of Richard both to heighten his villainy, as Meron argues, *and* to draw attention to his exercise of exceptional sovereign power. This question of sovereign power, as suggested in opening, preoccupies Shakespeare throughout his writing career. Here, in early form, Shakespeare explores how a lawless subject becomes the decisionist sovereign, determining procedure independent of legal process.

With Edward's death, England shifts to a state of political uncertainty. The country lives in 'fear of harm' (2.2.130). These times are 'dangerous' (126) since 'the estate is green and yet ungoverned' (127). In the power vacuum created by the king's passing, security must be established to allay fears and political unrest. It is, as citizens claim in the next scene, 'a giddy world', (2.3.5), a 'troublous world' (9), one suffering from 'untimely storms' (35). Hastings and Catesby agree it is a 'tottering state' (3.2.36), and a 'reeling world' (37). To quell such political unrest in the destabilized state, 'insulting tyranny' (2.4.52) takes centre stage. Richard and Buckingham seize Rivers, Grey and Vaughan, imprisoning them without a charge (2.4.48); Richard then attacks sanctuary, where the Queen and princes have taken refuge. The cardinal, reluctant to pull the Queen out of the protection of sanctuary, is told by Buckingham, 'You are too senseless-obstinate, my lord, / Too ceremonious and traditional. / Weigh it but with the grossness of this age' (3.1.44–6).The opposition here – between necessity ('the grossness of this age') and form ('ceremonious and traditional') – is a crucial political conflict in the play. The scenes with Anne and Clarence highlighted it, in the necessity for marriage and execution pleaded by Richard on the one hand, and in the forms of mourning, marriage and legal process invoked by Richard's victims on the other. To Richard, 'the age' requires suspension of the law. It is a time of corruption, demanding emergency measures. The legal, political and theatrical forms, which the majority of court members obey, yield under Richard to necessity and reason of state arguments.

Richard's manipulation of law reaches a climax with the execution of Hastings; here scenes of legal violation pile up in swift procession, as Hastings is executed, the Scrivener forges the indictment, and the citizens stand in mute response. What unites these scenes is Richard's simultaneous suspension of law, and claim to uphold it. When the Mayor queries Hastings' sudden execution, Richard responds, 'What? Think you we are

Turks or infidels? / Or that we would, against the form of law, / Proceed thus rashly' (3.5.41–3). Richard embraces deformity, not 'forms of law,' but his protest convinces the Mayor: 'But, my good lord, your graces' words shall serve / As well as I had seen and heard him speak' (62–3). He will, he claims, 'acquaint our duteous citizens / With all your just proceedings in this case' (65–6). Controlling the 'duteous citizens' (65) and the 'censures of the carping world' (68) through claims of due process and legal procedure, the Mayor aids Richard in simultaneously upholding and trespassing law. The play dramatizes such an imperative to uphold legal process even as it is undermined when the Scrivener draws up the 'indictment of the good Lord Hastings' (3.6.1).

Of course, the time gap – it took eleven hours to draw up the indictment, and Hastings has only been deemed guilty for less than five – illuminates the counterfeit nature of the charges. 'Who,' the scrivener asks, 'is so gross / That cannot see this palpable device? / Yet who so bold but says he sees it not?' (3.6.10–12). These lines draw attention to the opposition of law and power in the play; Richard's suspension of law is so established that no one, from mute citizens, to the Scrivener, to the Mayor, dares challenge him. Instead, the Mayor and the Scrivener help produce the 'palpable device', the open secret of the law's suspension. As Richard claims to acknowledge, sometimes procedure must be sidestepped; to protect law, the state must suspend it: 'The extreme peril of the case, / The peace of England, and our persons' safety, / Enforced us to this execution' (3.5.44–6). Richard upholds England as a state of law, he celebrates the 'form of law', *and* he deems this a special situation, of 'extreme peril'. Law must be suspended, during the state of emergency, in the name of safety.

Early on, Richard blames his recourse to necessity on the queen. The extra-legal measures that he takes to condemn Clarence he claims as the queen's: she is the upstart, she ignores custom, and she trespasses boundaries and law. 'This is it, when men are ruled by women' (1.1.62), he claims, preying upon the fears familiar from Goodman, Ponet, and other pamphleteers railing against the rule of female monarchs. She 'tempers' her husband to 'extremity' (65), terms that suggest both the way in which she uses emotional wiles to accomplish legal ends (arrest and imprisonment); and the way in which she ushers in an emergency or 'extremity'. Survival requires submission to female dominance: 'be her men, and wear her livery' (80). For Clarence this submission destabilizes the state: 'By heaven, I think there is no man secure, / But by the Queen's kindred' (1.1.71–2). This line of accusation culminates in Richard's claim that he and Clarence are the 'Queen's abjects' (106). The gender trouble Richard abhors allegedly justifies his closing of ranks with male courtiers; the Queen provokes the declaration of internal war. Her apparent threat prompts the emergency situation, and provides Richard with a ready excuse to marshal necessary power to restore the norms.

But of course, as I have argued, Richard's relation to norms is entirely tenuous. His physical, theatrical and legal distortion of forms is endemic. Richard claims that he suspends the law only to protect the state from the climbing Queen and her aspirational heirs, but we instead recognize his singularity as the play's supreme exception, evident from his opening speech. If the inadequate opposition of the court to Richard underlines his exceptional status, as the play unfolds, the further absence of any popular opposition reinforces it. As seen in the forged warrant, the fictive confession and the false wooing, the play creates a joke out of the law; not only do the characters seem misguided or mistaken in their belief in legal procedure, such as Clarence, but their faith in law is out of tune with the charismatic force of Richard. The humour, wit, fascination and villainous power of Richard stand in complete contrast to the bland, tedious, formalistic invocation of law by Richard's opponents.

Exceptions

How might one classify Richard's political position? Tudor commentators viewed him as a tyrant, and with good reason. Early modern political theorists from all sides of the aisle, from the absolutist Bodin to the resistance theorist Mornay, concur that there are two kinds of tyrants: one is a usurper; the other puts his own pleasure before the law. Richard seems to be both. He has murdered his way into his position as successor, and he suspends biblical and national law. Yet Richard nonetheless poses a political challenge. If a tyrant trespasses legal form, a legitimate ruler, by contrast, ascends the throne legally and rules under the law, except in a time of emergency. Richard, even as he tramples most rituals, assiduously obeys the rituals of succession, ascending the throne legally, as Carroll carefully explores. Further, Richard might suspend laws but he justifies doing so in the name of emergency, claiming to protect the state during wartime from its alleged enemies. Richard is thus at once a tyrant and a legitimate ruler.

The exception, as Andrew W. Neil writes, exposes the 'limit condition and a constitutive threshold' of political discourses and structures.[15] It is through the state of exception that the sovereign comes most forcefully into being, by suspending the law in favour of violence. In *Richard III* Shakespeare explores this state, and in doing so poses questions to which he returns again and again in subsequent plays: what are the costs of exceptional rule? How is a state compromised when a ruler suspends the law, even in the name of security? Such questions on exceptional sovereignty emerge most clearly, for the twentieth century, in the work of Carl Schmitt, who first theorized state of exception in *Political Theology*: 'Sovereign is he who decides on the state of exception', he writes. 'The authority to suspend valid law,' he elaborates, 'is so much the actual mark of sovereignty.'[16] For Schmitt, the sovereign stands outside the law. Indeed, it is precisely the ruler's exercise of extra-legal power that determines him as sovereign. But well before Schmitt, Shakespeare and his contemporary theorists were familiar with the crisis brought about by suspension of the law in the name of security, and the dangers of the decisionist sovereign, acting beyond custom. In *Richard III*, Shakespeare teases out precisely the practice and dangers of exceptional rule. Further, he perfectly represents the alluring and deeply troubling spectre of political charisma. Charisma is a quality Schmitt celebrates in a sovereign: it signals his mystical singularity. But charisma also lies at the heart of murderous dictatorships, at least according to Schmitt's primary modern critic, Giorgio Agamben. Richard's ability to disarm his audiences, and suspend law for violent ends, all the while seeming to uphold law in the form of succession and trial, exposes what Agamben writes of the relation of law to violence: the sovereign is 'the point of indistinction between violence and law, the threshold on which violence passes over into law and law passes over into violence'.[17]

The Ricardian position, of breaking the law allegedly to honour it, and endangering custom and rule of law to protect the state, anticipates Schmitt's decisionist sovereign. But, as Agamben highlights, such a political position is riven with contradiction. The state of emergency comes from the 'conviction that even fundamental law could be violated if the very existence of the union and the juridical order were at stake'; nevertheless the problem with such a conviction lies in the unleashing of violence which permanently threatens normative law: 'The normative aspect of law can thus be obliterated with impunity by a governmental violence that – while ignoring international law externally and producing a permanent state of exception internally – nevertheless still claims to be applying the law'.[18] Richard might invoke a state of emergency in his claims of necessity, and he might momentarily justify his own lawlessness in the name of security; but he equally attempts to mask over such emergency claims by recruiting the Mayor and Scrivener, for example, to attest to legal procedure. Richard is particularly eager to obey legal form in the name of 'the citizens, who haply may / Misconster ... and wail his [Hastings] death' (3.5.60–1), as Buckingham puts it.

Richard embodies Agamben's governmental violence – he allegedly breaks the law in order to uphold norms, return to laws and reinvigorate the damaged country – even as he might pretend otherwise. As he claims in his execution of Hastings, he must resort to emergency measures to protect the state but he must also, after the fact, cover his tracks. In his portrait of

Richard's duplicity, Shakespeare is particularly astute in underlining the dangers of exceptional sovereignty, not least because
the state of emergency, he exposes, is a subjective one – rather
than responding to significant political threat, Richard decries
an 'extreme peril' of his own invention. The enemies threatening
the state are his own opponents within the court. As Agamben
writes: 'Far from being a response to a normative lacuna [namely,
the insufficiency of the law in the time of crisis] the state of
exception appears as the opening of a fictitious lacuna in the order
for the purpose of safeguarding the existence of the norm and its
applicability to the normal situation.'[19] Richard creates a fictitious
threat, which the law seems incapable of addressing; and he then
suspends the law to protect the state against the very threat he
devises. He both invents legal evidence, such as the false warrant,
the doctored confession and the feigned battle; and he insists that
laws be set aside in this gross age.

Why does Richard, who flagrantly violates national and biblical
law, go to such lengths to issue warrants and indictments for
characters that are dead or powerless? Why does he continue to
obey legal form when everyone comes to recognize his villainy?
Here Agamben helps illuminate precisely the stakes in such
seeming obedience to law. As Agamben writes: 'What the law can
never tolerate – what it feels as a threat with which it is impossible
to come to terms – is the existence of a violence outside the law;
and this is not because the ends of such a violence are incompatible
with law, but because of "its mere existence outside of law." '[20]
Specifically, were Richard to expose his own lawless violence,
he might open a space outside of the law for other citizens and
subjects to act – his own reactionary violence might prompt an
opposite but equal reaction in the form of revolutionary violence,
against himself and the entire rotten state. Benjamin addresses
precisely this issue in 'Critique of Violence':'[i]f violence is also
assured a reality outside the law, as pure immediate violence, this
furnishes proof that revolutionary violence – which is the name
for the highest manifestation of pure violence by man – is also
possible' (1996: 252).[21] In the case of Shakespeare's Richard, as

analysed through Benjamin's insight, his resolute turn to law even in his moments of most egregious violence helps to mask his own lawlessness, thereby ensuring that his opponents continue to operate within the bounds of norms he simultaneously pretends to uphold and successfully undercuts.

The obedience of citizens to law and custom, contrasted with the licence of Richard in breaking it, produces political silence. The very subjects who Richard claims to protect instead cower under his authority, as we learn when Buckingham reports on his speech to the citizens: 'The citizens are mum, say not a word' (3.7.3); 'They spake not a word, / But like dumb statues or breathing stones / Stared each on other and looked deadly pale' (24–6). This silence and indeed fear of the citizens is worth investigating. Shakespeare often registers popular discontent to political tyranny in his plays: the grain riots in *Coriolanus*, Cade's rebellion in *2 Henry VI*, the London crowds celebrating Bolingbroke in *Richard II*, and the revolt of nature in *Macbeth* stage extra-governmental opposition against the errant, or even legitimate, ruler. But in *Richard III* citizens stand as mute witnesses to the sovereign's theatrical tricks. Of course, citizens offer intelligent critique of the times in the inset conversation in 2.3. But the most articulate of them, Citizen 3, resolves on a 'take shelter' mentality, saying 'wise men put on their cloaks' (2.3.32) when storms arise, and it is best to 'leave it all to God' (45). The most the citizens can do is hunker down.

At court, Richard faces a greater degree of opposition than in the streets; but he uses the threat of war as a means to silence unwanted critique: 'Either be patient and entreat me fair, / Or with the clamorous report of war / Thus will I drown your exclamations' (4.4.152–4), he tells the Duchess and Elizabeth. In threatening wartime measures so boldly, however, Richard's power begins to slip. For his exceptional sovereignty depends entirely on the lawfulness of his subjects, in contrast to his own transgressions. When his subjects recognize his own exercise of naked power, and when they shift as a result from sincere to cynical speech, and from customary to innovative behavior, then

Richard's downfall begins. At precisely the moment when he believes only he has extra-legal recourses, others grasp the upper hand in learning to violate forms as well. Thus, when the Duchess seems to promise her daughter to Richard, only to grant her hand to Richmond, and when Stanley seems to obey Richard, only to collude with the enemy, Richard is undone. What Richard's opponents learn is to harness the state of exception, and the distortion of forms, for themselves.

Conclusion

In overturning the law, Richard reveals to his audience the inadequacy of a legal solution. How can Clarence, Anne and Hastings plead law, how can Buckingham plead the contract of a promise, when faced with Richard? The only adequate response to Richard is to suspend law in kind, to answer cunning with cunning, and force with force. But this answer lies at the heart of the play's dilemma. Can rulers undermine law in the name of law? Can subjects illegally snare Richard in the name of the state? Richard's charisma, his power and his tyranny invites us as the audience to demand a suspension of law and custom, to demand a state of emergency in response to Richard's own emergency politics. As Meron writes: 'Richmond presents strong justification for the right of revolt against a tyrant, especially one that usurped the Crown and is thus an illegitimate monarch. By comparing Richard III to Machiavelli, the counselor of evil, Shakespeare emphasizes that in Elizabethan times Richard was an approved target and a ruler against whom rebellion was, exceptionally, justified.'[22] Even if the play justifies such rebellion, however, it equally reveals the dangers of the pattern established by Richard, one that undermines law and custom in such a way as to compromise it permanently. The state of exception, as Benjamin writes, threatens to become the rule or norm. Thus, even as the invading Richmond answers a fantasy – in terms of our desire for retribution and revolt against Richard – his ascension reinforces some of the more troublingly lawless aspects of Richard's reign.

Richmond is not the people's prince. Instead, undermining the law and legal recourse, Richmond's invasion signals the embrace of necessity by a handful of elite men.

Indeed, the play's two triumphant sovereigns, Richard and Richmond, stand in parallel relation to one another. Both seek the hand of Elizabeth; both usurp the crown from a ruling prince; both dream of their own exceptionalism the night before battle, one imagining himself exceptionally worthy, the other exceptionally condemned; and both deploy nationalist rhetoric based in emotion and instinct, rather than law and reason. Fight, as Richmond says, 'against this country's foes' (5.3.257) against 'God's enemy' (252, 253) the 'bloody tyrant' (246) and to save our 'children's children' (262). Fight, as Richard declares, to defend England against 'bastard Bretons' (333), a 'scum of Bretons'(318) who seek to 'ravish our daughters' (337).The play does not then end with Richard's excision from the kingdom as its sole pariah or its predetermined villain. Richard might represent a particularly stark form of exceptionalism, drawing on physical and political distortion of forms. But the play does not contain Richard's threat in his villainous body. Instead Richard's opposition becomes increasingly cunning, and men like Richmond lay claim to an exceptional status, coming from foreign exile to usurp the throne. Richard thus pollutes sovereign power, inviting even the audience to sanction lawless resistance to counter him, thereby ensuring a permanent state of exception for England. The criminality becomes, thanks to Richard's cunning, endemic.

This point puts a degree of pressure on the thesis by René Girard, that the sacrifice, the sacrificial victim, is separated and exceptional, but is also paired to the audience and community. Charnes brilliantly follows this logic to show how Richard uses the opposition of monster and king to escape his own abjection: 'The reflection Richard sees and hears in the eyes and words of others is that of a monster. To escape this constituting reflection, Richard attempts to achieve the camouflage of royal authority and see reflected back at himself the king's divine body'.[23] But this attempt at transformation fails. Richard is already scripted by sources, Charnes argues, and only confirms expectations. Yet rather than seeing Richard's role as monster and king in opposition to each other, as Charnes does (following Girard), instead we might, through Agamben, consider how pariah and sovereign function as reflections of each other. The source of Richard's charismatic power as king comes precisely from his exceptional status as 'monster'. As Richard says in *3 Henry VI*, 'I am myself alone' (5.5.83). He has 'no brother', and is like 'no brother' (80). Finally, he fails to understand 'love' a feeling 'resident in men like one another' (82), but not in him. He is the exception to the rule of love, family, and fellow feeling. Richard's suspension of familial as well as moral and legal ties is so sustained he makes a mockery of them. He instead merges charismatic power with exceptional legal claims, ushering in a state of exception that the Tudor regime proceeds to exercise with unparalleled vigour.

CHAPTER 6

New Directions: 'Some tardy cripple'[1]: Timing Disability in *Richard III*

David Houston Wood

The very need for a story is called into being when something has gone amiss with the known world, and thus the language of a tale seeks to comprehend that which has stepped out of line. In this sense, stories compensate for an unknown or unnatural deviance that begs for an explanation.[2] David Mitchell and Sharon Snyder, *Narrative Prosthesis: Disability and the Dependencies of Discourse*.

Shakespeare and Disability Studies

Disability pervades Shakespeare's literary output; whether stigmatized representations of human variation manifest inwardly or outwardly, they are ubiquitous within the Shakespearean oeuvre. Extending beyond 'Crookback Richard' Gloucester (ultimately Richard III)[3] – perhaps the most infamous example of disability in the Western tradition – Shakespeare's creative output encompasses a broad scope of disabled selfhood: from instances of blindness to limping, from alcoholism to excessive fat, from infertility to war wounds, from intellectual incapacity to epilepsy, from senility to 'madness,' from congenital deformity to acquired impairment, and from feigned disability to actual. To be sure, Shakespeare consistently treats disability in thematic gesture, but such metaphorical reliance upon disability, as pervasive as it is, and familiar or otherwise, is only part of the story.[4] Recent scholarship on medieval and early modern Europe, influenced by the groundbreaking work of disability activists and scholars leading up to and in the wake of the landmark 1990 Americans with Disabilities Act (ADA), has begun to address the methodological challenges we confront in engaging the various significations of disability within these periods.[5] This chapter begins by engaging the arc of this scholarly conversation in order to provide the groundwork for a disability reading of Shakespeare's *Richard III*. While Richard serves as the most familiar of Shakespeare's engagement with disability, his representation draws upon social stigmatization that involves a range of psycho-physiological aberrations drawn from a list of Elizabethan socio-cultural norms. Indeed, Richard's achievement in *Richard III*, such as it is, functions politically in situating his deformities at the nexus of the particularities of oppression, in that disability, as it is deployed in the play, signifies against a background that includes classical concepts of the aesthetic (the Beautiful as the Good); medical concepts of pathology (the aberrant as the monstrous); medieval concepts of the marvellous (the fear of the other); a theological tradition that situates disability as a problem requiring the miracle of healing; and in the full range of other stigmatizing traditions that reflect the complexities of non-normative embodiment and selfhood in early modern England.

These varying concepts of disability, even the very term itself, must come under keen scrutiny, however, if we are to consider their application within an early modern concept of selfhood that differs demonstrably from the subsequent Cartesian and still more recent biomedical models that have supplanted it. Early modern disability scholarship has been aided in this regard by the recent discussion of these methodological matters within medieval studies. Indeed, groundbreaking work on medieval disability representations, by scholars ranging from Irina Metzler to Edward Wheatley, from Joshua Eyler to Tory Vandeventer Pearman, clarifies some of the most significant methodological challenges a focus on Shakespearean disability must address. As manifestations of late medieval and early modern selfhood, Shakespearean concepts of identity can be construed in large part as explorations of psycho-physiological variation and difference that highlight both the complexities involved in categorizing disability in sixteenth-century England and the implications of such representations, figurative or otherwise. In this way, they confirm Lois Bragg's crucial observation that different cultures define disability differently.[6] Since human variation has always existed, however, although the meanings, metaphors, and stigmatizations that have adhered to it have varied, it will be helpful to explore here the specific ways in which early modern disability is no anachronism.[7] Disability scholarship of any period thus must begin with the premise that the disabled self is indeed a cultural product of what Rosemarie Garland-Thomson suggests are 'material, discursive, and aesthetic practices'.[8] Charting these various practices in an early modern English context enables us to engage Shakespeare in significantly new ways, and in doing so to engage this historically remote cultural imagination of disability through the topical complexities of these overlapping concerns.

One way of grappling with the scope of these topical complexities, of course, is to diminish or even to ignore them. The epigraph for this essay, for example, centres on the most valuable contribution disability studies has yet made in the field of narratology, a term called *narrative prosthesis*, which was introduced by David Mitchell and Sharon Snyder. Their definition for the term offers something approaching a universal theory of disability narrative, in which aberration from the norm, at the level of character, serves as a catalyst for narrative emplotment that seeks to account for that deviancy. Drawing on the children's tale of a conspicuously one-legged toy soldier, entitled *The Steadfast Tin Soldier*, in which a child protagonist selects to engage with this disabled soldier's story over those of the countless able-bodied soldiers, Mitchell and Snyder offer that the prosthetic narrative involves the figurative situatedness of fictional representation: 'a narrative prosthesis evolves out of this specific recognition: a narrative issues to resolve or correct ... a deviance marked as abnormal or improper in a social context'.[9] In this sense, Richard's deformities in *Richard III* might serve transhistorically as a narrative prosthetic within a play that resolves to eradicate him as a sign of deviancy.

Mitchell and Snyder proceed to suggest that the schematic of a prosthetic narrative structure is frequently four-part:

• deviance is exposed to a reader;
• narrative calls for the origin of deviance and formative consequences;
• deviance is brought to centre-stage; and
• there is rehabilitation or an effort to fix the deviance in some manner, shape, or form.[10]

There are two ways Mitchell and Snyder propose narratives grapple with such devices: since 'Disability cannot be accommodated in the ranks of the norm(als) ... there are two options for dealing with the difference that drives the story's plot: a disability is either left behind or punished for its lack of conformity'.[11] This formulation has come to be known as the 'cure or kill' phenomenon of difference as it is deployed in such narratives. It is not hard to think of the frankly apparent way in which Richard's corporeality poses an aberration within his culture, the very culture which expunges him (not *cure* but *kill*) at play's end. The overlap between disability as metaphor (as narrative prosthetic) and as embodied verisimilitude (as approaching a stable identity-category), though, is one that disability theory has been engaging productively for some time now: it will be helpful to explore how Shakespearean's representation of a narrative prosthetic might function, and in what precise ways. In other words: how can we best explore this theory of disability narrative within the Elizabethan socio-cultural moment? *Richard III* presents a more complicated response to this question than we might assume.[12]

As this overview of narrative prosthesis suggests, disability studies is interested in cognitive, physical, or sensory manifestations of difference, and thus in examining the constructed nature of the term 'normal'. Within the humanities (and that burgeoning area of scholarship known as the medical humanities), scholarly interest increasingly lies in artistic representations of such difference. As Simi Linton suggests, 'disability studies takes for its subject matter not simply the variations that exist in human behavior, appearance, functioning, sensory acuity, and cognitive processing but, more crucially, the meaning we make of those variations'.[13] Tory Vandeventer Pearman concurs, engaging disability 'as a process wherein cultural standards for normalcy dictate whether those who do not fit such standards can fully participate in their societies'.[14] In exploring what a given culture regards as 'normal', disability studies thus involves a range of applications, drawn from several fields of inquiry including medical rehabilitation, special education, social services, civil rights, the arts and the humanities. Indeed, as Linton points out, disability studies promotes a wide-ranging audience in large part because of its interdisciplinary and intersectional nature. Pursuing disability, especially within the humanities, allows us to experience what Mitchell and Snyder have described as a 'new historicism of disability representations'.[15]

Accordingly, disability studies has theorized difference in a range of ways, first explaining the meanings associated with disability by responding to the 'medical model' of disability. Joshua Eyler observes (optimistically, in the past tense) that within the medical model, 'disability was seen only as a "problem" that needed to be solved or an illness that needed to be cured'. He expresses the most significant problems with such a view: '1) this model reduces people with disabilities to objects of study, and 2) it certainly does not take into account those with disabilities who do not seek or even wish for a cure'.[16] Constructivist models of disability, as a reaction to this model, have resisted this pathologizing of difference. Such models engage disability, and disabled people, as a socio-political category defined by common experience. As Allison Hobgood and I illustrate in *Recovering Disability in Early Modern England*, these reactionary constructivist models have led to a 'New Disability Studies' which, according to Rosemarie Garland-Thomson, 'conceptualizes disability as a representational system rather than a medical problem, a discursive construction rather than a personal misfortune or a bodily flaw, and a subject appropriate for wide-ranging cultural analysis within the humanities instead of an applied field within medicine, rehabilitation, or social work'.[17] However, the New Disability Studies is not uniform in its handling of disability representations.

Two of the dominant critical perspectives in the New Disability Studies are the 'social' and 'cultural' models of disability. As Eyler explains, these constructivist models 'acknowledge both the specific, individual realities of people with disabilities and the role played by society in constructing disability by imposing definitions of normativity and ability onto the social world, which consequently limits access, in all its forms, for people with physical and mental differences'. The social model notably separates 'impairment' from 'disability', suggesting that impairment connotes corporeal difference that only becomes disability when social obstruction denies access or accom-modation for that difference.[18] Irina Metzler, in *Disability in Medieval Europe*, offers a foundational account of the social model in a premodern context. Her work, accordingly, differentiates impairment from disability, which leads her, while acknowledging the pervasiveness of impairments in medieval Europe, to make the perhaps startling claim that 'there were very few medieval disabled people'.[19] Similarly, and following Metzler, though in a Shakespearean context, Abigail Elizabeth Comber maintains in equally jarring fashion that based upon his lack of impairment the Richard of *Richard III* is not possessed of a disability: 'He forces the audience to question whether or not he even has a disability: A hunchback, the text tells us, yes; but a disability, the text tells us, no.'[20] In contrast to such stark categorizing, the cultural model of disability helpfully removes such distinctions between impairment and disability.

The cultural model, as Mitchell and Snyder observe, 'prefer[s] to use the term "disability" to include both the reality of corporeal differences as well as the effects of social stigmatization'.[21] In doing so, the cultural model treats the meanings and consequences of disability within a context determined by the ways that cultural narratives, language, and representations engage embodiment. As Eyler notes, the cultural model 'allows us to take into account the entire spectrum of experience for people with disabilities and does not force us to focus on constructed perceptions of disability at the expense of real, bodily phenomenon'.[22] In this way, the cultural model of disability, as Allison Hobgood and I suggest, 'emphasizes the reciprocity between body and culture, between lived corporeal difference and social perception of that lived difference'.[23] Eyler argues that, 'going forward', the cultural model offers what he feels to be the 'best template' for future medieval disability studies due to its 'even-handed' approach.[24]

A final way in which medieval scholarship has productively engaged disability representations shares affinities with the cultural model; identified as the 'religious model' by Edward Wheatley, it provocatively links medieval religious experience with modern medical views.[25] Wheatley identifies

> resemblances between [the] discursive power of religion in the Middle Ages and that of medicine in the modern world. At its most restrictive, medicine tends to view a disability as an absence of full health that requires a cure; similarly, medieval Christianity often constructed disability as a spiritually pathological site of absence of the divine.

Where modern medicine 'holds out the possibility of cures through development in research; medieval Christianity held out the possibility of cure through freedom from sin and increased personal faith … Thus in both 'there is a tacit implication that somehow the disabled person is to blame for resisting a cure.'[26] While Eyler rightly points out that medieval Christianity was undoubtedly far more multi-faceted than this top-down approach suggests, the link Wheatley proposes here between medieval religion and modern science is one I believe we might find helpful in grappling with the representation of disability in *Richard III*.[27] Indeed, as we turn to the early modern period, one of great transition on both religious and medical fronts, Wheatley's model offers a unique take on the explanatory power of these two concepts and their perception and treatment of disability.

But can such constructivist models of early modern disability (engaged as they are in the socio-cultural embeddedness of embodiment within a text) work in tandem with an ostensibly totalizing narrative theory of disability like narrative prosthesis? While Mitchell and Snyder encourage us to be attuned to representations of characterological difference as spurs to narrative, in other words, it is also helpful to acknowledge, as they do, that historical forms of difference manifest differently. Narrative prosthesis, too, can and must be historicized, in other words, in order to account for varying socio-cultural concepts of stigmatization. The implicit danger, as Eyler suggests, lies in forcing a set disability template and ignoring cultural context entirely: 'we must listen to what the texts have to tell us and then gauge the applicability of disability theory'.[28] So while Richard's *apparent* disabilities within the text may seem self-evident, on the one hand, his obvious stigmatization in the socio-cultural context of Shakespeare's play may mask additional historical markers of disability, on the other. These markers are undoubtedly less apparent to us today, if not invisible; and pursuing them necessitates the insights a twenty-first-century reading of the play can offer in treating *Richard III* as a disability narrative. Doing so permits us to explore the topical complexities of early modern views on disability and to demonstrate the suppleness of these views by exploring their seamless integration within a topically-informed, prosthetic narrative device.

Inwardness and Disability in *Richard III*

I cannot weep, for all my body's moisture
Scarce serves to quench my furnace-burning heart;
Nor can my tongue unload my heart's great burden,
For selfsame wind that I should speak withal
Is kindling coals that fires all my breast,

And burns me up with flames that tears would quench.
To weep is to make less the depth of grief;
Tears, then, for babes – blows and revenge for me!
(3 Henry VI 2.1.79–86)

Fascination with the 'shape' of Richard Gloucester, who dies as Richard III in 1485, continues to pervade our culture. Al Pacino's insightful documentary, *Looking For Richard* (1996), for example, offers a popular view of Richard III through a focus on the link Shakespeare demonstrates in him between embodiment and morality. Pacino's dyspeptic aide, Frederic Kimball, notably offers that 'Shakespeare has exaggerated [Richard's] deformity in order to body forth, visually and metaphorically, the corruption of his mind'.[29] In this sense, Richard's 'notorious identity' serves as the warped icon, the 'designated symptom', of the political tendentiousness of the Tudor Myth.[30] As Linda Charnes explains:

In *Richard III*, all the political monstrosity developed in the first tetralogy is "embodied" in the deformed figure or Richard. Shakespeare's audience would immediately have recognized Richard's physical deformity and moral depravity as a synechdoche for the state; and there are frequent references in the play to the "unnatural" state of political affairs and their connection to the monstrous and unnatural Richard.[31]

Charnes's stress here on the monstrous, and, still more so, on the *unnatural* – that expansive early modern English category of terror – obtains across Shakespeare's canon in the categories of prodigiousness and monstrosity by which he populates his dramatic work. Monstrosity and unnaturalness signify outwardly, of course, in corporeal representation: Stephen Greenblatt observes that Shakespeare's reliance upon characterological difference lies in the very boundary-confusion such figures generate. Indeed, the cross-dressing gender confusion deployed and displayed by Viola in *Twelfth Night*, for example, leads her to assert 'I [am a] poor monster' (2.2.32), one who decides she must leave it to 'time' to 'untangle this ... knot' (38–9).[32] It is crucial to observe, however, that Shakespeare frequently deploys such representations both outwardly and *inwardly*: as outward monstrosity based on an inward prodigious constitution.[33]

Such 'monstrosity' derives, etymologically at least, from the two Latin infinitive verbs *monere* (to warn, advise, or caution) and *monstrare* (to demonstrate, show, or note). Examples of Richard's prodigiousness and deformities, of course, famously pervade the play: by his own admission, Richard is

> not shaped for sportive tricks, / ... rudely stamped, ... /
> ... curtailed of this fair proportion, / Cheated of feature
> by dissembling nature, / Deformed, unfinished, sent before
> [his] time / Into this breathing world, scarce half made up,
> / And that so lamely and unfashionable / That dogs bark at
> [him] as [he] halt[s] by them (*Richard III* 1.1.14–23).

These deformities, as Richard enumerates them, include an arm like a 'withered shrub', a back like a 'mountain', and legs 'shape[d]' of an 'unequal size', so that he is 'disproportione[d]'[...] 'Like to a chaos' (*3 Henry VI* 3.2.156–60). Indeed, by others' accounts, Richard is an 'elvish-marked, abortive, rooting hog' (*Richard III* 1.3.227), a 'poisonous bunch-backed toad' (1.3.245), a 'bottled spider, that foul bunch-backed toad' (4.4.81), a 'hedgehog', a 'cockatrice' and a 'cacodemon' (1.2.104, 4.1.54, 1.3.143), and, repeatedly, a 'dog', a 'hog' and as his own mother addresses him: 'Thou toad, thou toad' (4.4.145). These are the familiar terms that ring in our ears – and generate uncomfortable laughter – in any given performance of the play.

Prodigiousness and monstrosity, though, accounted for a range of reactions in early modern Europe. The stigmatization of psycho-physiological impairments in the early modern period stems at least in part from what Charnes has referred to as the 'moral semiology' at work in reading deviant bodies in the early modern period: 'Since bodies *could* signify, it followed that if they can be understood as deviant they *must* signify.' In this way, Charnes maintains, from a theological perspective: 'God's warnings could also be read in the deformities of a town cripple, dwarf, leper, or hunchback.'[34] Prodigious births, as Ian Moulton has explored, generally served as God's warning or caution: but against whom? The 'marked' individual? As a threat to the culture of which the marked individual was nominally a part? While this affiliation between monstrosity and deformity, between evil and ugliness, manifests within Shakespeare's play, in other words, such views are not altogether stable during the early modern period. Indeed, writers like Michel de Montaigne and Francis Bacon offer a more secularized approach to disability, theorizing as to what Montaigne refers to as 'nature's *copia*'. While the stark, punitive view of deformity and impairment clearly signifies during the period, in other words, other views were possible. During the early modern period, there is movement away from discourses of marvellousness and wonder and a shift in attention to the medical conundrum such difference suggests.[35]

The correlation between a monstrosity that registers both outwardly and inwardly bears closer scrutiny, however, in that early modern medical texts employ 'unnaturalness' as a formal medical term, an humoral category for the psychosomatic workings of the self. Surely, that is, Richard's disability is fully apparent within the play: unless, of course, it isn't. In somatic terms, the excess heat Richard identifies within himself in my second epigraph – in his 'furnace-burning heart' and the 'coals that fires all [his] breast' – functions as a dangerous symptom that signifies medically in early modern England. Indeed, the relationship between that heat and Richard's lack of tears hinges upon the dynamic construct of embodied selfhood espoused by humoral theory, which blossomed in the early modern period from classical origins. It is worth noting that the very concept of the material self as understood within humoral theory, in the relative mixture of the four principal humours (choler, sanguinity, melancholy and phlegm), is implicitly based upon aberration: excesses or deficiencies of these humoral components, early modern medical theorists insist, manifestly explain the very concept of character, as well as health and illness.[36] The normative states of flux and volatility that characterize early modern selfhood within humoral theory, after all, centre upon their involvement with a range of environmental stimuli – such as relative caloric and moisture registers – that is especially worthy of consideration in a disability context.

Indeed, the very porousness by which such humoral selves were conceived grants them what can best be understood as a nearly unattainable ideal of normalcy; while the salubrious goal of individual health is an apparently rare humoral equipoise, such moments of stasis are belied by the ostensible norms of humoral imbalance. The principal feature of humoral constitution, then, involved a tendency towards often sudden and dangerous alteration. The etymologically derivative concepts *tempus, temperatura, temperamentum* (time, temperature, and the humours) thus figured humoral selfhood as an uneasy construct that established early modern selves as emotionally volatile beings. In fact, early modern theorists categorized each of the humours into 'natural' and 'unnatural' forms in order to account for alterations in character. Outside agents such as wine and music, drawn from the Galenic non-naturals, were understood to introduce a potentially dangerous volatility to early modern selves. The sudden caloric escalations associated with wine-drinking, for example, were thought to increase heat and thus to promote health in many, but, for others, to lead to an humoral scorching, or adustion, by means of wine's sudden action upon the humours. It was perceived, that is, as a causative agent in promoting 'unnatural' humours that could facilitate horrific acts of rage and bloodshed.[37]

In this sense, early modern categories of disability, like early modern selves, must be perceived as far more labile and open to external influences than we today presume them to be. Indeed, diurnal and seasonal regimens prescribed by late medieval and early modern physicians – that of 'purging' choler through bleeding, for example – indicates that before the discovery of the circulation of the blood by William Harvey in 1628, and the gradual implementation of such observation-driven science over the course of the latter half of the seventeenth and eighteenth centuries, the interactive flux of self and environment that constitutes early modern selfhood bears heavily on concepts of embodied disability, as well. As Gail Kern Paster and John Sutton have shown, the shift from the humoral concept of the self to the Cartesian mode, while far from immediate, was remarkable. With this shift, the concept of the self changed from one of an essentially open apparatus enmeshed with its environment, to an estranged concept of the self that stressed both its mind–body duality and its isolation from the environment.[38]

Richard's reaction to his father's death involves such a self-narrative of humoral dynamism, hinging upon caloric and moisture volatilities. In contrast to Macduff's explanation in *Macbeth*, for example, regarding his ostensibly healthy need to shed tears at news of his family's slaughter or to Laertes's in *Hamlet* as he views the 'distracted' Ophelia or to Lear's in *King Lear* based upon his daughters' betrayal, Richard claims he feels the pang of his father's loss so severely that his tears have dried up altogether. He can yield none: 'I cannot weep', he exclaims, a point Ian Moulton addresses:

> After his father's death Richard's physical abnormality – his monstrosity – obtains inwardly as well as outwardly: his humoral imbalance, his excessive heat, is just as monstrous as his crooked back and withered arm. His physical monstrosity manifests itself as social monstrosity.[39]

Subsequently, of course, in *Richard III*, Richard proudly recalls this moment in which he had mastered his tears. Reflecting on that moment of his father's death, in *3 Henry VI*, Richard here proudly observes:

> all the standers-by had wet their cheeks
> Like trees bedashed with rain – in that sad time
> My manly eyes did scorn an humble tear...
>
> (*Richard III* 1.2.165–7)

His hypermasculine heat, he claims, had dried up his effeminate tears. According to Moulton, Richard 'believes his deformity sets him apart from others, but instead it is his aggressively masculine singularity that constitutes his monstrosity'.[40] Recognizing that this prodigiousness manifests both inwardly and outwardly, that it capitalises on both physical deformity and his self-narrated, inward humoral 'unnaturalness', helps broaden the scope of the ways in which we might examine his prodigiousness as a narrative prosthetic.

The ostensible depth Shakespeare grants Richard here should not surprise us, though. Richard, after all, is famous for serving as Shakespeare's first 'dense' character, and, as in this passage, a great part of what makes him so involves his soliloquies. Although the inwardly dynamic, humoral drama Richard narrates in this passage explores that inwardness, this ostensible representation of inwardness cannot, nor should not, be divorced from his fundamental role as the stock villain and Vice figure in the play, as Charnes has shown: Richard is possessed of a form of inwardness paradoxically *because* he can play off such a stable, 'notorious identity'.[41] And it is paradoxically his identity as deformed recipient of Tudor outrage which permits Shakespeare to complexify him as a character. In constructing a Richard that pushes beyond the established bounds of the figure of the medieval Vice, in other words, Shakespeare appears both to deploy and then to counter the religious model of medieval disability offered by Edward Wheatley, which suggests that medieval literature generally features 'exemplary texts featuring characters with disabilities [that] do not engage in what readers would call "characterization" of them; they remain flat and emblematic, the site where God's work can be made manifest'.[42] Since such characters tend not to alter or to demonstrate great depth within the medieval tradition, according to Wheatley, Shakespearean narrative prosthesis appears to signify differently. Accordingly, if Shakespeare's *Richard III* adheres in any sense to Mitchell and Snyder's theory of narrative prosthesis, then in doing so it must hinge upon a unique, Shakespearean form of characterization;

a unique, Shakespearean form of narrative prosthesis; or both. Where these concerns conjoin in *Richard III* hinges upon the overlap between plot and character (Aristotle's *mythos* and *ethos*), and thus centres, quite pointedly, upon the matter of time.

Time, Narrative and Disability in *Richard III*

Richard's self-identification as childlike – in framing himself 'as a child' (2.2.153), as 'too childish-foolish for this world' (1.3.141), as 'the infant that is born to night' (2.1.73), and in the sentiment evoked subsequently by a citizen (speaking of Prince Edward) as a curse: 'Woe to that land that's governed by a child' (2.3.11) –relies upon a form of temporal idealization, of nostalgia, that we see most profoundly perhaps in Shakespeare's haunting link with the past between the 'twinned lambs', Leontes and Polixenes, in *The Winter's Tale* (1.2.69).[43] In figuring himself with the moral probity of a child, Shakespeare's Richard uses time both metaphorically and subjectively. Such expressions of time are a distinct feature of the apparent density of Shakespearean characterization and are abetted by an early modern medical theory whose reliance upon, and manipulation of, temporal concepts is just recently coming under scrutiny.[44] However, rather than focus on the play's representations of historiography, Christian eschatology, and providentialism – in tracing Fortune's wheel, for example, or in Queen Margaret's representation as history's return of the repressed – it will be helpful to address the ways that Shakespeare employs time and temporality within the narrative prosthesis that fans out across the play in a subjectively-charged manner.

Whether in tracing its arc as narrative, its role in shaping prophecy, or its subjectifying impulse with regard to respective characters, time functions in a range of ways in *Richard III*. Intriguingly, each helps us account for Shakespeare's handling of narrative prosthesis in the play. In doing so, the play, and especially Richard's depiction, confirms Cathy Yandell's thesis that the early modern period formulates what she identifies as the 'secular subjectivization of time'.[45] Indeed, as we have seen, early modern medical texts stress an embodied overlap involving the terms *tempus, temperatura, temperamentum* (time, temperature, and the humours); tracing their deployment in *Richard III*, and in Richard, in particular, directs us still more closely to the play's entwined representation of time, narrative, and disability. From the first, Shakespeare calls attention to the way in which the subjectifying of time and temporal experience illuminates the play's representations of physical deformity. The opening speech in 1.1 of *Richard III*, for example, famously relies upon the rhetorical use of the term *now* – as in 'Now [1] … now [5] … now [10]' – to codify the dilemma Richard faces at the outset of the play in starkly temporal terms. In juxtaposing the displacedness that the war-minded Richard feels, trapped within a body, he claims, ill-suited for the amorous days of his brother Edward's reign, this opening speech highlights for us in miniature so much of Richard's ethos that it has rightly acquired the status as a sort of distilment of Shakespeare's talents as both a writer and dramatist.

Yet the temporalities highlighted in this speech point toward time's representation and –just as often – manipulation throughout the play. As Charnes has observed, discussions of Richard's character in the play contrast overgestation or belatedness – in that he was apparently born with a full set of teeth, 'gnaw[ing] a crust at two hours old' while possessed of a full head of hair [*Richard III* 2.4.27–30]) – with his self-styled prematurity, in that he suggests he was 'sent before his time', 'unfinish'd', 'scarce half made up', or, as King Henry VI addresses him in *3 Henry VI*, as an 'indigested and deformed lump' (5.6.51). His mother confirms such a view, suggesting that, in his boyhood, he was 'So long a-growing and so leisurely' (*Richard III* 2.4.19). Richard addresses this subjective temporality in a remarkable self-assessment of his prodigiousness in *3 Henry VI*:

> For I have often heard my mother say
> I came into the world with my legs forward.
> Had I not reason, think ye, to make haste,

And seek their ruin that usurped our right?
The midwife murmured and the women cried
"O Jesus bless us, he is born with teeth!" –
And so I was, which plainly signified
That I should snatch and bite and play the dog.
Then, since the heavens have shaped my body so,
Let hell make crooked my mind to answer it.

(5.6.70–9)

Richard's manipulation of time here as supple, manipulable, and thus radically subjective serves as a large part of Shakespeare's great feat of characterization in constructing him.[46] Indeed, each of these examples stresses a temporal 'out of joint'-ness that captures his displacedness quite thoroughly. Yet couched as these concepts are within Richard's corporeal form, the play deploys temporalities that are themselves more radically individuated – hinging as they do upon specific early modern medical concepts – than have yet been addressed. In evoking the varying temporalities Shakespeare associates specifically with Richard's disabilities, Richard's dense characterization evinces one method that Shakespeare will turn to again and again in framing early modern lives in time. Such temporal strategies demonstrate Shakespeare's cogent conceptualizing of Richard's disabled early modern selfhood, even as they necessarily point to the narrative emplotment, and the narrative prosthesis, of the play itself.

In this sense, and to review, Richard's textual portrayal centres upon a caloric economy that both signifies his otherness inwardly and that prefigures later Shakespeare representations of the complexity of the self. Richard's excess of corporeal heat serves as an internal index of his monstrosity within early modern humoral theory,[47] but this caloric monstrosity manifests with distinct temporal ramifications at the level of character and in the emplotment of *Richard III* as a whole. In this sense, *tempus*, *temperatura*, and *temperamentum* (time, temperature and the humours), as Shakespeare deploys them, obtain both at the level of character and of narrative. But there are additional, temporal issues at work here, since early modern medical theory links the vehement emotions with dual attributes: first, with caloric escalations; and second, with a temporal urgency that also has keen characterological and narrative effects. In other words, where early modern medical theorists associate humoral coldness with grief, effeminacy and temporal delay, they associate humoral heat with rage (or lust), hypermasculinity and temporal urgency.[48] Richard's characterization makes this link clear; after the death of his father in *3 Henry VI*, as we have seen, Richard stresses that he cannot weep as the thermal dynamics of his sudden caloric escalation have repressed the 'wind' that tears require. He concludes: 'To weep is to make less the depth of grief. / Tears, then, for babes; blows and revenge for me!' (2.1.79–86).

Shakespeare works from this groundwork in *Richard III* to frame time, temperature, and the humours within a specific disability context. Indeed, Richard repeatedly deploys disability, rhetorically, as temporally-driven. He does so, first, by registering it as a physically embodied cause for narrative delay that permits him to 'bustle' in the world (1.1.152). In 2.1, as well, Richard employs a Machiavellian belatedness as courier with news of Clarence's pardon, concocting a delay he associates with his own disability:

Richard	Who knows not that the gentle duke is dead?
	They all start …
King Edward	Who knows not he is dead? Who knows he is? …
King Edward	Is Clarence dead? The order was reversed.
Richard	But he, poor soul, by your first order died,
	And *that a winged Mercury* did bear.
	Some tardy cripple bare the countermand,
	That came too lag to see him buried.
	(*Richard III*, 80, 82, 87–91 emphasis added)

Richard's rhetorical focus in this passage upon a strategic delay, in this sense, redirects our attention to his extraordinary and ruthless agency in pursuing power across the whole of the play.

Richard proceeds to enact additional rhetorical deployments of disabled dilatoriness, paradoxically, to rouse himself to battle with Richmond in Act 5 of *Richard III*. Again, he couches disability as a temporal construct, a delay that hinders swiftness:

> Come, I have heard that fearful comments
> Is *leaden servitor* to *dull delay*;
> *Delay* leads *impotent* and *snail-pac'd beggary*.
> Then *fiery expedition* be my wing,
> Jove's *Mercury*, and herald for a king ...
> We must be brief when traitors brave the field.
>
> (4.3.51–5, 57 emphasis added)

Richard here evokes the delays he has associated with disability in a still more subtle way than to fall back upon the victimhood status he might suggest. The rhetorical link Richard establishes in this passage between delay and begging – with 'snail-pac'd beggary', for example – shrewdly maintains a series of links Shakespeare has outlined in *Richard III* regarding disability and the discourses of charitable begging starting in 1.2, in which, as Lindsey Row-Heyveld has shown, Richard positions himself in wooing Anne as a disabled beggar who appeals repeatedly to Saint Paul, patron saint of charity; in 3.4, too, in which Richard demands strawberries ostensibly to brighten the physical mark of his disability; and in 2.1, as well, in which Richard presents himself as a 'tardy cripple' (2.1.90). These rhetorical ploys demonstrate that Richard simply will not permit himself to be passively expunged, as might the deviant element in a standard prosthetic narrative.[49] More than just a 'wry joke against himself', as has been asserted of Richard's self-identification as a 'tardy cripple', these passages display a rhetorical manipulation of time which fleshes out Richard's character even as it formulates a timing of disability within the text that clarifies far more than it obscures.[50]

This attention to time and disability in *Richard III* reflects Richard's agency in other ways, as well: in 3.4, for example, linked with his demand for strawberries, Richard also accuses

Queen Elizabeth and Mistress Shore of witchcraft in order to lure Hastings to his death. In doing so, according to Charnes, Richard

> performs a breach of decorum that stuns the men into silence: a performance in which anyone who dares to regard his deformed body as *proper to him* is a traitor to the new solidarity that has been rhetorically fostered around complicitous misogyny. Richard eclipses his 'difference' from the other men by invoking the 'differences' of gender. Selectively dispossessing and deploying his deformity, Richard speaks it in terms that he purports to control by displaying himself as the target, rather then the origin of malignity.

It is here, Charnes observes, that Richard offers a 'preposterous revisionism – of history, of physiognomy, even of ontogeny' in accounting for his deformity.[51] After all, are *we*, are *they*, to understand that Richard's arm has *suddenly* withered? This agency, which must be seen to operate both in terms of character and narrative emplotment, manifests elsewhere, as well.[52]

Towards the play's conclusion, in a similar manner, Richard notes that his martial spirits are flagging. To revive them, he twice demands wine: 'Fill me a bowl of wine' (5.3.63), he insists; and 'Give me some wine' (72). He does so, he informs us, for medical reasons: in order to warm his chilled spirits with heat, and thus to stoke himself physiologically into action:

> I have not that alacrity of spirit
> Nor cheer of mind, that I was wont to have (5.3.73–4).

As we have seen, Elizabethan medical texts support this view regarding the impact of caloric escalations within humoral theory, and the links they make between heat with action, and coldness with delay. But we have also observed that it is precisely Richard's excess of heat that has constituted his inward monstrosity. Richard thus demonstrates in his demand for wine, topically speaking, a form of medically-tenable self-empowerment, and thereby yet another refusal of a deterministic, victimhood status. Here he thoughtfully takes overt steps, in other words, cogent within early modern medical theory, to restore himself. In the acknowledgment of his demand for wine, we learn something about his emotional constitution that is sorely missing in other views of him as a disabled character.

In this sense, wine itself serves as a prosthesis for Richard, an agent, perhaps paradoxically, to exercise an historicized form of self-control via corporeal heat to facilitate the pursuit of valour. Such a pursuit, of course, links back again to his calorically-charged vow after his father's death in *3 Henry VI*. And thus it is that Richard makes an effort to maintain his own identity in a way that proves him to be actively seeking to maintain his inward monstrosity. This view of Richard ultimately refutes those which suggest Richard serves merely as a narrative symbol or as a political symptom, a narrative prosthetic within his cultural moment whose function is simply to be eradicated. What we can learn from Richard about early modern disability narratives is that time and emotion – the link between time, temperature, and the humours – can play a foundational role in representing crucial aspects of subjective identity, including the way in which corporeal difference, as inwardly and outwardly constituted, combine with social perception of such difference to produce stigma: the social stigmatization upon which Richard's own rhetoric relies.

A final way in which this relationship between time, temperature, and the humours signifies in *Richard III* involves the play's obsession with dramatic narrativity, especially involving stops and terminations. This focus coalesces in Richard's stage-managing a series of narrative (or temporal) emplotments that push through to the play's conclusion. In 1.1, Richard famously suggests the multiple 'Plots' he has 'lain, inductions dangerous' (1.1.32); subsequently, he offers a masterful rhetorical shift in conversation with Anne (and still later with Elizabeth) into a 'slower method' (1.2.119). These narratological features demonstrate

Shakespeare's cogent conceptualizing of the relationship between emplotment and character (again: Aristotle's *mythos* and *ethos*) in the play itself and push through to its conclusion. Take, for example, Richard's interaction with Buckingham as they discuss the performance of tragic acting in notably narrative terms:

Richard	Come, cousin, canst thou quake and change thy colour,
	Murder thy breath in middle of a word,
	And then again begin, and stop again … ?
Buckingham	Tut, I can counterfeit the deep tragedian …
	(*Richard III* 3.5.1–3, 5)

Such an awareness highlights, meta-theatrically, the crucial role time and terminations manifest in the play as a whole. For a while, Richard understands power as the control of time and its shaping in narrative form. But as the play unfolds, events dictate Richard's (and others') accelerated inability to master his time. Hastings, for example, soon to face the chopping-block, requests 'What is't o'clock?' (3.2.4); Richard, bereft of all else as an object in swearing his 'love' for his niece and would-be bride, Elizabeth – Queen Elizabeth derides his choices of swearing by the world (4.4.374), his father's death (376), and God (377) – settles almost hopelessly upon 'the time to come' (387); and where Richmond observes that 'True hope is swift and flies with swallows' wings' (5.3.23), Richard obsessively iterates in the same scene: 'what is't o'clock' (47), 'give me a watch' [a time-marking candle] (63), and 'Tell the clock there. Give me a calendar' (276). The contexts in which these phrases arise matter somewhat less than their increasing frequency and force: this focus on time in the latter half of the play links Richard's medically tenable preoccupation with time and his emotional state. Indeed, Richard's mocking interaction with the disfavoured Buckingham – 'what's o'clock'; 'Well, but what's o'clock' (4.2.107, 109) – yields finally to a very real concern with discerning the time, Richard's time, even as his clock, as in Christopher Marlowe's *Doctor Faustus*, ineluctably runs out its course.

Narrative Prosthesis and the Cultural Model of Disability

In tracing the implicit humoral dynamism of early modern selves, and the unique volatility of a specific Shakespearean self, I have been demonstrating some specific ways in which markers of embodied non-normativity register in various Elizabethan socio-cultural contexts. In doing so, I have been engaging Mitchell and Snyder's assertion that a narrative prosthesis evolves 'to resolve or correct ... a deviance marked as abnormal or improper in a social context'.[53] But the metaphor of narrative prosthesis, as I have engaged it, apparently registers differently within this Shakespearean context than in medieval tradition. Indeed, within the medieval texts Edward Wheatley considers, Mitchell and Snyder's concept of narrative prosthesis only obtains in a strained manner: 'Rarely do [medieval] authors sketch a disability's "origins and formative consequences"', Wheatley observes; 'rather, they seem to assume that disability simply exists [...]'. In fact, a disability representation, he maintains, 'is often under-girded by the religious model whereby punishment for sin is implied'.[54] We are left in some sense where we began, then, asking what exactly Richard is doing within this text of *Richard III* and the first tetralogy as a whole. On whom lies the blame for Richard's wickedness? Is he the marked individual bearing God's anger? Is he an agent of God sent to punish? As Harry Berger shrewdly illustrates, from Margaret's perspective, the murder-ousness Richard wreaks on the House of York serves as an overtly political punishment against the Yorks. That is, the theological implications of one so marked could lead to the belief of the prodigy's evil nature, or to the prodigy's role as God's agent in destroying wickedness on earth.[55]

Accordingly, Richard's ubiquitous appellative as 'the devil' would appear to yield over the course of the play to some early modern approximation of Wheatley's religious model. In this sense, Richard frankly serves as the 'spiritually pathological site of absence of the divine', and thus comes to serve as an evil that must be annihilated.[56] In *Richard III*, however, as I have been charting, Shakespeare introduces his version of Wheatley's 'modern medicine', too – the well-developed humoral theory – as a contemporary link that complexly presents Richard not within an exclusively religious context in which he either is the devil or he is not, but rather within a different context altogether: Richard comes to serve as *both* a 'spiritually pathological' image of the demonic *and* simultaneously medically explicable. That is the horror of the play, ultimately, in my view. Of course, in accepting that explanation, hinging as it does upon an humoral medical theory that would come to be utterly discredited in subsequent centuries, we see in Richard's self-narration of his inner humoral 'unnaturalness' a complex representation of disability that both confirms a cultural model of early modern disability even as it displays the complex value of Mitchell and Snyder's narrative prosthetic model, when suitably historicized. Wheatley's final assessment of medieval narrative prosthesis, however, should give us pause: 'What is striking about the options that Mitchell and Snyder list in their fourth step is that "the extermination of the deviant as the purification of the social body" almost never occurs in medieval literature'.[57]

It certainly does so in *Richard III*, however. In spite of its inapplicability within medieval tradition, a pressing sense of early modern narrative prosthesis here obtains. The play offers representation of characterological deviance, just as does Mitchell and Snyder's tale of the tin soldier, deviance which begs for explanation. In this sense, Mitchell and Snyder's suggestion that the schematic of a prosthetic narrative structure is frequently four-part is thus readily workable in the context of *Richard III*. One way Richard engages this template is that:

- Richard reveals his physical deformity (deviance is exposed);
- Richard's non-normativity is couched as both literal and figurative monstrosity (origin of deviance is explored);
- Richard's ethical deformity is made manifest (deviance is brought to centre-stage); and
- Richard is killed (deviance is rehabilitated).

But insofar as *Richard III* relies upon inwardly disabling humoral forms, the clarity of this schema, unlike in Wheatley's religious model, becomes more fully embodied than the schema itself might suggest. Indeed, the palpable drama of difference staged in *Richard III* comes to centre on non-normativity conceived equally to be pointing backward to a medieval religious model that stigmatizes Richard based on his outward prodigiousness, and simultaneously to be medicalizing Richard's monstrosity as inwardly constituted. The correlation the play maintains between the caloric and such psycho-physiological deformities thus demonstrates the efficacy of reading the play within the cultural model of disability: and in doing so, to point to the narrative complexities involved in representing the multidimensional, embodied realities of early modern lives.

Shakespeare's representation of Richard's deformities ultimately indicates the limitations of the social models of disability that would seek to parse elements of disabled experience, such as Richard's ostensible lack of physical impairment. Simply put, I disagree with the overly restrictive view that the textual Richard does not display a disability: 'A hunchback, the text tells us, yes; but a disability, the text tells us, no.'[58] In response, I suggest that *Richard III* can be read most successfully within the 'less divisive'[59] cultural model of disability, a model that elides differences between impairment and disability by engaging both corporeal difference and social stigmatization under one term: disability. Discounting the effects of stigmatization on physical difference in *Richard III* – whether derived from inward manifestations, outward manifestations, or both – appears in my view to impose modern disability theory upon an early modern text in too limiting a manner. At the same time, as I have been suggesting, it would be a mistake to focus exclusively on systems of stigma as merely symbolic: to do so would be to miss entirely the realities of non-normative early modern embodiment and the stigmatizations associated with human variation. Charting how Shakespeare's construction of Richard ultimately hinges on his effort to mark this character in time and narrative clarifies much about the Shakespearean strategy of characterization as a whole, and that is the final payoff of a reading of *Richard III* within the cultural model of disability. Shakespeare's representation of Richard centres upon the relationship between forms of time that singularize Richard's embodied, disabled selfhood even as they necessarily point to the narrative emplotment of the play itself. Mitchell and Snyder's formulation of narrative prosthesis in this sense proves to be a remarkably subtle model which elicits the vibrant ways in which stigma and corporeal difference unfold in a Shakespearean context. That is what makes this play so remarkable as an early Shakespearean play over any other, to my mind: the subtlety and the novelty of its representation of narrative prosthesis.[60]

Charnes's observation that Richard's deformities serve as a textual production introduced and maintained by Tudor historians, whereby Richard comes to serve as the literal embodiment of York treachery, remains to me fundamental to any reading of the play. And yet, as with so many of Shakespeare's dramatic personations, Richard is more than the mere sum of his political parts. Although Richard admittedly achieves a 'density' of character by means of an inwardness that achieves depth against the identity of the stock villain, or Vice, Shakespeare's representation of inwardness enlists outward significations of deformity even as it embodies them with terrific intensity by means of a psychosomatic dynamism that helps produce a Richard imbued with both a chilling and singular coherence. That Shakespeare achieves this end by deploying Richard's 'unnatural', adust humours happily links such unnaturalness with the 'unnatural deviance' which Mitchell and Snyder require as the force that propels all prosthetic narratives. In this sense, Richard's charismatic qualities stem from his representation as demonstrably disabled, but also from an inward disability that clarifies the agency he deploys in the play insofar as he makes use of prodigious heat – in his rhetoric, in his vehement emotions, and in his wine – to promote a hypermasculine valour where, naturally, he comes to find none.

CHAPTER SEVEN

New Directions: 'Put[ing] on Some *Other* Shape': *Richard III* as an Arab V.I.P.

ADELE LEE

In *3 Henry VI* the Duke of Gloucester brags about his ability to 'frame his face to all occasions' (3.2.185) before proving in the next/last instalment in Shakespeare's history cycle that he is indeed a consummate chameleon and Machiavellian villain *par excellence*.[1] At once the good-natured uncle, the Stalin-like schemer, the holy ruler and the smooth seducer of women, Richard is an ever-changing role-player who revels in his virtuosity and range. It seems fitting, then, that there has been a 'wide spectrum of screened Richards' and that the history of filmic adaptations of *Richard III* has similarly borne witness to the protagonist's protean qualities since he has appeared (both on the small and the silver screen) in numerous different, constantly-shifting guises throughout the twentieth and twenty-first centuries.[2] In fact, Shakespeare's antagonist-as-central-character has been reincarnated in a seemingly infinite variety of fashions on-screen, fashions dependent on which context – historical, political and geographical – the *play* is being 'framed' to suit, and on which actors and directors are involved.

Richard III's multiple metamorphoses on-screen – and it is worth just pointing out here that the first screen adaptation of the play (the now extant Vitagraph starring William Ranous [1908]) is widely claimed to be the film that also marks the birth of the movie industry – are appropriate given that as a character he ultimately lacks a fixed identity. Sent into the world 'scarce half made up',[3] Richard has no 'character' as such, but 'the unique freedom of the self-creating actor'.[4] It is not surprising, therefore, that the part has been and continues to be a particularly appealing one to actors, often attracting and requiring the finest in the profession. Indeed, *Richard III* is commonly regarded as a 'star vehicle' for actors, as is evident in the following overview of Richard's most notable screen appearances. But it is the most recent and, arguably, fascinating form Richard III has taken in the medium of film to date – that of an Arab V.I.P. – which will be explored in-depth here. Focusing on directors Shakir Abal's and Tim Langford's 2011 documentary film about a pan-Arab theatre company founded by Sulayman Al-Bassam (director of the RSC's first-ever Arabic-language play), this chapter evaluates the extent to which both the play and its eponymous hero have, for perhaps the first time, literally taken 'some *Other* shape' (4.4.286).[5] Put another way, this chapter, through detailed analysis of *Richard III, An Arab V.I.P.*, considers whether Richard – a figure who has always, to an extent, been Other due to his physical deformity and general singularity – in his latest cinematic incarnation can be labelled as racially and/or radically distinct from his predecessors: has Richard found yet another genuinely different guise in which to masquerade? And if so, what exactly is it that this new, foreign, twenty-first century Richard can reveal to us about Shakespeare's play and its current critical reception?

Richard III's Multiple Metamorphoses Onscreen

The role of Richard III was perhaps most famously played by Laurence Oliver in the 1955 film that is frequently dubbed the 'definitive' adaptation.[6] In it, Olivier, who donned a heavy black wig and wore a prosthetic nose, played the part as a limping hunchback who nevertheless oozed charisma and 'flaunted sexual magnetism and athletic rigour'.[7] Forming an intimate rapport with the audience through the use of several direct addresses to the camera, Olivier's Richard is an almost Byronic figure – dark and brooding – whose shadow often engulfs the space on the screen. As Michael Anderegg nicely puts it, '[Olivier's] *Richard III* resembles a *danse macabre*, with Richard leading and almost

everyone and everything else following, harnessed to his will'.[8]
By contrast, Ian McKellen, in a version described by Douglas
Brode as a 'stylized art-deco wallow, an outrageous thirties
retro fashion extravaganza' that 'not just updates but *undermines*
Olivier's film', presents Richard as a fascist tyrant, who, despite
being smug and ruthless, is made to seem pitiful by suggestions
that he is a repressed homosexual, deprived of maternal care.[9]
Released in 1995 and directed by Richard Loncraine, this film's
Richard is an immaculately-dressed, cigarette-smoking military
Duke, clearly modelled on historical figures like Adolf Hitler
and Oswald Moseley. Meanwhile, in Al Pacino's 'docudrama',
Looking for Richard (1996), Shakespeare's eponymous hero-villain
is portrayed as a character who, like the Bronx-born Pacino
himself, has street as well as sex appeal.[10] Moreover, as Barbara
Hodgdon comments:

> In the savage blankness of [Pacino's] face, the slightly
> hooded eyes, the slight twitch of the mouth, evanescent
> as smoke, before he turns on his prey, his performance as
> *The Godfather*'s Michael Corleone (1972) comes into view,
> generating a productive collision between roles.[11]

In other words, Pacino's earlier, better known roles as mafia dons
and drug dealers in films like *The Godfather* (1972), *Carlito's
Way* (1993) and *Scarface* (1983) – a movie itself believed to be
indebted to *Richard III* – shape and inform his performance of
Shakespeare's anti-hero.[12] And even though Pacino, in general,
attempts to maintain a distinction, primarily through the use of
music and costume, between himself – and his filmic past – and
the character, there are several moments when it is not apparent
whether Pacino is representing himself or Richard. For instance,
when Pacino extravagantly enacts the death of Richard on the
streets of New York while wearing a leather jacket and sporting
a baseball cap, it is obvious that the actor's and the character's
identity has become merged. Such a fusion results in, to re-quote
Hodgdon, a 'productive collision of roles', with Al Pacino's

Richard becoming reminiscent of and perhaps modelled on the street gangsters typically associated with the actor.

Richard III's onscreen metamorphosis into a 'tough guy' in Al Pacino's *Looking For Richard*, albeit momentarily, marks a significant juncture in filmic adaptations of the play. And although Loncraine/McKellen's *Richard III*, it should be noted, likewise resonates with the gangster genre, with Richard Corliss going so far as to describe the film as 'Hitler as Scarface', it is Al Pacino's documentary film that heralds the emergence of an increasingly 'street' and, no less significantly, *American* Richard III (the one being commonly conceived as synonymous with the other).[13] Of course, the Shakespeare film and the Americanization of culture are in many respects inseparable, as Denise Albanese has convincingly argued, and Shakespeare simply 'must meet America at the movies', so it comes as little surprise that the adaptation of *Richard III* into the medium of film has steadily led to the growing Americanization of its central character.[14] In the New Millennium two more filmic versions of *Richard III* have been produced that pay testimony to the rise of a Richard who is American and 'of the street': James Gavin Bedford's *The Street King* (a.k.a. *King Rikki*, 2002) and Scott Anderson's *King Richard III* (2008).[15]

'Channelling *Richard III* to fit the rhythms of Chicano gang subculture in Southern California (specifically LA's east side), and the cinematic and televisual conventions that characteristically represent them', Bedford's *The Street King* stars former-boxer Jon Seda as Rikki Ortega, a macho gang leader who is 'more hunk than hunchback'.[16] This Richard III's only physical deformity is a large scar on his face, a scar that makes explicit the link between *Richard III*, *Scarface* and the gangster genre *per se* (the film ends with a typical gangster showdown). But links to other, well-known screen adaptations of the play are also apparent; in particular, *The Street King* shows parallels with Loncraine's film through suggesting that lack of maternal love is to blame for Richard's coldness and that the Richmond figure – corrupt cop Juan Vallejo (Mario Lopez) – is 'just a smarter version of Rikki'.[17]

However, far from being 'camp' like McKellen's Richard, Seda's is aggressively masculine, which, according to Mark Thornton Burnett, can be read as indicative of the instillation of 'vulgarised American values' onto the source material.[18] What is more, Seda's Richard seems to operate as 'a precursor to the Horatio Alger type, or what has been termed "the self-made man," a figure who finds profit in disadvantage and who fashions himself according to the principles of promotion and self-improvement'.[19] This type, of course, can be identified as specifically American, highlighting once more the ways in which Richard III is not just being translated into modern American vernacular onscreen, but being infused with and transformed by the values of American popular culture.

The second twenty-first-century screen adaptation to explicitly Americanize the play and its central character is the little-known and never-officially-released 2008 film directed, produced and starring Scott M. Anderson. Anderson is an amateur filmmaker, and currently works as a veterinarian in Los Angeles, the place in which his low-budget (and by all accounts, lowbrow) adaptation is set. In it, the York and Lancaster families are 'rival branches of the former England [Film] Studios' who 'exert a mafia-like control of the city and local politics/law enforcement' and Duke Richard, 'lounging on his sun deck' and aided by his sinister counsellor Buckingham, 'plots to eliminate the hated Lancaster dynasty'.[20] Set primarily in nightclubs and health spas (i.e. the preferred hangouts of the wealthy and decadent), Anderson's film, like Bedford's, suggests contemporary, downtown Los Angeles – associated with street crime and gang warfare – constitutes an appropriate equivalent to the world of feudal England. The analogy is no doubt a tenuous, albeit entertaining, one; for, even as suggested by the promotional poster, which features a medieval dagger superimposed against the backdrop of the iconic Hollywood sign, the two worlds are obviously incongruous. Indeed, the juxtaposition of these two symbols underpins the deeper sense that, in Robert Shaughnessy's words, there is a 'potentially irreconcilable antagonism between cinematic and Shakespearean values'.[21]

Scott Anderson's *Richard III* was a critical and commercial failure, but a useful example of what qualifies as a 'bad Shakespeare film'. More specifically, the failure of Anderson's filmic adaptation of *Richard III* suggests that the Americanization of Shakespeare is, indeed, gradually resulting in 'dumbed-down' versions that have been 'rewritten in the idiom of mass culture'.[22] It also suggests that when the role is literally performed by the man on the street (as opposed to a well known celebrity playing the part as 'street') it loses the charisma and star-quality perceived essential to the part. So, regardless of whether Richard is envisaged as aristocratic, regimental or 'street', as a hunchback or a hunk, or as a repressed homosexual or an uninhibited heterosexual, the actor required to play him must hail from certain stock. This argument perhaps applies to all filmic versions of Shakespeare's play which are typically associated with acting royalty. Even in the film on which this chapter will now focus, despite its foreign and marginal status – the company fashions itself as a 'rogue outfit' – Richard is played by Syrian star Fayez Kazak, an actor who enjoys immense popularity and acclaim in his homeland. Thus while the guises in which he appears, and the masks with which he covers his face, may be ever-changing, the calibre of actor likely to perform Richard III is consistently high. One other constant, stable factor in the history of filmic adaptations of the play is the enduring appeal and fascination of the figure of Richard to filmmakers and movie-goers alike.

Put[ting] on an Other Shape?

Richard III, An Arab V.I.P. (dir. Shakir Abal and Tim Langford, 2011), like most 'new wave' Shakespeare films to emerge in the twenty-first century, is difficult to label in terms of genre.[23] An international 'docudrama' or 'documentary road movie', it follows a pan-Arab theatre troupe as they discuss, rehearse and perform *Richard III* at two seemingly very different venues: the Kennedy Centre, Washington DC, and Al Jahili fort in Al Ain, United Arab Emirates. Similar to Al Pacino's *Looking for Richard* (1996) in that it, too, is a bricolage of interviews with the cast and crew, shots of the actors-in-rehearsal and performances of selected scenes, *Richard III, An Arab V.I.P.* is a 'frantic' (4.4.68), tension-filled and fast-paced production which includes a dizzying array of scene changes.[24] Stylistically 'kaleidoscopic' in the sense that it derives its visual and auditory cues from multiple, non-site and non-genre-specific sources, it also, like other Middle Eastern Shakespeares, offers insight into not just Shakespeare's play, but the history, culture and politics of the Arab world; as Monadhil Daood (Catesby) states, the implied Western viewer 'get[s] to know the Other through Shakespeare'.[25]

What is particularly interesting about this film, however, is its contention that the figure of Richard is a familiar one in the oil-rich Middle East: here, it is asserted throughout, Richard the Thirds still exist. In fact, it was Saddam Hussein that was 'the first hook', writer and director of the stage version Sulayman Al-Bassam explains, and the piece was originally going to be called *Baghdad Richard*; however, 'before we knew it Saddam was hanging from a rope'. The film's central conceit is not just that 'Richard is still here in every Arab country' (Nadine Jomaa/Lady Anne), but that Shakespeare has more to say about the contemporary Middle East than he does about the West: 'if you take Shakespeare's plays and look at them through the times we are living in the Arab world, you'll find Shakespeare is practically writing about *us*', claims the actor who plays Hastings, Nicolas Daniel.[26]

Such opinions are becoming increasingly commonplace (the late Libyan leader, Muammar Al-Gaddafi, even argued that Shakespeare was a sixteenth-century Arab sheik named Shaykh Zubayr), especially given the rise in Arabic-language productions of Shakespeare. At the 2012 World Shakespeare Festival, for instance, there featured Arabic versions of *Richard II*, *Cymbeline* and *Romeo and Juliet*, the last of which, incidentally, was directed by Monadhil Daood – the actor who plays Catesby in *Richard III, An Arab V.I.P.* The critical reception of all three productions tended to focus on the ways in which these Arab theatre companies explored (and in some cases forged) parallels and found equivalencies and correlates between their world and Shakespeare's. For example, Daood's *Romeo and Juliet* rooted the story in post-war Iraq – 'a loathsome world' (5.1.81) – and turned Romeo into a Shiite and Juliet into a Sunni, but the analogy risked becoming glib when Paris was conceived as an Al-Qaeda suicide bomber. At this point, the production seemed to become trapped in 'the empty enumeration of meaningless parallels, [and] the loss of specificity in a tangle of woolly generalities'.[27]

Furthermore, linking Shakespeare's world to the contemporary Middle East, and viewing the one as analogous to the other, reveals some dubious assumptions about Arab culture and society; the notion that the latter embodies the qualities that characterized Shakespeare's time suggests the Middle East is stuck in a time warp and that 'the spatial movement from West to East parallels the temporal movement from twenty-first century rationalism (Logos) to Renaissance pre-Cartesian Mythos'.[28] This is a decidedly Orientalist idea of what differentiates the 'East' from the 'West', and one which is still perpetuated in the Western media today as well as, interestingly/alarmingly, in *Richard III, An Arab V.I.P.*

A Rogue Outfit

The opening scene of *Richard III, An Arab V.I.P.* takes place, at night, outside a desert fort called Al Jahili in Al Ain (an oasis in Abu Dhabi). Al Jahili, constructed in the late 1890s under Sheikh Zayed the First, is one of United Arab Emirates' most historic buildings and a place of significant military and trading importance. It is owned by the ruling Al Nahya family, a branch of the House of Al-Falahi (Āl Bū Falāḥ), related to the House of Al-Falasi (from which the ruling family of Dubai, Al Maktoum, descends), and who, according to Forbes, are currently estimated to possess a fortune of $150 billion collectively. This fort, then, is a symbol of the extraordinary wealth and power of a ruling Arab family, a family that, like that the Houses of York and Lancaster,

Figure 7.1   Surreal Margaret, 'hungry for revenge'

has been engaged in on-going and often bloody struggle with rival families for centuries.

Outside this fort, and surrounded by flickering candles which create a mystical and almost ethereal atmosphere, stands Margaret (Amal Omran) (Figure 7.1), centre-screen, staring directly at the camera with striking, kohl-lined eyes. 'I am Margaret,' she announces, in a challenging and haunting voice, 'you needn't be concerned about me: we lost.' Exactly who, in the context of this film, 'we' are and what they have lost is not spelt out, but it is clear that this is the voice of a bitter and dispossessed Middle Eastern woman speaking to – it is strongly implied – a Western viewer in an accusatory and, at times, threatening tone. Her marginalized status is highlighted by her position outside the fort – the Arab equivalent of the tower or palace – and her appearance, mannerisms and setting endow her with all the qualities associated with a witch. Moreover, costume designer Abdullah Al Awadhi claimed, 'Margaret was my only chance to go

beyond reality because that was her character. We went through
to the surreal element'. A 'prophetess' (1.3.300), with the power
of foresight – 'I see', she warns – Margaret is wearing a dress
upon which are sewn shells, beads and coins – items commonly
used for witchcraft and fortune-telling. Against the background
sound of faint and ghostly howling, she continues, 'it is your
right to ignore me: I would ignore myself, if my history would let
me'. Margaret is haunted by a past to which she has fallen victim
and from which she cannot escape.[29] Her very dress consists of
layers of chiffon representing the distinct chapters in her life and
is elaborately embroidered with words which underscore what
Louis Montrose refers to as 'the textuality of history'.[30]

Arguably, and at the risk of pandering to stock images of
the contemporary Middle East, Margaret is a figure Western
audiences – who, it is implied, enjoy the 'rights' she does not –
will associate with the wailing widows and weeping mothers they
are accustomed to seeing in news reports on the wars in Iraq and
Afghanistan, and more recently, in Libya and Syria. These women,
deprived of their fathers, husbands and sons – figures on whom
they are, arguably, as dependent as the women in Shakespeare's
time were on their male relatives – are frequently filmed ululating
in grief at their loss, for 'many of the major religions established
in the Middle East are based on ritual lament'.[31] As such, they
share much in common with the women in Shakespeare's *Richard
III* whose roles all centre on loss and whose cries, curses and, not
to mention, conjurings, provide an important form of expression
and rebellion.[32] Like the Middle East's women – debatably, the
primary victims of the 'War on Terror' (according to Hilary
Clinton and other feminists) – Shakespeare's Margaret, Elizabeth
and the Duchess of York are the primary victims of the War of
the Roses and they spend the majority of the play lamenting their
fates and plotting their revenge. Some have even commented that
the gathering of mothers in the so-called 'wailing scene' (Act 4,
Scene 4), wherein they fill the air with '*heathenish* cursing and
chanting', is reminiscent of Seneca's chorus of women lamenting
the destruction of Troy in *Troiades*.[33] The non-Christian Middle

East, then, arguably constitutes a more fitting context for this scene than Shakespeare's England ever did.

Needless to say, Arab women are (commonly conceived, at least) as being, also similar to the female characters in *Richard III*, the victims of an oppressive patriarchal system that denies them either a voice or freedom. And when Margaret asserts that 'it is your right to ignore me', the camera cuts to an image of Richard III (Fayez Kazak) rehearsing his part, thereby indicating that it is this Eastern despotic male, as much as the West, to whom she feels she has fallen victim. She, and all the Muslim women in *Richard III, An Arab V.I.P.*, is doubly victimized by sexism and racism. However, interestingly, while Western film directors have tended to omit or minimize the roles and relevance of women in *Richard III* – Richard Loncraine and Laurence Olivier both as good as cut the figure of Margaret, for example – Sulayman Al-Bassam, the adherent to a religion frequently condemned for its (mis)treatment of women, grants Margaret – and the actress playing her – a principal role in the film: it is, after all, her face we see and her voice we hear first. And, in stark contrast to most filmmakers, who have, as Nathalie Vienne-Guerrin points out, adopted Richard's strategy to 'drown [their] exclamations', 'let[ting] not the heavens hear these tell-tale women/ Rail' (4.4.154; 150–1), Al-Bassam not only gives Margaret the 'seniory'(4.4.36) she seeks in Shakespeare's play and 'let[s] [her] griefs frown on the upper hand' (4.4.37), he allows her – as well as the other female characters – a voice and presence that actually threatens to 'smother' Richard's.[34]

This is indicative of Al-Bassam's liberal, forward-thinking views regarding women and gender, and of his 'mission' to use Shakespeare's play to enlighten Arab people and 'change expectations'. The audience at the Company's first performance in Al Jahili comprised 50 female students from the United Arab Emirates University who had to be persuaded by Al-Bassam, and their American English Literature professor, James Mirrione, to attend. Both men, it would seem, regard Shakespeare as the means through which Muslims can be educated to think in more liberal and enlightened terms – an attitude that is reminiscent of that of colonial administrators in the heyday of British imperialism.[35] It should be noted, too, that Al-Bassam appears to deem it necessary to cast an attractive actress in the role of Margaret in order for her to attain 'seniory'. Far from being a 'wither'd hag' (1.3.214), Amal Omran is a good-looking woman, free of wrinkles, thus Al-Bassam could be accused of putting the emphasis on physical appearance when it comes to female actors and of casting only the best-looking women in lead roles.[36]

Throughout *Richard III, An Arab V.I.P.*, Margaret forms a sort of double and shadow to Richard, with the opening scene, in particular, serving as the perfect counterpart to a later scene in which Richard rants outside the gates of the White House.[37] By having Richard deliver his 'Now is the winter of our discontent' speech (Act 1, Scene 1) outside the seat of Western power in the 'heart of the *new* empire', as Daood describes it, filmmakers draw attention to his minor status on the global political stage. Despite (or perhaps because of) being dressed in regimental uniform, this Arab Richard appears oddly pathetic, as indeed all the cast do when they are in Washington where they perform as part of the Arabesque festival: 'the cold huge buildings make you feel very small', Daood comments. Literally peeping at the White House through black railings (Figure 7.2) – recalling to mind the 'constantly spying and preying presence' of Laurence Olivier's Richard – this Richard has clearly only the power to victimize members of his own race: he 'preys on the issue of his mother's body' (4.4.57).[38] The bars in front of which he stands also serve as a reminder of the criminality of this Arab Richard and, more accurately, the historical figure upon whom he is modelled, Saddam Hussein, the Iraqi President who was imprisoned and subsequently executed in 2006.

Richard and Margaret inhabit separate, gendered spheres – Richard's locale is Western, modern, masculine and Margaret's is eastern, ancient, and (therefore, according to binary thinking) feminine – spheres which highlight the 'confrontation between tradition and modernity and between East and West [which]

Figure 7.2   Richard III outside the gates of the White House

are among the "perennial themes" in Arabic literature' and in this film too.[39] Nevertheless, despite the distinction, the two characters are portrayed as equally disenfranchised. Of course, Richard's deformed body alone aligns him with women, since in the Renaissance they were considered ' "unfinished" men, lacking enough spirit or heat to develop the ideal male body'.[40] Even Richard's chosen arms are feminine: gossip, rumour, 'inductions dangerous ... prophecies, libels, and dreams' (1.1.32–3).[41] But Shakir and Langford emphasize Richard and the women's shared sense of powerlessness and bitterness since they seem to echo one another in their laments: while Margaret bemoans that 'we lost', Richard, suffering from a pronounced nervous tic, complains that 'the earth has changed its robes' – a statement accompanied by a close-up of the 'stars and stripes' flying majestically.[42] Indeed, as an Arab, he and the whole cast and crew involved in this production are 'losers' in the sense that they have been defeated in innumerable wars over the last few decades and supplanted by America and the West *per se* in the new world order.[43] Even Al Jahili Fort, the building that serves as a symbol of Arab wealth and power in the opening shot, fell into disrepair in the 1950s when the British requisitioned it as a base for a unit of the Trucial

Oman Levies, thereby signalling the diminished status of the Arab people and the ruin of their 'house'.[44]

Twice in the course of the film, Al-Bassam refers to himself and his touring company as a 'rogue outfit', at odds with and in many ways at war with the world around them: 'we've been allowed in', he says sarcastically when the crew land in the USA. Due, in large part, to the fact 'Islam does not approve of acting' (Amal Omran) and it, just like in Shakespeare's day, 'is not a respected profession', the troupe is under-funded, marginalized and perceived as going against the authorities as a result of their desire to 'question and disturb': in the scene immediately following Margaret's speech, we glimpse a huge piece of roadside graffiti emblazoned with the words 'Art is meant to Disturb'. Interestingly, it is art in general and not Shakespeare in particular that is regarded in this film as providing the assembly – all of whom fashion themselves as vigilantes, airing their subversive opinions with passion on the streets and in the back of taxis – with the means to challenge oppression, both Eastern and Western. Shakespeare, as a matter of fact, is rarely ever mentioned. Indeed, the main reason Shakespearean material is used to transmit political statements, Al-Bassam admits, is because it guarantees Western attention.

In a revealing moment, while Al-Bassam shakes hands and exchanges niceties with American dignitaries after the troupe's performance of *Richard III* in the Kennedy Centre, he explains in a voiceover to the viewer that the company 'use Shakespeare so we are to be able to be understood'. Subscribing to the belief that one must adopt the master's tools in order to dismantle the master's house, Al-Bassam continues by saying, in a decidedly embittered tone, that he is aware that this renders them into a bit of 'art paraphernalia' that:

> They [Americans] can happily put on their shelves and say we're in dialogue with the Arab Islamic world and it's only extremists from that region that need to be dealt with and hence excusing the whole history of Western intervention and mismanagement and violence in the region.

Al-Bassam is acutely aware that indigenous adaptations of Shakespeare can be 'easily pilloried as a ploy to tickle foreign fancies', but they 'ensure a global platform for geo-specific cultural statements that could not otherwise be made'.[45] Nevertheless, securing an audience and fulfilling a political agenda are two different things, for Al-Bassam may have gained the global (read, American) platform he sought, but he and his company cannot claim to have successfully conveyed their message that the West is as much to blame for violence in the Arab world as native tyrants and madmen. The American audience in *Richard III, An Arab V.I.P.* leaves the auditorium, from Al-Bassam's perspective, looking smug and assured, thus proving that deploying Shakespeare to protest against Western cultural hegemony is fraught with difficulties.[46] Indeed, so disheartened has Al-Bassam become that in a recent interview in *Rolling Stone* magazine he revealed that he's decided to no longer produce political plays, since 'he has devoted so much of himself to his work without seeing it foster any kind of political change'.[47]

The US Ambassador for Women's Rights' rather patronizing response to the production, and her verdict that it represents 'the kind of thing *they* should think about over and over and over', highlights that Al-Bassam's stage version at the Kennedy Centre was interpreted as endorsing rather than criticizing American values and superiority. Of course, by simply choosing to 'do' Shakespeare, the 'outfit' are seen to be acquiescing with rather than questioning Western ideas and values. Perhaps it is because of Al-Bassam's sense of having failed to convey adequately the message on the stage alone, and to this small rather elite audience, that he decided to make this film in the first place. The medium of film not only guarantees increased attention and longevity, but it allows filmmakers to exert more control over the viewer, forcing the latter to interpret the action how the director wants them to:

> [T]he filmmaker in the movie genre has far more potential control over the spectator's attention than does the theatre director … [for] the movie spectator is always looking where

he or she should be looking, always attending to the right
details and thereby comprehending, nearly effortlessly, the
on-going action precisely in the way it is meant to be
understood.[48]

The documentary film genre is, naturally, more didactic in nature
as the primary purpose of a documentary is usually to present
the audience with an argument and reinforce a certain ideological
position. Originally emerging out of the travelogue and developed
as a means of introducing viewers to exotic locations (which
is arguably the intention of the directors of *Richard III, An
Arab V.I.P.*), the documentary form privileges the political and
ethical stance of the filmmaker, providing him/her with the
means to make audiences conscious of a problem and to win
their support.[49] As a result, the aesthetic dimension tends to get
neglected in docu-films and, more significantly, 'the sense of an
aesthetic remove between an imaginary world in which actors
perform and the historical world in which actors live no longer
obtains'.[50] This is certainly the case in regards to *Richard III, An
Arab V.I.P.*, a film that aims more at making a political statement
than engaging creatively with Shakespeare.

Theatre is Political and Politics is Theatre

Al-Bassam and his company's decision to perform Shakespeare
was predominantly a political rather than an artistic one. And the
choice of *Richard III* in particular was because, as mentioned, it
seemed to fit neatly the context of the contemporary Middle East.
So accurately, in fact, does the play speak to the history, concerns
and culture of the Arab world that throughout *Richard III, An
Arab V.I.P.* the distinction between the 'real' world and the world
of the play, and between members of the cast and the characters
they perform, frequently becomes blurred. When Syrian-born
actress and drama instructor Amal Omran preaches about the
importance of sexual and religious freedom; tells her interviewer
'you have to be strong enough to say you're not scared'; instructs a

female student, rehearsing the part of Anne in the 'wooing scene', to 'hit him when he corners you and gets hold of your finger'; and, while smoking a cigarette, brands Saeed Ghabra, who burnt down Khali Qabani's theatre, 'an animal', it is impossible to determine whether or not she's still 'in character'. Margaret's likening of Richard to a 'bunchback'd toad' (4.4.81) and 'elvish-mark'd, abortive, rooting hog' (1.3.227), and the play's general association of Richard with the bestial, in particular, the porcine, makes it impossible not to view this moment, as well as others featuring the outspoken and angry Omran, who rants and cackles throughout the film, as meta-fictional, in that, they breach the so-called 'fourth wall' – a technique Shakespeare himself frequently deploys in *Richard III*.[51]

Given Omran first performs the role of Margaret *off* stage and outside the company's designated playing-space – albeit the grounds of Al Jahili are rendered 'stagey' by the use of candles – it is evident that the film is blurring the lines of distinction between the theatre and the world and implying, like many Shakespeare plays, that the two are indistinguishable. Indeed, *Richard III, An Arab V.I.P.*'s motto is 'Theatre is Political and Politics is Theatre', so it endorses the distinctively Renaissance view that power is consolidated through spectacle and theatrical display.[52] The film also adheres to the Renaissance belief in the constructed and performative nature of all social roles: Fayez Kazak claims that when he puts on his military uniform, 'I become a general', a moment that emphasizes both this actor's *and* the character of Richard's capacity to slip into various, different roles as seamlessly as one would don a costume.

Like Al Pacino's *Looking For Richard*, *Richard III, An Arab V.I.P.* makes it difficult to determine when actors are in or out of character, and which parts constitute the 'drama' and which the 'documentary'. This blending of documentary and drama, according to Sebastian Lefait, makes perfect sense when it comes to *Richard III*, given its use of the play-within-the-play device – a device which always leads to the theme of *theatrum mundi*.[53] However, the porous nature of the relationship between

documentary and fiction in Shakir and Langford's film is intended
more to emphasize the similarities between Shakespeare's play
and the twenty-first-century Middle East.

Gradually, we are introduced to all the actors individually
before they congregate in Kuwait to begin rehearsals. The female
ones, by virtue of their very occupation, are similar to their
fictional counterparts in that they are perceived as subversive
figures, and their passions and dispositions frequently mirror
that of the characters they play. All three of them – Nadine
Jomaa, Carole Abbound and Amal Omran – openly express their
(dissenting) political views, often in a highly emotional manner:
with eyes filled with bitter tears, for instance, Jomaa confesses
during one interview that 'I have hate and anger' and 'I was
happy with the shoe thrown at [George W.] Bush'. After Jomaa
utters these sentiments, the camera then pointedly cuts to scenes
of her hurling abuse at Richard. Again, the film suggests the lives
of these actors are intricately entangled with the parts they play.

This is particularly evident in the case of the actor playing
Catesby, Monadhil Daood – a rather menacing figure who at
one point even threatens to kill an administrator in a theatre in
Baghdad for being late. Emotionally scarred by the bombing of
his home city – a place frequently and unexpectedly plunged into
darkness – Daood, it is suggested, like the character he plays, is
the product of a violent world and spends his evenings drowning
his sorrows in Ouzo. One particularly memorable scene features
him delivering an acerbic speech about the bombing of Baghdad,
during a power cut, with his face illuminated only with a torch à
la *The Blair Witch Project* (1999). The effect of this is to give him a
creepy, conspiratorial appearance and to create a level of intimacy
with the audience which makes viewing uncomfortable.

The most intriguing 'character' in *Richard III, An Arab
V.I.P.*, however, is arguably the clever and charismatic theatre
director, Al-Bassam, who himself possesses and exhibits distinctively 'Ricardian' qualities – knowingly or otherwise. Al-Bassam
is a British-born Kuwaiti with the uncanny ability to switch
subject positions depending on context and company. Attired in

Western clothing – a suit and tie – and speaking with a polished BBC accent (he was raised in England and educated at the University of Edinburgh), in one scene, and appearing in the next in traditional Arab robes speaking fluent Arabic, Al-Bassam, it would seem, has indeed 'entertain[ed] some score or two of tailors, / To study fashions to adorn my body' (1.2.259–60). He also spends the majority of the film discussing the production while seated in the back of a chauffeur-driven car, making one wonder who's the real V.I.P. His attitude towards his cast, from whom he remains at a noticeable distance, is disquieting: 'actors perform better with little food or sleep and should be kept on a tight regime', he states in a way that makes it difficult to discern if he is being tongue-in-cheek. Further, the intimate relationship Al-Bassam forms with the viewer – letting them in, for instance, on his true opinions about the American dignitaries that attend his production in Washington and with whom he sipped wine under a sparkling chandelier, is decidedly 'Richard-like'. After 'flatter[ing] and speak[ing] fair' to them, 'smil[ing] in their faces' and (almost) 'duck[ing] with French nods and apish courtesy' (1.3.47–9), Al-Bassam, as noted earlier, reveals in a voiceover his resentment at having to 'play the system' in this manner in order to 'give the Other a voice'.

Al-Bassam has been accused of being a Westernized traitor by some, and of 'wash[ing] out differences between [...] personal and local backgrounds', by others.[54] What is more, he has been criticized for producing *Al-Hamlet Summit* for the sole purpose of 'shock[ing] and implicating his Western audience' by creating a 'voyeuristic thrill' and a 'sense of strangeness in familiarity'.[55] There is no doubt Al-Bassam is an (self-confessed) opportunist, a sophisticated trans-national who, capitalizing on his hybridity, knows how to play both sides. He possesses 'the kind of superior cultural intelligence owing to the advantage of in-betweeness, the straddling of two cultures and the consequent ability to negotiate the difference', Homi Bhabha famously celebrates.[56] It could also be claimed that Al-Bassam belongs to a group that is 'able to profit by the cultural advantages of the system they are attacking';

although, how many activists cannot be accused of this? After all, as Gayatri Spivak and other critics have convincingly argued, the subaltern cannot speak: 'for "the true" subaltern group, whose identity is its difference, there is no subaltern subject that can "know and speak" itself'.[57]

Al-Bassam's Ricardian nature, finally, reinforces the film's central argument that Richard IIIs are 'everywhere in the Arab States' and that the reason for this can be attributed to their disenfranchised condition which necessitates recourse to a combination of charm and cunning in order to be heard or achieve power. While, as H. R. Coursen points out, Richard III's tyranny was 'not really an exception, but part of a pattern' in Shakespeare's 'original', Arab Richards' actions and behaviour are similarly products of their geo-political context; for, the unstable and troubled Arab world is a breeding ground, it is implied, for corrupt and violent despots like Richard to flourish.[58] More specifically, the film controversially concludes by suggesting that American intervention in the region has been responsible for planting Richards in the first place: Saddam Hussein, upon whom the Arab Richard III is modelled, was (debatably) allowed, nay, helped into power by US President, Richard Nixon.

'Battered, Beaten, Buckled and Underdone'

At the beginning of *Richard III, An Arab V.I.P.* a voiceover announces that 'Richard III is no stranger to the Arab world. A ruthless king, poisonous[ly] charm[ing], [and a] bloodthirsty tyrant, [he represents] kings in this region since time immemorial'. Richard, then, from the very outset, is not conceived as a unique individual which would explain why, unlike other Richards (who feature in almost every scene), Fayez Kazak is not the centre of attention throughout, starring in relatively few scenes and often fading into the background in others. This is not to say that this Arab Richard is not, in many respects, an intriguing character – Kazak has been widely praised for his onstage performances – but the whole film's *raison d'être* seems to be to make a case for the commonality of such figures in the Arab world. The entire company's conceptualization of itself as a 'rogue outfit' might also serve to erode Richard's distinctiveness, for usually he alone is supposed to be the character at odds with the society he is in.

Traditionally, too, as Ben Brantley reminds us, Shakespeare's play is rendered as a portrait of a *singular* sociopath, with actors like Laurence Olivier and Ian McKellen digging deep for psyche-warping motives.[59] Not so in the case of Kazak's Richard, who 'looks like a dapper blend of Alan Ladd and Omar Sharif'.[60] Brantley has a point here, but he is overstating the case: this Richard is still a grotesque and, indeed, crazed figure. Suffering from several pronounced nervous tics, his body is constantly in motion and his facial muscles are permanently contorted, making it seem like there is something almost frenetic about him and making it difficult to tell if he has a disability. (One imagines if he does have a limp, it is the result of a gunshot to the leg, rather than of a disability with which he was born). He darts out his tongue lizard-like when he speaks and his head flicks dramatically from side-to-side, while sweat streams from every pore. What's more, the directors are at pains to emphasize his, and indeed his enemies', porcine qualities through his use of words and actions. For, when he is not dubbing his opponents 'bastard heathens ... who swill in [life's] iniquities and vice as animals' (words, note, one would expect to hear from a holy man [an Imam] rather than a military leader thus illustrating Richard's ability to dress himself up in religion), he is himself swilling in rainwater while crawling on all fours in obvious reference to his oft-commented upon bestiality. In light of the particular revulsion Muslims have for pigs and pork-eating, and the common use of the term as a form of insult, Richard's behaviour seems even more vile and unnatural.

As might be expected, Kazak is a mesmerizing figure even when out of character, never losing his ability to thrill the audience when he makes an appearance. He winds his way through the narrow, labyrinthine streets of Damascus as he is interviewed and one cannot help but assume this is an allusion to his ability to negotiate/manoeuvre his way through intricate, complex court intrigue: film, after all, permits the concretization of motifs to an extent the stage cannot. Next we see him in Damascus' Academy of Arts, watching a group of young, female dancers as they practise their moves, seemingly oblivious to his leering presence. He turns to the camera, still smirking and slightly off-frame, and says, 'these are my students, I love them a lot. They love me too' which implies a level of control and ownership over them – sexual and financial. The cameramen then follow Kazak as he leads them out of this room (he possesses control over them too) and into another which he says proudly is 'also new and modern', thereby imitating a king showing off his newly-acquired castle.

Kazak is the most enigmatic actor in the film and he stays 'in character' the majority of the time, managing to perform all Richard's 'best bits', including the 'Now is the winter of our discontent' soliloquy; the 'My horse, my horse!' line – performed while wearing jeans and standing in a desert; and the 'cut off his head!' command, delivered in the film's final scene which features Kazak playing Richard in an empty auditorium in the middle of a storm. This storm, apparently, is 'the pay-off to the opening scene when the play's director Al-Bassam speaks, in jest, of entering 'the eye of the storm'.[61] Yet surely it has as much to do with the 'deluge most unnatural' (1.2.61), Richard's 'inhuman and unnatural' (1.2.60) deeds are thought to provoke? As pathetic fallacy, the storm is in keeping with the pessimistic note on which the film closes: 'modernity is a façade', and 'the situation in the Arab world has lost all forms of stability', are the last, unscripted words uttered.

The cause of the instability is evident throughout and it is less the Richards who are to blame and more America. Perceived by Richard in his closing speech as a 'gang of heretics', 'a grand conspirator who holds the Bible aloft', who

> Saw you owning oil and blessed with astonishing wives,
> And they want to molest the one and rape the other.
> And who leads them but a paltry heathen?
> An infidel and a follower of Sykes Picot[62]

Straying further and further away from the source material in order to make a political statement, Al-Bassam's rewriting of the script points the finger of blame squarely at the British and Americans. And by the end of the film the question proposed earlier by Carole Abbound (Queen Elizabeth), 'who is the oppressor and who is the oppressed?' has become impossible to answer. The conflation of Richard's identity with that of former President Richard Nixon in the latter half of the film – through the shots of Watergate – seems to highlight that both sides are equally corrupt. As a paranoid, unethical 'ugly man' who refused to view tapes of his 1960s debates with Kennedy because he could not stand the way he looked on TV and who infamously beat his wife and taped conversations with suspected opponents, Nixon is often likened to Richard III.[63] Indeed, in 1972 Charles S. Preston wrote a play explicitly linking the two called *The Tragedy of King Richard the Third: 'My Kingdom for a Bomb'*.[64]

But it was, of course, during Nixon's term as President that Saddam Hussein came to power, and many in the Arab world impute the former for the rise of the latter: support for Hussein's Ba'ath Party, it is claimed, was provided by the CIA. Indeed, 'two CIA military coups brought the genocidal Ba'ath party, and with it Saddam Hussein, to power, in order to protect US strategic and economic interests'.[65] In *Richard III, An Arab V.I.P.*, it is an Americanized Buckingham who gives Richard arms in return for 'reforms' – a deal reminiscent of the type thought to have been carried out between Hussein and the US government in the 1970s. 'Palace advisor' and political puppeteer, Buckingham (Raymond Hosni) is as treacherous a figure as Richard, if not more so, suggesting that Richards are ultimately to be found everywhere – not just in the Middle East. This fact is underscored by the scene featuring Buckingham in silhouette while he boasts about his ability to 'flatten countries with the cock of a brow'. Sounding exactly like the self-inflated Richard in Act 3 Scene 2 of *3 Henry IV*, Buckingham becomes a figure whose identity merges with that of Richard III and Richard Nixon: it is impossible to differentiate one from the other at this point. All are similarly 'shadowy'.

'I am I': Conclusion

Ironically, then, the film which embarks on proving that Richard III 'belongs' to the contemporary Middle East – that he is a specifically Arabic figure and it is this world that can now be viewed as the play's 'cultural home' – concludes by presenting us with a character lacking any distinctive features: he is, like the use of silhouette implies, not a member of any particular race, colour or creed, but exists universally. Richard's lack of a concrete, fixed identity thereby also reinforces the widely held view of him as being unable to establish an 'essential being anterior to performance'.[66] His latest onscreen incarnation as an 'Arab V.I.P.', in a film that promised to show audiences the anti-hero 'putting on some Other shape', in the end, serves to present Richard as the (Same) archetypal, albeit fascinating, villain he has been throughout the history of film adaptations. Finally, his metamorphosis (or disintegration?) into shadow form – a word, notably, that was once rhetorically applied to an actor – recalls to mind Olivier's Richard whose shadow hovers over everyone in the 1955 film, and whose performance has cast a shadow over actors and directors in subsequent years. The conflation of Olivier's Richard with Kazak's Arab Richard highlights that rather than providing the viewer with a genuinely new Richard, *Richard III, An Arab V.I.P.* resurrects the old, familiar, Western one.

CHAPTER EIGHT

Resources for Teaching and Studying *Richard III*

Daniel Cadman

Richard III is one of Shakespeare's most enduringly popular plays, both on stage and in the classroom. The appealingly amoral villain and the shrewd, manipulative schemes he initiates in order to gain the English crown have helped to cement the play's popularity, yet challenges to these received views, primarily from feminist critics, have also ensured that the play continues to generate a robust range of critical responses. While it is undoubtedly an appealing object for both teaching and study, the sheer volume of criticism and the diverse range of performances it has generated can be daunting; similarly, the length of the text and the wide range of issues it examines can make it difficult to choose topics for teaching the text. In this chapter I aim to provide an accessible starting point for those about to begin teaching the text and for those about to embark upon in-depth research on the play. The resources and topics I highlight are by no means exhaustive; the purpose of this section is to stimulate ideas about the profitable ways in which the play can be researched and taught. For ease of use, the chapter is divided into sections which will focus upon potential teaching strategies as well as providing a survey of scholarly editions of the text, a summary of available audio and visual resources, a survey of internet resources and an annotated bibliography containing examples of scholarship with a dedicated section for studies of the play in performance.

Teaching the Play

The purpose of this section is to stimulate ideas about teaching the play by providing some potential strategies for exploring it with undergraduate students and suggesting potential topics for discussion. A common barrier to a student's understanding of the play is the difficulty in ascertaining what is actually going on. As with any other Shakespearean or early modern play, this is largely attributable to the difficulty in understanding the language of the play. A widely recommended solution to this problem is for students to see a performance of the play either in the theatre or on film which allows them to get a sense of the language and to see how the action is progressing. While it is not always possible to see theatrical productions of the play, there are numerous film and audio recordings, as detailed in the 'Audio and Visual Resources' section below. A number of theoretical writings on the teaching of early modern texts have emphasized the importance of integrating performances and film into the teaching of dramatic works.[1] Matthew C. Hansen has argued that one useful method of encouraging students' understanding of a play is ensuring that their first reading of the text takes the form of a group reading in which students will read individual parts aloud on the grounds that 'students' first reading of Shakespeare shouldn't be silent, internal and solitary, it should be audible, external and collaborative. The first time our students read Shakespeare should parallel the theatrical read-through rehearsal.'[2] Such an approach emphasizes the importance of the play as a performance text as well encouraging the students to be more receptive to the language. The group setting may also help to make the student's first reading of the Shakespeare play less intimidating. Students struggling to get to grips with the play may also benefit from the advice offered in David Bevington's *How to Study a Shakespeare Play* (Oxford: Blackwell, 2006), which does not focus specifically on *Richard III* but offers some useful strategies for getting started on Shakespearean plays. Similarly, Chris Coles's *How to Study a Renaissance Play* (Houndmills: Macmillan, 1988) does not provide specific advice on Shakespeare but the introduction offers some helpful tips which can be applied to a wide variety of early modern plays.

The problems students may have with understanding the language of the play are exacerbated in *Richard III* by the complex relationships of the various characters to one another, many of which are established in the *Henry VI* plays. This can be seen in such elements of the play as the presence of two Edwards in the dramatis personae and in the references to events from the *Henry VI* plays such as Richard's views on the legitimacy of the princes and in the dialogue between Margaret, Elizabeth and the Duchess of York and in the scene in which Richard is haunted by the ghosts of his previous victims. In common with many editions of the play, this chapter contains a family tree which should help students to appreciate the historical significance of many of the characters and to understand the problematic nature of the succession in this period. It may also be necessary to provide students with details about the historical background to the events in the play and possibly a sheet of quotations from the *Henry VI* plays to help clarify the events taking place in *Richard III*. There are also a number of introductory books which may help students to understand the play in the context of Shakespeare's histories.[3]

Another preliminary consideration to be taken into account when teaching *Richard III* is the fact that there are two distinct texts of the play and editors have adopted different policies when it comes to using the quarto and folio texts (see the Survey of Editions below). It is therefore advisable for anyone designing or teaching on a course that includes *Richard III* to settle upon a particular edition of the play and recommend it for purchase, thus avoiding any potential problems which could be caused by students consulting a range of different editions based upon different texts (it will also make life easier when it comes to marking student papers). It is also worth ensuring that the chosen edition is affordable for the typical student and readily available online, in local bookshops and in the institution's library.

Once these preliminary considerations have been addressed, an approach to teaching the play can be developed. The kinds of strategies tutors will wish to develop for this play will be dependent upon the kind of syllabus on which it appears and whether it is a general course on early modern drama, a course on Shakespearean drama, or a module with a specific theme, such as the history play or the representation of the body in the early modern theatre. On this basis, some of the potential topics for discussion will be more pertinent than others. If the play is being taught as part of a course on early modern drama which includes texts from a variety of authors, there are a number of ways in which *Richard III* can be used in conjunction with contemporary plays, depending upon the focus of the module. One obvious way is to compare the treatment of the Machiavellian protagonist with similar figures in other plays, such as Christopher Marlowe's *The Jew of Malta*, Iago in *Othello* and Lorenzo in Thomas Kyd's *The Spanish Tragedy*. There are also solid grounds for comparing the treatment of political power and ambition with the analyses of the same themes delivered in *Macbeth*. Another option is to open up space to compare Richard with other characters in early modern drama who are marginalized because of their appearance or because of a disability: one option includes comparing Richard with De Flores in Thomas Middleton and William Rowley's *The Changeling* who, like Richard, emerges simultaneously as an object of repulsion and, on one level, one of sexual attraction. It is also possible, depending on how ambitious you want to be, to compare the treatment of disability in *Richard III* to that which is represented by the character identified by the speech prefix of 'Stump' in the non-canonical play *Alarum for London*, an approach which can usefully be informed by Patricia Cahill's recent work on trauma in the early modern history play.[4]

As well as the representation of his body, there are a number of other potentially fruitful topics relating to Richard. One possible exercise is to show film clips and photographs from performances of the play and asking students to comment on the particular elements upon which each production concentrates and how they illuminate certain potential aspects of his character: McKellen's performance, for example, focuses upon his fascistic nature; David Troughton's incarnation of him as a court jester adds a metatheatrical element to the character and emphasizes his ability to manipulate others in a theatrical manner; and Antony Sher's 'bottled spider' highlights his physical disability. This exercise should also encourage students to think about the ways in which performance as well as text can convey meaning and to consider what elements of the text might have provided the inspiration for these performances. The group can then take the ideas that have emerged from the exercise and have them contribute to a discussion of the characterization of Richard, as well as examining extracts from critics such as Rossiter and Charnes (see annotated bibliography below). Another possible topic of discussion relating to Richard is how he compares to Richmond. Is Richmond a desirable alternative to Richard? Can he be viewed as an agent of providence ushering in a new era of stability under the Tudors, or are there elements which complicate this view? Such a discussion will provide another opportunity for the students to consider how the views they have developed relate to the debates in which critics such as Tillyard, Howard and Rackin and Hunt have intervened. This approach also represents a good opportunity to get students to examine the play in relation to theoretical trends, in this case new historicism and cultural materialism. The importance of this kind of approach in the teaching of *Richard III*, combined with an emphasis upon performance, has been voiced by Martine van Elk who argues that the historical and ideological factors that determine individual views of the progress of history must be taken into account.[5]

The representation of Richard and Richmond can also contribute to discussions about Shakespeare's use of his sources. In spite of its age, Geoffrey Bullough's *Narrative and Dramatic Sources of Shakespeare: Volume 3, Earlier English History Plays* (London: Routledge, 1960) is still a useful resource for this purpose. The introduction to James R. Siemon's Arden edition of the play also includes an overview of Shakespeare's use of his sources and other editions of the play, including those produced by Levine and Cartelli, contain extracts of the source material which could be consulted in seminars (see the survey of editions below). A helpful piece of secondary reading would be the relevant chapter in Goy-Blanquet's book on the sources of the first tetralogy. This can also lead on to the question of genre; students can be encouraged to think about the significance of the fact that the play's title proclaims it as a tragedy, yet it is usually viewed in the context of the first tetralogy of history plays. What do students understand about the nature of the two genres? What distinguishes them from one another? To what extent does Richard conform to classical and Aristotelian ideas about the tragic hero and how helpful is it to think of him as a tragic protagonist? Discussions arising from these questions can be complemented by engaging with the critical views of the likes of Garber and Marche.

A number of themes in the play represent potentially profitable topics for discussion in seminars. If undergraduate teaching is to reflect the prominent trends in criticism, as it arguably should, then it is important to encourage students to engage in debates about the role of women in the play. Jane Donawerth has shown that she found this to be a particularly profitable approach to the play in the seminar room in which the group 'emphasized the misogyny of the male characters and the division between the worlds of men and women as a sign of social malfunction'.[6] Donawerth goes on to point out that encouraging students to approach the play in this manner leads them to 'question the long-standing interpretation of Richard as the "villain you love to hate" and ask whether women in the audience feel the same rapport with Richard, despite his evil, that men do'.[7] Discussing the role of women in the play can therefore be a rewarding activity and one which can be supplemented by critical readings of the works of Adelman, French and Levine, among others.

A Survey of Editions

Bate, Jonathan and Eric Rasmussen (eds), *Richard III* (Houndmills: Macmillan, Royal Shakespeare Company, 2008). An individual edition of the text based principally upon the first folio which appears in the RSC's ambitious *Complete Works*. The text is supplemented with a useful introduction along with additional information on Shakespeare's theatrical career, a scene-by-scene analysis, recommendations for further reading, and a performance history which includes interviews with actors Simon Russell Beale, Bill Alexander and Tom Piper. The text is well set out and is supplemented by concise footnotes.

Bevington, David and Peter Holland (eds), *Richard III: Shakespeare in Performance* (London: Methuen, Sourcebooks Shakespeare, 2007). This is an edition with an emphasis upon the play in performance. The text is richly illustrated and prefaced by essays on the performance history of the play from William Proctor Williams and from Lois Potter on the 1990 National Theatre production and its development into Richard Loncraine's 1995 film. The book also includes a discussion of the 1984 production by Antony Sher and a voice coach's perspective of the play by Andrew Wade, along with a CD featuring audio excerpts from a number of plays featuring Sher, Kenneth Branagh and Peter Finch.

Cartelli, Thomas (ed.), *Richard III* (New York: W. W. Norton, 2009). The text is based principally upon the 1597 quarto and is supplemented with comprehensive annotations. This edition also contains extracts from a number of Shakespeare's key sources and excerpts from Colley Cibber's text, along with extracts from contemporary reviews of nineteenth-century stage productions, a performance history and essays on the key film adaptations by Saskia Kossak, Barbara Hodgdon and Peter S. Donaldson. The 'Criticism' section also contains extracts from early critics like Edward Dowden and modern studies by Wilbur Sanders, Linda Charnes, Harry S. Berger and others.

Davison, Peter (ed.), *The First Quarto of 'King Richard III'* (Cambridge: Cambridge University Press, 1996). This edition of the first quarto text of *Richard III* will be of interest primarily to scholars and students specializing in the textual issues relating to the play, especially the lucid introduction which discusses the origins of the first quarto text and related issues such as memorial reconstructions, the composition of various companies, the practices of touring companies and the implications they have upon the text.

De Somogyi, Nick (ed.), *Richard III / The Tragedie of Richard III* (London: Nick Hern Books, The Shakespeare Folios, 2002). This parallel edition of the play includes a facsimile of the folio text on the right-hand page and a modern spelling text of the play on the left. It is supplemented by a short introduction discussing textual matters and is appended by a set of textual notes explaining the reasoning behind the editorial decisions that have been taken. This is likely to be of interest mainly to specialists in textual scholarship but it can also give students an insight into the processes involved in producing a modernized edition of an early modern text.

Hammond, Anthony (ed.), *King Richard III: Playgoer's Edition* (London: Thomson, The Arden Shakespeare, 1999). The text of the second series Arden Shakespeare edition is accompanied by an introduction providing a detailed performance history of the play.

Hankey, Julie (ed.), *Plays in Performance: Richard III* (Junction Books, 1981; revised, Bristol: Bristol Classical Press, 1988). In spite of being somewhat out of date, this edition of the play will still prove useful to those interested in the play in performance. A detailed commentary appears alongside the text which relates how various instances in the text have been realized in past performances. This edition also includes several illustrations from notable productions and an engaging introduction with a stage history of the play up until the mid-1980s.

Honigmann, E. A. J. (ed.), *Richard III* (London: Penguin, 1968, reprinted 2005). Honigmann's text is reissued with a detailed new introduction by Michael Taylor and an essay on the play in performance by Gillian Day. There is also a useful guide to further reading and a set of genealogical tables covering the principal characters in the history cycle. The major disadvantage of this edition is that the commentary has not been updated and, unlike most other editions, it appears at the back of the book making it less convenient for students of the play; however, the fact that the notes are separate from the text is often viewed as an advantage by those interested in performing the play.

Jowett, John (ed.), *The Tragedy of King Richard III* (Oxford: Oxford University Press, 2000). John Jowett's edition of the play is based upon the first quarto text on the grounds that this is the version closest to the play as it would have first been staged. A substantial introduction includes comment upon the textual and performance history, as well as material on the cultural and historical context of the play and photographs from notable productions of the play. The text is also supplemented with detailed on-page notes.

Levine, Nina S., *Richard III* (Boston: Cenage, The Evans Shakespeare Editions, 2011). Levine's new edition contains a text accompanied by detailed explanatory notes as well as sections with excerpts from key source materials and extracts from critical writings, including works by Rossiter and Charnes.

Lull, Janis (ed.), *King Richard III* (Cambridge: Cambridge University Press, 1999; revised, 2009). Lull's edition for The New Cambridge Shakespeare series is based upon the folio version of the play. It contains useful on-page explanatory notes and a solid introduction which contains information on *Richard*

III as a history play, comparisons with *Macbeth*, the language of the play, the play in performance and an overview of recent films, performances and criticism. It also contains a helpful essay discussing the textual issues and the differences between the quarto and folio texts of the play.

Siemon, James R. (ed.), *King Richard III* (London: Methuen, The Arden Shakespeare, 2009). As well as a reliable edition of the play, Siemon's excellent work includes a lengthy, detailed and generously illustrated introduction covering such matters as the representation of various characters, the sources of the play, the continuity of the character of Richard from the *Henry VI* plays, and a stage history. There is also a discussion of the various texts of *Richard III* and a number of useful appendices including a potential casting and doubling chart and a genealogical table.

Audio and Video Resources

The enduring popularity of *Richard III* means that there are a number of notable film and audio versions of Shakespeare's play available. The first of the two major film adaptations of *Richard III* is the 1955 version produced and directed by Laurence Olivier who also leads the cast as Richard. This version is not quite as ambitious as Olivier's earlier Shakespeare adaptations and lacks the inventive verve of his *Henry V* (1944) and the brooding mood of his *Hamlet* (1948), but it does boast a spirited performance from Olivier, if somewhat mannered by today's standards, and an impressive supporting cast which includes John Gielgud, Claire Bloom and Ralph Richardson. The UK DVD release (Network, 2006) includes a restored version of the film and, as part of the special features, *The Trial of Richard III*, a docu-drama from 1984 in which the reputation of the historical figure is scrutinized. The film is also available as a region one DVD as part of the acclaimed Criterion Collection (Criterion, 2004). This release boasts a specially restored high-definition transfer of the film and a number of extras including an audio commentary by playwright Russell Lees and Shakespeare expert John Wilders and an essay by film historian Bruce Eder along with archive material, including an interview with Olivier conducted by Kenneth Tynan. The other major film adaptation of the play is Richard Loncraine's 1995 film starring Ian McKellen as Richard, which is only currently available as a Region 1 DVD release (MGM Video and DVD, 2000). In this adaptation, the play is set in a fictionalized version of England in the 1930s with Richard as the fascistic ruler of a totalitarian state. Loncraine's film is a skilfully adapted version of Shakespeare's play which boasts some inventive set-pieces, most notably the climactic battle which takes place in the environs of Battersea Power Station, and some sterling performances from a cast which also includes Annette Benning, Kristin Scott-Thomas, Jim Broadbent and Robert Downey Jr. Also of interest is Al Pacino's *Looking for Richard* (Fox, 2005). Part documentary, part screen adaptation, this provocative film follows Pacino as he sets out to explore a number of issues and, in Pacino's words, to 'communicate a Shakespeare that is about how we feel and how we think today' and to make the play more accessible to the general American public, thus counteracting what he perceives as the dominant influence of the academy and the British establishment. Viewers also have the opportunity to see the earliest filmed production of *Richard III*, thanks to the BFI's *Silent Shakespeare* compilation DVD (BFI, 2004). The version of *Richard III* which appears on this DVD is a recording of an acclaimed performance by the notable British actor, Frank Benson. Unfortunately though, as the film historian Judith Buchanan points out in her illuminating audio commentary, the film is decidedly unadventurous in its approach, using a single static camera to capture that which emerges, by today's standards, as an old fashioned and mannered stage performance, making little of the potential offered by the new medium. As an additional feature, the *Silent Shakespeare* release also includes a useful introduction by Dr Buchanan providing an insightful overview of the relationship between Shakespeare and the early cinema.

Two notable television productions of the play, both from the BBC, have also been released on DVD, the first of which is from the 1960 series *An Age of Kings* (BBC Video, 2009). All the plays from Shakespeare's two history tetralogies are presented over thirteen episodes, each approximately 60 minutes in length. *Richard III* is divided over the final two episodes of the series, 'The Dangerous Brother' and 'The Boar Hunt', with Paul Daneman as Richard. The box-set of this series is currently only available as a Region 1 release. A later attempt at filming *Richard III* for television is also available on DVD. First transmitted in January 1983 as part of the BBC's ambitious endeavour to make television productions of all the plays in the Shakespearean canon, Jane Howell's production follows on directly from her productions of the *Henry VI* plays and is characterized by a repertory approach, using largely the same company of actors who had appeared in the previous three plays and having the action take place on the same studio set which is dressed to appear increasingly dilapidated as the sequence progresses, reflecting the deterioration of the state. Ron Cook reprises his role as Richard to head a cast that also includes Annette Crosby, Zoë Wanamaker, Brian Protheroe and Paul Jesson. Clocking in at just under four hours, this is without doubt the most comprehensive version of the play committed to film. It is currently unavailable as a standalone release but is available on region 2 as part of *The BBC TV Shakespeare Collection*, a 37-disc set which contains all the BBC adaptations, and on region 1 as part of the *BBC Shakespeare Histories* collection which also includes various other versions of the history plays from the same series. A 30-minute animated version of the play suitable for younger children was also produced as part of S4C's *Shakespeare: The Animated Tales* series. Adapted by Leon Garfield and featuring the voices of Antony Sher, Michael Maloney and Tom Wilkinson, it is available as part of the complete box-set, or individually as *Shakespeare: The Animated Tales (Act 4: 'A Midsummer Night's Dream' and 'Richard III')*.

The play is also available on various audio releases, including an old recording available on CD featuring much of the cast of

Olivier's film (Saland Publishing, 2010). There is also a version based upon the New Cambridge edition of the text which stars Kenneth Branagh as Richard and features a strong supporting cast which includes Michael Maloney, Geraldine McEwan, Nicholas Farrell and Stella Gonet (Naxos, 2005). Another recent adaptation on CD is available as part of the *Complete Shakespeare* range from Arkangel starring David Troughton, reprising his acclaimed performance as Richard, and featuring Saskia Wickham, Mary Wimbush and Philip Voss (Arkangel, 2005); this production can also be heard in MP3 format by subscribers to the *Literature Online* database by visiting their multimedia page.

Internet Sources

The sheer volume of information proliferated on the internet means that no section on web-based resources is going to be anywhere near exhaustive. The purpose of this section is therefore to provide information on a relatively small number of websites on Shakespeare in general and on *Richard III* in particular which should act as a starting point for further research. I will begin by providing details of some databases of which any student with a serious interest in the study of early modern literature should be aware. The first of these is *Early English Books Online* (*EEBO*), an indispensable resource containing electronic versions and digital facsimiles of a vast range of texts published in England. Thanks to *EEBO* it is now easier than ever to access early printed texts. There is also a useful facility which allows users to carry out a keyword search of the texts within a particular date range, enabling users to research the abundance and recurrence of individual words within a certain period. Another useful database is Chadwyck-Healey's *Literature Online* (*LION*) site which contains a wide range of electronic texts, links to criticism, and a number of multimedia resources. Another indispensable resource for literature students is JSTOR, a vast searchable database containing digitized articles from a wide range of journals.

There is a tendency for students to be drawn towards online study guides like SparkNotes (http://www.sparknotes.com), Gradesaver (http://www.gradesaver.com) and Bibliomania (http://www.bibliomania.com). While these guides can be quite useful in providing plot summaries and basic information, they are unlikely to encourage the depth of critical insight necessary in undergraduate study. Similarly, Wikipedia (http://www. wikipedia.org) is becoming an increasingly prominent presence in student research; again, this will provide some useful basic information but the entries are not necessarily written by recognized experts in the field, nor are they subject to any kind of formal peer review meaning there is no guarantee that the information provided is completely accurate or reliable. In short, these sites are no substitute for the depth and variety of critical interpretations available from other sources.

A handy starting point for researchers in Medieval and Renaissance literature is the Luminarium site (http://www. luminarium.org), a database containing information on Renaissance history and culture along with biographical information on various authors, e-texts of their works, and links to criticism available online. A number of journals are also taking advantage of the opportunities offered by the internet. While many exist as both online and print journals, *Early Modern Literary Studies* (http://extra.shu.ac.uk/emls) operates solely on the internet and has been widely recognized as a leading innovator in online scholarship. As well as publishing peer reviewed articles, *EMLS* also hosts and provides links to a range of excellent online resources including hypertext editions of early modern works and a number of useful databases.

It is also worth looking at the websites for various institutions. The Folger Shakespeare Library website, for instance, offers a wealth of material on Shakespeare, including information on individual plays, contextual details, teaching resources and over 40,000 images in their Digital Image Collection which is available to view online (http://www.folger.edu). The British Library website also contains information on *Richard III* in its Shakespeare in Quarto section (http://www.bl.uk/treasures/shakespeare/richard3.html) where there are details about the play in print, its sources and a link to detailed bibliographical descriptions of the various quarto versions of the text held by the British Library.

Other useful online sources include the *Internet Shakespeare Editions* database which contains e-texts of Shakespeare's plays, including transcriptions of the first quarto and folio texts and modernized editions of the play (their edition of *Richard III* is edited by Adrian Kiernander). There are also facsimiles of early editions of the plays as well as a wealth of biographical and contextual material, including some particularly useful information on the early modern theatre and the kinds of plays Shakespeare is likely to have seen and read (http://internetshakespeare.uvic. ca). More Shakespeare e-texts are available on Open Source Shakespeare (http://www.opensourceshakespeare.org), a useful database with user-friendly advanced search facilities and helpful tools such as concordances and an option to view all the lines of any individual speaking character in one place. Another database containing useful material is The Internet Archive (http://www. archive.org) which contains digitized versions of public domain texts, including a number of old editions of *Richard III* and Colley Cibber's version.

There are a number of sites available for those who are keen to keep informed of developments in Shakespeare studies. Shaksper: The Global Electronic Shakespeare Conference (http://shaksper.net) is one of the best; it provides a useful forum for news, discussion, comment and reviews, with a range of participants including academics, students and general enthusiasts. The community of Shakespeare scholars and enthusiasts have also taken advantage of the emergence of the blog as another source of news and comment. One of the most engaging is Blogging Shakespeare (http://bloggingshakespeare.com) which provides a space for the views of an impressive range of scholars and specialists. There is also a useful list of related websites for further exploration.

Moving on to some sites with a specific interest in *Richard III*, the website of The Richard III Society (www.richardiii.net), the society dedicated to rehabilitating the reputation of the historical Duke of Gloucester, contains a good deal of historical detail and useful information on publications and other websites. The American branch of the society has a separate website which boasts, amongst other things, a rich online library containing hypertext editions of Shakespeare's texts, source material and other historical sources (http://www.r3.org). Both obviously have a particular agenda to promote, but they still contain a great deal of useful information between them. Another recommended site is '*Richard III*: A Virtual Dramaturgical Casebook' (www.richardiiicasebook.blogspot.com), a richly detailed blog that was developed by Corinna Archer between Febrary and May 2010 in conjunction with a production of the play at Carnegie Mellon University, primarily as a means of collating the research undertaken for the production. It contains information on the historical context of the play, details of criticism and provides an insight into the process of producing a Shakespeare play. Another interesting internet source with a particular emphasis upon performance is a part of the National Theatre's 'Stagework' project which provides an interview with Sir Ian McKellen in which he discusses Shakespeare and, in particular, *Richard III*; the website has an interactive element in which McKellen's responses are determined by the options you choose when posed certain questions: (http://www.stageworkmckellen.com).

Annotated Bibliography

General Scholarship

Adelman, Janet. *Suffocating Mothers: Fantasies of Maternal Origin in Shakespeare's Plays, 'Hamlet' to 'The Tempest'* (London: Routledge, 1992). Janet Adelman's hugely influential study examines the ways in which Shakespeare's plays interrogate ideas of maternal power and the problems it poses to masculine subjectivity. In her introduction, she reads *Richard III* as a play in which the aggressively ambitious masculine forces in the play repudiate any feminine influences, resulting in the complete absence of female characters in the play's closing scenes.

Brooks, Harold F. '*Richard III*, Unhistorical Amplifications: The Women's Scenes and Seneca', *The Modern Language Review*, 75.4 (1980): 721–37. Brooks explores the possibility that Shakespeare was influenced by a number of Senecan texts, particularly *Troades* and *Hercules Furens*, in his treatment of scenes featuring the female characters, especially the wooing of Anne and in the spectacle of three generations of mourning women.

Burden, Dennis H. 'Shakespeare's History Plays: 1952–1983', *Shakespeare Survey* 38 (1985): 1–18. A useful overview of mid-twentieth century criticism on Shakespeare's history plays, with a number of helpful suggestions for secondary reading on *Richard III*.

Campana, Joseph. 'Killing Shakespeare's Children: The Cases of *Richard III* and *King John*', *Shakespeare* 3.1 (2007): 18–39. Campana reacts to the tradition of sentimentalizing childhood characters in Shakespeare's plays by focusing upon the ill-fated princes in *Richard III* and Prince Arthur in *King John* and arguing that the child characters create a 'series of affective, sexual and temporal disturbances' (19) which ultimately result in their deaths.

Charnes, Linda. *Notorious Identity: Materializing the Subject in Shakespeare* (Cambridge: Harvard University Press, 1993). This study examines Shakespeare's appropriations of various historical figures and argues that the characters as realized in the plays are responding to the notoriety which they had gained. In a substantial chapter on *Richard III*, Charnes argues that Richard attempts to repudiate his reputation by fusing his roles as vice figure and a psychologically complex individual, questioning the extent to which regal power can negate Richard's physical deformity.

French, Marilyn. *Shakespeare's Division of Experience* (New York: Ballantine Books, 1983). Contains a section on the character of Richard in both the *Henry VI* plays and *Richard III* in which French argues that he represents a form of masculinity 'completely unmitigated by any tinge of the feminine' (58) through whom the plays are reflective of a misogynistic culture beset by anxieties about the potential erasure of masculinity.

Garber, Marjorie. *Shakespeare's Ghost Writers: Literature as Uncanny Causality* (New York: Routledge, 1987). The second chapter of Garber's study argues that *Richard III* is decidedly self-conscious about its historiography with the physical deformity of the protagonist reflecting the way in which history itself has been deformed in Shakespeare's narrative.

Goy-Blanquet, Dominique. *Shakespeare's Early History Plays: From Chronicle to Stage* (Oxford: Oxford University Press, 2003). Goy-Blanquet's book contains a wealth of information on the early chronicle plays and, in particular, their sources. The book contains detailed comment on Shakespeare's use of his source material in the first tetralogy of history plays and the ways in which he appropriated, re-emphasized, re-ordered and omitted material from his sources at various points in the plays. Essential reading for those interested in Shakespeare's treatment of his sources.

Howard, Jean E. and Phyllis Rackin. *Engendering the Nation: A Feminist Account of Shakespeare's English Histories* (London: Routledge, 1997). The chapter on *Richard III* in this feminist reading of Shakespeare's history plays argues that the female characters are marginalized and that their powers of agency and transgression are appropriated by male characters such as Richard and Richmond.

Hunt, Maurice. 'Ordering Disorder in *Richard III*', *South Central Review* 6.4 (1989): 11–29. Hunt's essay engages with ideas of providence by tracing a pattern of disorder paving the way for a new period of order; in this way, Richard emerges as a figure whose 'motivation for his cruelty arises from his bitter desire to deface, to disorder the beautiful handiwork of the God who has malformed him. Regarded from this perspective, their antagonism becomes a terrific contest in which God finally orders the defacement wrought by his seemingly successful disorderer' (11).

Jackson, Ken. ' "All the World to Nothing": Badiou, Žižek and Pauline Subjectivity in *Richard III*', *Shakespeare* 1.1–2 (2005): 29–52. Jackson scrutinizes the fact that Richard is Shakespeare's only character to invoke St Paul and engages with figures such as Derrida, Badiou and Žižek to explore the play's views on Pauline subjectivity.

Levine, Nina S. *Women's Matters: Politics, Gender, and Nation in Shakespeare's Early History Plays* (Newark: University of Delaware Press, 1998). In her chapter on *Richard III*, Levine provides a lively and lucid new reading of the role of women in the play, arguing that they are much more proactive than had previously been acknowledged. She also argues that Richard's simultaneous misogyny and dependence on female characters is reflective of contemporary anxieties about female monarchy and issues relating to the succession.

Logan, Robert A. *Shakespeare's Marlowe: the Influence of Christopher Marlowe on Shakespeare's Artistry* (Aldershot: Ashgate, 2007). The second chapter in Logan's study of Marlowe's influence upon Shakespeare looks at *Titus Andronicus* and *Richard III* in relation to the fragmentary play, *The Massacre at Paris*. Logan argues that its influence can be discerned in the overreaching Machiavellian villains in each of the plays and in the elaborate plots they concoct in order to achieve their goals.

Lull, Janis. 'Thirteen Ways of Looking at a Blooper: Some Notes on the Endless Editing of *Richard III*' in Linda Anderson and Janis Lull (eds), *"A Certain Text": Close Readings and Textual Studies on Shakespeare and Others* (Cranbury: Associated University Presses, 2002): 50–64. Taking as its starting point the textual crux in which Buckingham is due to be executed on All Soul's Day in November when the Battle of Bosworth (which, of course, comes later in the play) takes place in August of the same year, this thought-provoking essay examines some of the complex editorial issues provoked by the play and Shakespeare's work in general.

Marche, Stephen. 'Mocking Dead Bones: Historical Memory and the Theater of the Dead in *Richard III*', *Comparative Drama* 37.1 (2003): 37–57. Marche argues that the tension in the play's generic status between history and tragedy requires further examination in the light of recent research in Renaissance attitudes towards death. The play's discussions about death contribute to the mingling of genres, as they represent anxieties which are prominent in both historical and tragic narratives. Marche concludes that Richard's theatrical manipulations of events will eventually be overtaken by the onset of history with the appearance of the ghosts on the eve of battle confirming to him that 'dead men do tell tales' (53).

Moulton, Ian Frederick. '"A Monster Great Deformed": The Unruly Masculinity of Richard III', *Shakespeare Quarterly* 47.3 (1996): 251–68. This essay examines the links between gender and the ways in which power is exercised in Shakespeare's play, arguing that the 'characterization of Richard III functions as both a critique and an ambivalent celebration of excessive and unruly masculinity and, in so doing, highlights the incoherence of masculinity as a concept in early modern English culture' (255).

Neill, Michael. 'Shakespeare's Halle of Mirrors: Play, Politics, and Psychology in *Richard III*', *Shakespeare Studies* 8 (1976):

99–129. This elegant article engages with some of the psycho-logical issues surrounding Richard and argues that he uses theatricality as a synthesis to compensate for his lack of a self and the absence of love in his life.

Olson, Greta. 'Richard III's Animalistic Criminal Body', *Philological Quarterly* 82.3 (2005): 301–24. Olson examines the ways in which criminals were often associated with animals in the early modern period by focusing on Shakespeare's charac-terization of Richard III and explores the significance of the comparisons made between him and certain animals at various points in the play to denote not only his criminality, but also his intelligence and strength.

Rabkin, Norman. *Shakespeare and the Problem of Meaning* (Chicago: University of Chicago Press, 1981). The third chapter of this lucid book, entitled 'Tragic Meanings: The Redactor as Critic', examines the ways in which adaptations of Shakespeare's plays act as vehicles for critical comment and views *Richard III* in relation to Colley Cibber's adaptation, arguing that Cibber places much more emphasis upon Richard's political ambition, something which, he argues, remains implicit in Shakespeare's play.

Rackin, Phyllis. *Stages of History: Shakespeare's English Chronicles* (Ithaca: Cornell University Press, 1990). An engaging study combining elements of new historicist and feminist literary theory to demonstrate the ways in which Shakespeare's history plays challenge the official orthodoxies conveyed in his sources. *Richard III* is brought into Rackin's analyses when she argues that Richard's conscious Machiavellianism clashes with the play's emphasis upon plots, prophecy and providence, as well as focusing upon treatment of the previously marginalized female characters from the sources.

Rossiter, A. P. *Angel with Horns and other Shakespeare Lectures*

(New York: Theatre Arts Books, 1961). Based upon his lecture on *Richard III*, Rossiter's entertaining and engaging essay rejects E. M. W. Tillyard's view of the play as a 'moral history' by emphasizing the theatrical nature of the central character who contributes instead to the play's status as a 'comic history'.

Sanders, Wilbur. *The Dramatist and the Received Idea: Studies in the Plays of Marlowe and Shakespeare* (Cambridge: Cambridge University Press, 1968). Sanders's book argues that previous critical orthodoxies relating to the plays of Shakespeare and Marlowe have presented an overly simplistic view of those texts. In his chapter on *Richard III*, he begins by examining Richmond's final speech and goes on to argue that the providential rhetoric contained within it deflects the factors which serve to complicate such an outlook that had been scrutinized earlier in the play.

Smidt, Kristian. *Unconformities in Shakespeare's History Plays* (London: Macmillan, 1982). Smidt's chapter on *Richard III* looks at the significance of plots and prophecies in the play, paying particular attention to their dramaturgical effects upon the most 'non-realistic' of Shakespeare's history plays.

Smith, Kristin. 'Martial Maids and Murdering Mothers: Women, Witchcraft and Motherly Transgression in *Henry VI* and *Richard III*', *Shakespeare* 3.2 (2007): 143–60. Smith's article explores how the use of language associated with witchcraft is aligned with feminine vice and corruption in the first tetralogy. In this reading, Richard's body is a manifestation of this feminine corruption which must be purged by Richmond, who is symbolic of masculine virtue, in order that the Tudor myth may be realized.

Taylor, Neil and Bryan Loughrey (eds). *Shakespeare's Early Tragedies: 'Richard III', 'Titus Andronicus', 'Romeo and Juliet': A Casebook* (Houndmills: Palgrave Macmillan, 1990). A useful collection which includes early and pre-twentieth-century essays on *Richard III*, from critics such as George Steevens, Charles

Lamb and Henry James, along with more recent essays. These include essays contributed by Irene G. Dash, who argues against the frequent directorial decision to cut the material featuring Margaret from productions, and Peter Reynolds, whose essay looks at performing Richard on stage and rejects the style of performance dating back to Cibber and promulgated by Olivier, as well as examining the significance of the actions of the marginalized group of minor characters in the play.

Torey, Michael. '"The Plain Devil and Dissembling Looks": Ambivalent Physiognomy and Shakespeare's *Richard III*', *English Literary Renaissance* 30.2 (2000): 123–53. This engaging essay contextualizes the play's emphasis upon Richard's deformity by viewing it alongside early modern theories of physiognomy promulgated by Francis Bacon and Michel de Montaigne as well as such lesser known theorists as Thomas Hill and James Ferrand.

Urkowitz, Steven. 'Reconsidering the Relationship of Quarto and Folio Texts of *Richard III*', *English Literary Renaissance* 16.3 (1986): 442–66. In this important intervention in the area of textual studies of the play, Urkowitz rejects the prevailing idea that the quarto is the product of a memorial reconstruction and suggests that its departures from the folio could be a result of authorial revision rather than the faulty recollections of actors.

Wheeler, Richard. 'History, Character, and Conscience in *Richard III*', *Comparative Drama* 5 (1971): 301–25. This article comments upon the ways in which Richard makes use of theatrical methods in order to manipulate others, particularly his cynical use of his physical deformity as a means of explaining his motives, a strategy which ultimately fails when the theatrical world he has created is broken down by the onset of reality.

Performance and Film Criticism

Colley, Scott. *Richard's Himself Again: A Stage History of Richard III* (London: Greenwood Press, 1993). A lively and erudite stage history of *Richard III* which covers all the major American and British productions of the play up to the date of publication, *Richard*'s *Himself Again* provides a narrative of the evolution of the play in theatrical tradition as well as viewing notable realizations of the role from David Garrick to Antony Sher, as well as some significant departures from established tradition.

Coursen, H. R. 'Filming Shakespeare's History: Three Films of *Richard III*' in Russell Jackson (ed.), *The Cambridge Companion to Shakespeare on Film* (Cambridge: Cambridge University Press, 2000): 99–116. This essay focuses upon the film versions of *Richard III* directed by Laurence Olivier and Richard Loncraine, along with Al Pacino's *Looking for Richard*, arguing that each of these film seek to establish themselves as essentially cinematic artefacts by taking advantage of the potential of the medium, rather than emerging simply as film versions of the play.

Day, Gillian. *Shakespeare at Stratford: Richard III* (London: Thomson Learning, The Arden Shakespeare, 2002). This volume is part of The Arden Shakespeare's *Shakespeare at Stratford* series which makes use of materials in the theatre archive of the Shakespeare Birthplace Trust at Stratford-Upon-Avon to provide a stage history of the play in Stratford since the World War II. Day's richly illustrated volume contains a wealth of information helpfully divided into three sections focusing, respectively, on political, psycho-social and metatheatrical realizations of the play.

Donaldson, Peter S. 'Cinema and the Kingdom of Death: Loncraine's *Richard III*', *Shakespeare Quarterly* 53.2: 241–59. Donaldson examines the established idea that the cinema is an art form which engages in the *memento mori* tradition, forcing the audience to encounter death rather than overcome it, and argues that this is reflected in Loncraine's film of *Richard III* which 'uses allusions to and techniques characteristic of silent cinema as emblems of death, framing the story of Richard as an allegory of the role of cinema and other modern media in the institution and maintenance of death-dealing social regimes' (244).

Freedman, Barbara. 'Critical Junctures in Shakespeare's Screen History: The Case of *Richard III*' in Russell Jackson (ed.), *The Cambridge Companion to Shakespeare on Film* (Cambridge: Cambridge University Press, 2000): 47–71. Freedman's chapter in this collection looks at four film adaptations of the play: a rediscovered silent film starring Frederick Warde; a segment in the 1929 film *Show of Shows*; Olivier's 1955 film version; and the Richard Loncraine version from 1995. Freedman argues that these films are reflective of their situation at critical moments in the development of film, both from a technological and a commercial point of view.

Hassel, R. Chris. *Songs of Death: Performance, Interpretation, and the Text of 'Richard III'* (Lincoln: University of Nebraska Press, 1987). Hassel's study examines the role of performance in the interpretation of Shakespeare's play. With a particular emphasis on the theological and providential elements of the play, Hassel looks at certain elements of the play in detail – such as the opposition between Richard and Richmond, the wooing of Elizabeth, and the scene in which Richard appears before the citizens – as well as focusing upon textual cruxes and outlooks on Providence. While he does not fully endorse the idea that the play is Tudor propaganda, his reading remains decidedly pro-Richmond.

Hatchuel, Sarah and Nathalie Vienne-Guerrin (eds). *Shakespeare on Screen: 'Richard III'* (Rouen: Publications de l'Université de Rouen, 2005). This lucid collection of essays includes contributions from a number of eminent Shakespearean scholars. The essays cover individual films such as Laurence Olivier's version,

Jane Howell's television adaptation and Al Pacino's *Looking for Richard*, as well as more general topics such as the representation of children, 'Englishness' in the film versions of the play, and the ways in which the play has been parodied.

Hodgdon, Barbara. *The End Crowns All: Closure and contradiction in Shakespeare's History* (Princeton: Princeton University Press, 1991). Using a methodology which appropriates elements of new historicism and performance studies, Hodgdon's chapter on *Richard III* considers as part of her analysis productions including those by Bill Alexander (1984), Peter Hall (1963), Terry Hands (1970) and Michael Bogdanov (1988), among others, to argue that performance as well as criticism participates in the social and cultural discourses in which the plays are engaged.

Hoenselaars, Ton (ed.). *Shakespeare's History Plays: Performance, Translation and Adaptation in Britain and Abroad* (Cambridge: Cambridge University Press, 2004). This collection of essays examines the appropriation and adaptation of Shakespeare's history plays both in Britain and overseas, discussing the effect of performance and translation upon the texts. There is much material on various productions of *Richard III* throughout; of particular interest in relation to *Richard III*, though, are Mariangela Tempera's chapter on Italian responses to the history plays from 1800–1950 and Hoenslaars's essay on Dutch and Belgian adaptations of the plays in the late 1990s.

Kossak, Saskia. *Frame My Face to All Occasions: Shakespeare's 'Richard III' on Screen* (Vienna: Wilhelm Braunmüller, 2005). A detailed study of adaptations and appropriations of *Richard III* in the cinema from versions of the play itself to other films which exhibit its influence and that of Colley Cibber's version.

McKellen, Ian and Richard Loncraine. *William Shakespeare's 'Richard III': A Screenplay* (London: Doubleday, 1996). The screenplay of the 1995 film based upon the National Theatre's

1990 production with an introduction detailing the development of the film. The material has been uploaded on McKellen's website where it is available to view free of charge: http://www.mckellen.com/cinema/richard/screenplay/index.htm.

Sher, Antony. *The Year of the King: An Actor's Diary and Sketchbook* (1984; revised edition, London: Nick Hern Books, 2004). A newly revised edition of Antony Sher's memoir of his award-winning performance as Richard at the RSC in 1984 in which he gives an insight into the process through which he created the role. Widely regarded as one of the best accounts of the experiences of an actor appearing in a theatrical production.

Wilkinson, Kate. ' "A Woman's Hide": The Presentation of Female Characters in Michael Boyd's *The Histories*', *Shakespeare* 7.1: 56–69. Kate Wilkinson's article looks at Michael Boyd's productions of the cycle of Shakespeare's history plays staged between 2006–8 and argues that the chronological order in which the plays are presented reveals that 'the development of the women characters is positive, from voiceless oppression in *Richard II* to anguished agency in *Richard III*' (57).

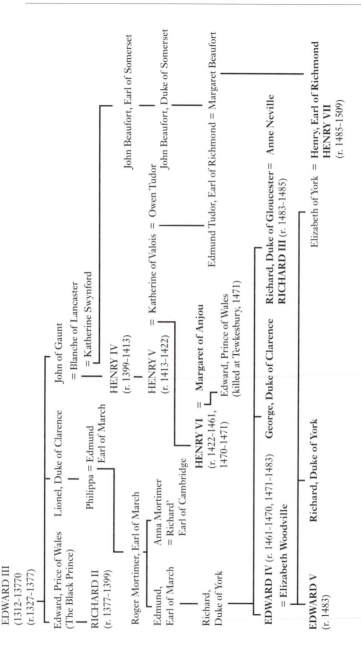

A family tree covering the major characters in *Richard III* and detailing the succession leading from the Plantagenet to the Tudor dynasty. Speaking characters in the play appear in bold.

NOTES

Introduction

1   For information about 'The Search for King Richard III' project under-
     taken by the University of Leicester see the University of Leicester's
     website *The Search for Richard III Press Materials* http://www2.le.ac.
     uk/offices/press/media-centre/richard-iii and David Baldwin, 'King
     Richard's Grave in Leicester', *Transactions of the Leicestershire
     Archaeological & Historical Society*, vol. 60 (1986), 21–4.

2   For Holinshed's account of the return of Richard's corpse into Leicester
     see Holinshed's *Chronicles of England, Scotland and Ireland* (1587) vol. 3:
     79, at *The Holinshed Project* http://www.english.ox.ac.uk/holinshed/texts.
     php?text1=1587_0504

3   For discussion of the influence of Marlowe on Shakespeare, particu-
     larly *Richard III*, see Robert A. Logan, *The Influence of Christopher
     Marlowe on Shakespeare's Artistry*, (Aldershot: Ashgate, 2007), 31–54.
     Further discussion of *Richard III* and *Doctor Faustus* can be found in
     Bernard Beckerman, 'Scene Patterns in *Doctor Faustus* and *Richard III*',
     in *Shakespeare and his Contemporaries: Essays in Comparison*, E. A. J
     Honigmann (ed.), 31–41.

4   William Shakespeare, *King Richard III*, James R. Siemon (ed.), (London:
     Bloomsbury Publishing, 2009), 5.3.179–81, 193–201. All further quota-
     tions from the play will be taken from this edition and reference will be
     given in the text.

5   Christopher Marlowe, *Doctor Faustus*, John D. Jump (ed.), (Manchester:
     Manchester University Press, 1982), Scene 19, lines 169–71.

6   For further discussion of the relationship between *Richard III* and *Macbeth*
     see Janis Lull 'Introduction' to William Shakespeare, *King Richard III*,
     Janis Lull (ed.), (Cambridge: Cambridge University Press, 1999), 16–19,
     Abraham Stoll 'Macbeth's equivocal conscience', in *Macbeth: New Critical
     Essays*, Nick Moschovakis (ed.), (London: Routledge: 2008), 132–50 and
     John S. Wilks, *The Idea of Conscience in Renaissance Tragedy* (London:
     Routledge, 1990).

7   *Warren Chernaik, The Cambridge Introduction to Shakespeare's History
     Plays* (Cambridge: Cambridge University Press, 2007), 7–11. See also

Scott McMillin and Sally-Beth MacLean, *The Queen's Men and their Plays* (Cambridge: Cambridge University Press, 2006).

8 See Chernaik, *The Cambridge Companion to Shakespeare's History Plays*, 106–25.

9 *A Mirour for Magistrates being a true chronicle historie of the vntimely falles of such vnfortunate princes and men of note, as haue happened since the first entrance of Brute into this iland, vntill this our latter age.* (London: F. Kyngston, 1610), 750–51.

10 *A Mirour for Magistrates*, 751.

11 John Jowett (ed.), 'Introduction' to William Shakespeare, *The Tragedy of King Richard III* (Oxford: Oxford University Press, 2000), 31.

12 See Jowett, 'Introduction' to William Shakespeare, *The Tragedy of King Richard III*, 59.

13 For the dating of the play see Peter Ure, 'A Pointer to the Date of Ford's *Perkin Warbeck*', *Notes and Queries* 17 (1970) 215–17.

14 S. J. Gunn, 'Warbeck, Perkin (c. 1474–1499)' *Oxford Dictionary of National Biography*. Oxford: Oxford University Press 2004.

15 John Ford, *Perkin Warbeck* in *'Tis Pity She's a Whore and Other Plays*, Marion Lomax (ed.), (Oxford: Oxford University Press, 1995), I.1.11. All further quotations from the play will be taken from this edition and reference will be given in the text.

16 See Lisa Hopkins, *John Ford's Political Theatre* (Manchester: Manchester University Press, 1994), Willy Maley, 'The Incorporation of Identities in *Perkin Warbeck*: A Response to Lisa Hopkins', *Connotations* 7.1 (1997/98) 105–15 and Joseph Candido, 'The Strange Truth of *Perkin Warbeck*', *Philological Quarterly* 59:3 (1980): 300–16.

17 'Tey, Josephine', in *The Oxford Companion to Crime and Mystery Writing*, Rosemary Herbert (ed.), (Oxford: Oxford University Press, 1999), 450–51 and Gillian Avery, 'MacKintosh, Elizabeth (1896–1952).' *Oxford Dictionary of National Biography*. Oxford: Oxford University Press, 2004. 17 January 2013 http://www.oxforddnb.com/view/article/37714 [accessed 17 Januuary 2013].

18 Susan Baker, 'Shakespearean Authority in the Classic Detective Story', *Shakespeare Quarterly* 14 (1995): 424–48.

19 Josephine Tey, *The Daughter of Time* (Harmondsworth: Penguin, 1975), 83.

20 Tey, *The Daughter of Time*, 29.

21 Tey, *The Daughter of Time*, 76.

22 Deborah Mitchell, '*Richard III*: Tonypandy in the Twentieth Century', *Literature/Film Quarterly* 25 (1997): 133–45.

23 Tey, *The Daughter of Time*, 94.

24 Tey, *The Daughter of Time*, 95.

25 David Pownall, *Richard III Part Two* in *Plays One* (London: Oberon Books, 2000), Act 1, p. 142. All further quotations from the play will be taken from this edition and reference will be given in the text.

The Critical Backstory

1   *The Diary of John Manningham of the Middle Temple*, Robert Parker Sorlien (ed.), (New Hampshire: University Press of New England, 1976), 75.

2   *The Three Parnassus Plays*, J. B. Leishman (ed.), (London: Ivor Nicholson & Watson, 1949).

3   *The Poems of Richard Corbett*, A. W. Bennett and H. R. Trevor-Roper (eds), (Oxford: Clarendon Press, 1955), 43.

4   *Complete Prose Works of John Milton*, Merritt Y. Hughes (ed.), (New Haven and London: Yale University Press, 1962), 8 vols, III, 361.

5   Milton's first publication was the poem, 'On Shakespeare', which had appeared in the Second Folio (1632). Milton, at this point, was unknown. See Gordon Campbell and Thomas Corns, *John Milton, Life, Work and Thought* (Oxford: Oxford University Press, 2008), 54. On Charles I's familiarity with Shakespeare and his ownership of a Second Folio, see Eric Rasmussen, *The Shakespeare Thefts: In Search of the First Folios* (Houndmills and New York: Palgrave Macmillan, 2011), 114.

6   Cited in Michael Dobson, *The Making of the National Poet* (Oxford: Clarendon Press, 1992), 26–7.

7   *Shakespeare Made Fit: Restoration Adaptations of Shakespeare*, Sandra Clark (ed.), (London: Dent, 1997), lxx.

8   George C. D. Odell, *Shakespeare From Betterton to Irving* (New York: Charles Scribner's Sons, 1920), 2 vols, I, 75–6.

9   *An Apology for the Life of Mr Colley Cibber Written by Himself*, Robert W. Lowe (ed.), (London: John C. Nimmo, 1889), 2 vols, I, 139–40.

10   *Apology*, I, 182.

11   *Apology*, I, 182. One of Cibber's finest performances was thought to be his Justice Shallow.

12   *Shakespeare: The Critical Heritage*, Brian Vickers (ed.), (London: Routledge, 1981), 6 vols, VI, 59–45.

13   John Jowett (ed.), 'Introduction' to William Shakespeare, *The Tragedy of King Richard III* (Oxford: Oxford University Press), 80.

14   *Eyewitnesses of Shakespeare: First Hand Accounts of Performances, 1590–1890*, Gāmini Salgādo (ed.), (London: Sussex University Press, 1975), 96.

15   *The Romantics on Shakespeare*, Jonathan Bate (ed.), (London: Penguin, 1992), 502.

16   William Hazlitt, *The Round Table and Characters of Shakespear's Plays*, Catherine Macdonald Maclean (ed.), (London: Everyman, 1936), 300–1.

17   Jowett's edition, 93.

18   George Bernard Shaw, *Our Theatres in the Nineties* (London: Constable and Co., 1932), 3 vols, II, 287.

19   Shaw, *Our Theatres in the Nineties*, II, 291.

20   Joseph Knight, *Theatrical Notes* (London: Lawrence and Bullen, 1893), 168.

21   Knight, *Theatrical Notes*, 169.

22   Knight, *Theatrical Notes*, 170.

23   Cited in *Richard III: Plays in Performance*, Julie Hankey (ed.), (Bristol: Junction Books, 1988), 2nd edition, 65.

24   *Romantics on Shakespeare*, Bate (ed.), 139.

25   *Romantics on Shakespeare*, Bate (ed.), 254.

26   *Romantics on Shakespeare*, Bate (ed.), 255.

27   Wilhelm Hortmann, *Shakespeare on the German Stage: The Twentieth Century* (Cambridge: Cambridge University Press, 1998), 3.

28   Hortmann, *Shakespeare on the German Stage*, 3. It is worth noting that *Shakespeare-Jahrbuch* has been published in Germany since 1865. *Shakespeare Quarterly* (the journal of the Shakespeare Association of America) was founded in 1950 and *Shakespeare* (the journal of the British Shakespeare Assocation) was first published in 2005.

29   J. A. R. Marriott, *English History in Shakespeare* (London: Chapman and Hall, 1918), 236.

30   Harold Jenkins, 'Shakespeare's History Plays: 1900–1951', *Shakespeare Survey 6* (1953), 1–15, 3.

31   Jenkins, 'Shakespeare's History Plays', 6.

32   Kingsley Amis, *Lucky Jim* (London: Victor Gollancz, 1954).

33   Jenkins, 'Shakespeare's History Plays', 9.

34   E. M. W. Tillyard, *The Elizabethan World Picture* (Harmondsworth: Penguin, 1979), 20, 22.

35   E. M. W. Tillyard, *Shakespeare's History Plays* (London: Chatto and Windus, 1974), 17.

36   Tillyard, *Shakespeare's History Plays*, 199.

37   Tillyard, *Shakespeare's History Plays*, 200–1.

38   'Laurence Olivier in interview with Kenneth Tynan', in *Great Acting*, Hal Burton (ed.), (London: British Broadcasting Corporation, 1967), 24.

39   Kenneth Tynan, *Theatre Writings*, Dominic Shellard (ed.), (London: Nick Hern Books, 2007), 4.

40   G. Wilson Knight, *Collected Works* (London and New York: Routledge, 2002), 12 vols, IV, 21.

41   Wilson Knight, *Collected Works*, IV, 23.

42   Wilson Knight, *Collected Works*, IV, 24.

43   E. M. W. Tillyard, *Shakespeare's Problem Plays* (London: Chatto & Windus, 1957), 13.

44   Dennis H. Burden, 'Shakespeare's History Plays: 1952–1983', *Shakespeare Survey 38* (1985), 1–18, 1.

45 A. P. Rossiter, *Angel with Horns and Other Shakespeare Lectures* (London: Longmans, 1961), 22.

46 Rossiter, *Angel with Horns*, 1.

47 Rossiter, *Angel with Horns*, 13–16.

48 Rossiter, *Angel with Horns*, 16.

49 Rossiter, *Angel with Horns*, 20.

50 Jan Kott, *Shakespeare Our Contemporary*, translated by Boleslaw Taborski (London: Routledge, 1991).

51 Peter Brook, Preface to *Shakespeare Our Contemporary*, x.

52 Brook, Preface to *Shakespeare Our Contemporary*, x–xi.

53 Kott, *Shakespeare Our Contemporary*, 3.

54 Kott, *Shakespeare Our Contemporary*, 45.

55 Kott, *Shakespeare Our Contemporary*, 8–10.

56 For a discussion of the political and educational context of the rise of materialist criticism, see Peter J. Smith, *Social Shakespeare* (Houndmills: Palgrave, 1995), 1–10.

57 *Political Shakespeare: New Essays in Cultural Materialism*, Jonathan Dollimore and Alan Sinfield (eds), (Manchester: Manchester University Press, 1985), viii

58 Jonathan Dollimore, 'Introduction: Shakespeare, Cultural Materialism and the New Historicism', in *Political Shakespeare*, 2–17 (1985) 5.

59 Graham Holderness, *Shakespeare Recycled: The Making of Historical Drama* (Hemel Hempstead: Harvester, 1992), 22.

60 Jonathan Dollimore, *Radical Tragedy: Religion, Ideology and Power in the Drama of Shakespeare and his Contemporaries* (Hemel Hempstead: Harvester, 1989), 177.

61 Phyllis Rackin, *Stages of History: Shakespeare's English Chronicles* (Ithaca, New York: Cornell University Press, 1990), 38.

62 Jowett's edition, 36.

63 Jean E. Howard and Phyllis Rackin, *Engendering a Nation: A Feminist Account of Shakespeare's English Histories* (London and New York: Routledge, 1997), p. 105.

64 Howard and Rackin, *Engendering a Nation*, 106.

65 Howard and Rackin, *Engendering a Nation*, 116.

66 Howard and Rackin, *Engendering a Nation*, 115.

67 Howard and Rackin, *Engendering a Nation*, 117.

68 'I began with the desire to speak with the dead' is the opening sentence of Greenblatt's *Shakespearean Negotiations: The Circulation of Social Energy in Renaissance England* (Oxford: Clarendon Press, 1988), 1. The latter quotation comes from Greenblatt's *Renaissance Self-Fashioning: From More to Shakespeare* (Chicago and London: University of Chicago Press, 1980), 256.

69 Greenblatt, *Shakespearean Negotiations*, 65.

Richard III on stage

1   Julie Hankey, *Richard III* (London: Junction Books, 1982), 12.

2   Hankey, *Richard III*, 13.

3   Janis Lull (ed.), 'Introduction' to William Shakespeare, *King Richard III* (Cambridge: Cambridge University Press, 1999), 24.

4   Prescott, *Richard III: A Guide to the Text and its Theatrical Life* (New York: Palgrave Macmillan, 2006), 104.

5   Julie Hankey's excellent 1982 'Plays in Performance' edition of the text includes all of these added speeches in an appendix to the text.

6   Lull, *King Richard III,* 25.

7   Hankey, *Richard III*, 31, 15.

8   Hankey, *Richard III*, 30.

9   *Laureat* quoted in Hankey, 31.

10 Aaron Hill quoted in Prescott, 105.

11 Thomas Davies, *Dramatic Miscellanies*, quoted in Hankey, 32.

12 *Laureat* quoted in Prescott, 105.

13 Hugh Richmond, *Shakespeare in Performance: King Richard III* (Manchester: Manchester University Press, 1989), 52.

14 Hankey, *Richard III*, 35.

15 Hankey, *Richard III*, 35.

16 Hankey, *Richard III*, 38.

17 Hankey, *Richard III*, 36.

18 Hankey, *Richard III*, 36, 37.

19 Prescott, *Richard III: A Guide,* 107.

20 Hankey, *Richard III*, 46.

21 Prescott, *Richard III: A Guide,* 106.

22 Alan Downer, Preface to *Oxberry's 1822 Edition of King Richard III*, (facsimile edition, Society for Theatre research, 1959), xi.

23 All references in this paragraph are from William Hazlitt in Stanley Wells, *Shakespeare in the Theatre: An Anthology of Criticism* (Oxford: Oxford University Press, 2000), 39–40.

24 Prescott, *Richard III: A Guide,* 115.

25 Hankey, *Richard III: A Guide,* 63.

26 Hankey, *Richard III: A Guide,* 64.

27 Prescott, *Richard III: A Guide,* 111.

28 Madeline Bingham quoted in Prescott, 114.

29 Madeline Bingham quoted in Prescott, 114.

30 Harold Hobson quoted in Richmond, 57.

31 Scott Colley, *Richard's Himself Again: A Stage History of Richard III*, (New York and London: Greenwood Press, 1992), 167.

32 Donald Wolfit quoted in Colley, 168.

33   Colley, *Richard's Himself Again*, 169.

34   The example of Olivier's Richard III is representative of how, even in the era
      of the directors' theatre, the lead actor in productions of *Richard III* become
      synonymous with the production in which they performed. More often than
      not when referring to this 1944 production it is termed Olivier's, however,
      Olivier only played the role – this production was directed by John Burrell.
      The slip may happen because Olivier would later go on to direct himself in
      his film version, but it is certainly symptomatic that most of the productions
      under discussion here are referred to by their actor not their director.

35   Lull, *King Richard III*, 28.

36   Kenneth Tynan in Wells, 231.

37   Kenneth Tynan in Wells, 231.

38   Kenneth Tynan in Wells, 233.

39   Kenneth Tynan in Wells, 231.

40   Kenneth Tynan in Wells, 232.

41   Hankey, *Richard III*, 68.

42   This was the only chance in this production for Thorndike to showcase
      herself here – the role was cut from Olivier's film of the play.

43   Williamson and Person quoted in Prescott, 122.

44   W. A. Darlington quoted in Hankey, 68.

45   Tynan in Wells, 233.

46   1963/4 *Wars of the Roses* RSC, 1980s *Wars of the Roses* ESC, 2006/8 *The
      Histories* RSC.

47   Robert Shaughnessy, *Representing Shakespeare: England, History and the
      RSC* (New York and London: Harvester Wheatsheaf, 1994), 41.

48   Peter Hall and John Barton, Introduction to *The Wars of the Roses: adapted
      for the Royal Shakespeare Company from William Shakespeare's* Henry VI,
      Parts 1, 2, 3 *and* Richard III (London, British Broadcasting Corporation,
      1970), x.

49   Hampton-Reeves and Chillington Rutter, *Shakespeare in Performance: The
      Henry VI Plays*, 55.

50   Hall and Barton, *The Wars of the Roses*, x–xi.

51   Colley, 222–3.

52   Hall and Barton, xi.

53   Hall and Barton, xi.

54   Shaughnessy, 122.

55   Colley, 226.

56   Colley, 226.

57   Peter Roberts, review in *Shakespearean Criticism*, 459.

58   J. C. Trewin, review in *Shakespearean Criticism*, 458.

59   Stanley Well review in *Shakespearean Criticism*, 486.

60   Antony Sher, *The Year of the King* (London: Nick Hern Books, 2004), 38.

61   Sher, *The Year of the King*, 38.

62   Sher, *The Year of the King*, 8.

63   While playing the Fool to Michael Gambon's King Lear, Sher had torn his Achilles tendon and spent six months unable to work, on crutches and in rehabilitation.

64   It is interesting to note that the skeleton which was found in a car park in Leicester and revealed to be that of Richard III in February 2013 did indeed have scoliosis.

65   Shaughnessy, 125.

66   Sher, *The Year of the King*, 129.

67   Sher, *The Year of the King*, 130.

68   Shaughnessy, *The Year of the King*, 122.

69   John Peter review in *Shakespearean Criticism* vol. 14, 486.

70   Michael Billington quoted in Colley, 239.

71   Michael Ratcliffe review in *Shakespearean Criticism* vol. 14, 485.

72   Giles Gordon, July 1984, 487.

73   Ratcliffe in *Shakespearean Criticism*, 485.

74   Ratcliffe in *Shakespearean Criticism*, 486.

75   John Peter *Shakespearean Criticism*, 486.

76   Giles Gordon August 1984 in *Shakespearean Criticism*, 489.

77   It may be significant that so many of these Richards have gone on to be knights of the realm – Olivier, Sher, McKellen – perhaps suggesting that Richard marks an important role in the career of great actors.

78   Peter Lewis, 'McKellen and his Foot Soldiers', *The Sunday Times*, 22 July 1990.

79   Robert Hewison, 'Parallel Portraits produce a Dark Double Vision', *The Sunday Times*, 29 July 1990.

80   Benedict Nightingale, 'A Very Modern Nightmare', *The Times*, 26 July 1990.

81   Nightingale, 'A Very Modern Nightmare', *The Times*, 26 July 1990.

82   Michael Billington, 'Enter Richard the Blackshirt', *Guardian*, 27 July 1990.

83   Hewison, *'Parallel Potraits Produce A Double Vision'*, 29 July 1990.

84   Hewison, *'Parallel Potraits Produce A Double Vision'*, 29 July 1990.

85   Hewison, *'Parallel Potraits Produce A Double Vision'*, 29 July 1990.

86   Peter Holland, 'Shakespeare Performances in England', *Shakespeare Survey 43* (Cambridge: Cambridge University Press, 1991), 186.

87   Billington, 27 July 1990.

88   'About Us', http://www.northern-broadsides.co.uk/?page_id=29 [accessed 6 October 2011].

89   Carol Chillington Rutter, 'Rough Magic: Northern Broadsides at Work at Play', *Shakespeare Survey* 56, 239.

90   Rutter, 'Rough Magic: Northern Broadsides at Work at Play', 239.

91   Holland, *English Shakespeares*, 152.

92   Peter Holland, *English Shakespeares: Shakespeare on the English Stage in the 1990s* (Cambridge: Cambridge University Press, 1997), 151.

93   Holland, *English Shakespeares: Shakespeare on the English Stage in the 1990s*, 152.

94   In 2002 Grandage directed Christopher Marlowe's *Edward II* with Joseph Fiennes.

95   Michael Dobson, 'Shakespeare Performances in England', *Shakespeare Survey 56* (Cambridge: Cambridge University Press, 2003), 276.

96   Benedict Nightingale, *The Times*, 19 March 2002.

97   Michael Billington, *Guardian*, 20 March 2002.

98   Carole Woddis, *Evening Standard*, 20 March 2002.

99   Dobson, *Shakespeare Survey 56*, 276.

100   Nightingale, 19 March 2002.

101   Paul Taylor, *Independent*, 20 March 2002.

102   Dobson, *Shakespeare Survey 56*, 277.

103   Dobson, *Shakespeare Survey 56*, 277.

104   Woddis, 20 March 2002.

105   Woddis, 20 March 2002.

106   Nightingale, 19 March 2002.

107   Nightingale, 19 March 2002.

108   Taylor, 20 March 2002.

109   Dobson, *Shakespeare Survey 56*, 277.

110   Billington, 20 March 2002.

111   Dobson, *Shakespeare Survey 56*, 278.

112   Dobson, *Shakespeare Survey 56*, 278.

113   Dobson, *Shakespeare Survey 56*, 278.

114   Woddis, 20 March 2002.

115   The Globe theatre on the Southbank in London is a replica of the theatre that has become synonymous with Shakespeare. The theatre was opened in 1997 and is as authentic a reconstruction as was possible with knowledge at the time.

116   The season of regime change was so called in part as a reaction to the war in Iraq and thus the productions at the Globe in the summer of 2003 were about misgovernment and battles leading to new leadership.

117   Claire Allfree, 'Enter His Majesty the Queen', *Independent*, 8 May 2003.

118   Allfree, 'Enter His Majesty the Queen', *Independent*, 8 May 2003.

119   Klett, 'Re-Dressing the Balance: All-female Shakespeare at the Globe Theatre', in Bulman (ed.) *Shakespeare Re-Dressed*, 176.

120   Kate Bassett, *Independent on Sunday*, 15 June 2003.

121   Klett, 'Re-Dressing the Balance', 177.

122   Klett, 'Re-Dressing the Balance', 147.

123   Lyn Gardner, *Guardian*, 13 June 2003.

124   Michael Coveney, *Daily Mail*, 13 June 2003.

125   Kate Bassett, 15 June 2003.

126   Lyn Gardner, 13 June 2003.

127   While Michael Coveney was explicit in calling the set a 'horror movie of a hospital' Lyn Gardner simply referred to the 'surgical masks and syringes' which conjured this image. Peter Kirwan saw the set as an 'abattoir', but it was Dominic Cavendish who saw the presence of both calling the set 'a cross between an abattoir and a First World War military hospital'.

128   Peter J. Smith, 'A Self, Reflected', *Times Higher Education*, (7 July 2011), 50.

129   Smith, 'A Self, Reflected', 50.

130   As Propeller's *Richard III* was seen as a conclusion, albeit ten years later, to the Company's production of the *Henry VI* plays titled *Rose Rage*, so Clothier's performance of Richard can also be viewed as a conclusion to the Gloucester which he performed in that earlier production. Clothier's Richard was extra-textually violent, committing a number of murders himself – of Clarence's murders, Tyrell and Lady Anne whose neck he broke while embracing her.

131   Smith, 50.

132   Michael Coveney, 'Two Plays Propelled by Fierce Energy', *Independent*, 7 February 2011.

133   Dominic Cavendish, 'Richard III/The Comedy of Errors', *The Telegraph*, 31 January 2011.

134   Peter Kirwan, '*Richard III* (Propeller) @ The Belgrade, Coventry', Bardathon blog, 10 February 2011. http://blogs.warwick.ac.uk/pkirwan/entry/richard_iii_propeller/ [accessed 20 October 2011].

135   Kirwan, '*Richard III* (Propeller) @ The Belgrade, Coventry'.

136   Kirwan, '*Richard III* (Propeller) @ The Belgrade, Coventry'.

137   Cavendish, 31 January 2011.

138   Queen Elizabeth was performed by Dominic Tighe, Lady Anne was performed by Jon Trenchard, and Queen Margaret was performed by Tony Bell in the Propeller production.

139   Ben Brantley, 'Old Stories, Spun Anew', *New York Times*, 11 July 2011.

140   Paul Taylor, 'Mendes, Spacey and a flick of Söze – this is not the usual Richard III', *Independent*, 30 June 2011.

141   Michael Billington, '*Richard III* – review', *Guardian*, 29 June 2011.

142   Quentin Letts, '*Richard III*: Showmanship Supreme but, Alas, Spacey is Hardly Olivier', *Daily Mail*, 30 June 2011.

143   Billington, 29 June 2011.

144   Billington, 29 June 2011.

145   Billington, 29 June 2011.

146   Sher, *The Year of the King*, 8.

The State of the Art

1   Marjorie Garber, *Shakespeare and Modern Culture: Literature as Uncanny Causality* (New York: Pantheon Books, 2008), 112.

2   Stephen Greenblatt, *Hamlet in Purgatory* (Princeton: Princeton University Press, 2001), 180.

3   Katharine Goodland, *Female Mourning in Medieval and Renaissance English Drama: From the Raising of Lazurus to King Lear* (Aldershot: Ashgate, 2005), 136.

4   Patricia A. Cahill, *Unto the Breach: Martial Formations, Historical Trauma, and the Early Modern Stage* (Oxford: Oxford University Press, 2008), 218.

5   Quoted in Philip Schwyzer, 'Lees and Moonshine: Remembering Richard III, 1485–635', *Renaissance Quarterly* 63 (2010), 880.

6   Wes Folkerth, *The Sound of Shakespeare* (London: Routledge, 2002), 8.

7   Kate E. Brown and Howard I. Kushner, 'Eruptive Voices: Coprolalia, Malediction, and the Poetics of Cursing', *New Literary History* 32 (2001), 548.

8   Harry Berger, Jr, 'Conscience and Complicity in *Richard III*', in *Richard III: A Norton Critical Edition*, Thomas Cartelli (ed.) (New York: W. W. Norton, 2009), 400–17, esp. 410.

9   Berger, 417.

10   Brian Walsh, *Shakespeare, The Queen's Men, and the Elizabethan Performance of History* (Cambridge: Cambridge University Press, 2009), 2.

11   Jeremy Lopez, 'Time and Talk in *Richard III* I.iv', *SEL* 45 (2005), 302.

12   Robert Weimann, *Author's Pen and Actor's Voice: Playing and Writing in Shakespeare's Theatre* (Cambridge: Cambridge University Press, 2000), 89.

13   Weimann, 90.

14   Andreas Höfele, *Stage, Stake, and Scaffold: Humans and Animals in Shakespeare's Theatre* (Oxford: Oxford University Press, 2011), 82.

15   David T. Mitchell and Sharon L. Snyder, *Narrative Prosthesis: Disability and the Dependencies of Discourse* (Ann Arbor: University of Michigan Press, 2000), 103.

16   Agnes Heller, *The Time Is Out of Joint: Shakespeare as Philosopher of History* (Lanham: Rowman and Littlefield, 2002), 277.

17   Sandra Bonetto, 'Coward Conscience and Bad Conscience in Shakespeare and Nietzsche', *Philosophy and Literature* 30 (2006), 512.

18   Bonetto, 516.

19   Joel Elliot Slotkin, 'Honeyed Toads: Sinister Aesthetics in Shakespeare's *Richard III*', *The Journal for Early Modern Cultural Studies* 7 (2007), 8, 18.

20   Barbara Hodgdon, 'Replicating Richard: Body Doubles, Body Politics', *Theatre Journal* 50 (1998), 208.

21   Robert McRuer, 'Fuck the Disabled: The Prequel,' in *Shakesqueer: A*

Queer Companion to the Complete Works of Shakespeare, Madhavi Menon (ed.) (Durham: Duke University Press, 2011), 299.

22   Peter Donaldson, 'Cinema and the Kingdom of Death: Loncraine's *Richard III*', *Shakespeare Quarterly* 53 (2002), 241.

23   Donaldson, 245.

24   Sarah Hatchuel, ' "But did'st thou see them dead?": performing death in screen adaptations of *Richard III*', in *Shakespeare on Screen: Richard III*, Sarah Hatchuel and Nathalie Vienne-Guerrin (eds) (Rouen: Publications de l'Université de Rouen, 2005), 270.

New Directions: Audience Engagement and the Genres of *Richard III*

1   For a review of this generic information see James R. Siemon, 'Introduction', Arden Third Series *Richard III* (London: Methuen, 2009) 1, 422. All citations of *Richard III* here will be taken from this edition.

2   History as a distinctive kind of drama was certainly recognized before this, as in, for instance, the discussion of types of plays in the 'Induction' to John Marston's *What You Will* (1601). But the table of contents for the First Folio is an important turning point in the formalizing of it in literary study as its own category.

3   The first major revisionist account of Richard's life is George Buck's *History of King Richard III*, c. 1622.

4   *Hamlet* 2.2.397, 398, Constance Jordan (ed.) (New York: Pearson Longman, 2004).

5   Lawrence Danson, *Shakespeare's Dramatic Genres* (Oxford: Oxford University Press, 2000) 15–16.

6   David Scott Kastan, *Shakespeare and the Shapes of Time* (Hanover, NH: University Press of New England, 1982) 133.

7   Danson, *Shakespeare's Dramatic Genres*, 7.

8   See Siemon, *Richard III* 'Introduction,' 17.

9   As printed in the Quarto. Siemon follows the Folio by assigning the entrance with the head to Lovell and Ratcliffe.

10   The classic elaboration of this argument can be found in Bernard Spivack, *Shakespeare and the Allegory of Evil* (New York: Columbia University Press, 1958).

11   Raphael Holinshed, *The Chronicles of England, Scotland and Ireland* (London, 1587) 730.

12   I discuss this issue at length in my book *Shakespeare, The Queen's Men, and The Elizabethan Performance of History* (Cambridge: Cambridge University Press, 2009).

13 Jeremy Lopez, *Theatrical Convention and Audience Response in Early Modern Drama* (Cambridge: Cambridge University Press, 2003) 18.

14 See Harbage, *Shakespeare's Audience* (New York: Columbia University Press, 1941), Cook, *The Privileged Playgoers of Shakespeare's London* (Princeton: Princeton University Press, 1981), Gurr, *Playgoing in Shakespeare's London*, 3rd edn (Cambridge: Cambridge University Press, 2004). Two recent noteworthy works on audiences that eschew sociology in favor of exploring the theoretical and practical implications of the play–playgoer dynamic are Tanya Pollard, 'Audience Reception', in Arthur Kinney (ed.) *The Oxford Handbook of Shakespeare* (Oxford University Press, 2012), and the collection *Imagining the Audience in Early Modern Drama, 1558–1642* (New York: Palgrave, 2011) Jennifer A. Low and Nova Myhill (eds). In the latter, see especially the editors' insightful introduction.

15 Lopez, *Theatrical Convention*, 18. I also do not mean to be theoretically sloppy in using terms like 'crowd' and 'assembly' as synonyms for theatrical audience. I am interested not in conflating these terms, but in the moments in a performance when an audience might imagine itself as something other than purposive playgoers; instead as, perhaps, something like a group of people massed for other purposes.

16 See, for instance, the overview of audience experience in Tiffany Stern, *Making Shakespeare: From Stage to Page* (London: Routledge, 2004) 26–7.

17 Tiffany Stern, *Documents of Performance in Early Modern England* (Cambridge: Cambridge University Press, 2009) 86.

18 See David Scott Kastan's classic article 'Proud Majesty Made a Subject: Shakespeare and the Spectacle of Rule', *Shakespeare Quarterly* 37 (1986): 459–75 for a compelling argument that audiences could learn from history plays to 'subject' kings to the will and judgment of the people.

19 On the importance of the female complaints as symbolizing the nation's 'conscience,' though, see Alison Thorne, 'O, Lawful Let It Be / That I have room … to curse awhile': Voicing the Nation's Conscience in Female Complaint in *Richard III*, *King John*, and *Henry VIII*', in Willy Maley, Margaret Tudeau-Clayton (eds) *This England, That Shakespeare: New Angles on Englishness and the Bard* (Surrey: Ashgate, 2010) 105–24.

20 Lukas Erne, *Shakespeare as Literary Dramatist* (Cambridge: Cambridge University Press, 2003).

21 For a summary of the Holinshed material and this stage direction, see Siemon, *Richard III*, 401.

22 Ramie Targoff, ' "Dirty" Amens: Devotion, Applause, and Consent in *Richard III*', *Renaissance Drama* 21 (2002): 61–84.

23 Targoff, ' "Dirty" Amens', 78, 79.

24 See Targoff, ' "Dirty" Amens', 79,

25 See the eponymous lecture in A. P. Rossiter's *Angel with Horns and other Shakespeare Lectures* (New York: Theatre Arts Books, 1961).

26 For an elaboration of this concept, see Walsh (2009), *Shakespeare, The Queen's Men, and the Elizabethan Performance of History*, 139–77.

New Directions: Tyranny and the state of exception in Shakespeare's *Richard III*

1 Walter Benjamin, 'Critique of Violence', trans. Edward Jephcott, in *Selected Writings*, Vol 1, *1913–26*, Marcus Bullock and Michael W. Jennings (eds), (Cambridge: Belknap Press, 1996), 697

2 William Shakespeare, *King Richard III: The Arden Shakespeare*, James R. Siemon (ed.) (London: Methuen Drama, 2009). All future references will be taken from this edition and cited in the text, unless otherwise noted.

3 For an excellent discussion of providentialism and identity see Martine Van Elk, '"Determined to Prove a Villain:" Criticism, Pedagogy, and *Richard III*', *College Literature* 34.4 (Fall 2007): 1–22.

4 See Francis Bacon, 'Of Deformity' (1612), in *Essays: Moral, Economical, and Political* (London: J. Johnson, 1807), 161 where he writes, 'Deformed persons are commonly even with nature, for as nature hath done ill by them, so do they by nature; being for the most part (as the Scripture saith) "*void of natural affection*" and so they have their revenge of nature.' But, Bacon goes on to argue, 'the stars of natural inclination are sometimes obscured by the sun of discipline and virtue' (162). Ian Frederick Moulton explores the range of interpretations of Richard's body in '"A Monster Great Deformed': The Unruly Masculinity of Richard III', *Shakespeare Quarterly* 47.3 (Fall 1996): 251–68, noting how for Montaigne, a physical deformity like a hunchback might a man extra virile whereas for Bacon, deformity is blight and leads to erotic 'perversion'. Linda Charnes, *Notorious Identity: Materializing the Subject in Shakespeare* (Cambridge: Harvard University Press, 1993), offers a particularly compelling, and highly influential, reading of Richard. In the end, she argues, Richard's attempt at self-determination is only a fantasy, insofar as his initial statement of villainy simply confirms the most deterministic model of the deformed criminal. He manages to assert and achieve only what audiences expected from the start: the man who cannot love will prove a villain.

5 See Ian Frederick Moulton, '"A Monster Great Deformed": The Unruly Masculinity of Richard III', *Shakespeare Quarterly* 47.3 (Fall 1996): 251–68; Joel Elliot Slotkin, 'Sinister Aesthetics in Shakespeare's *Richard III*', *JEMCS* 7.1 (2007): 5–32; Greta Olsen, 'Richard III's Animalistic Criminal Body', *Philological Quarterly* 82.3 (2005): 301–24.

6   Linda Charnes, *Notorious Identity*; Marjorie Garber, *Shakespeare's Ghost Writers: Literature as Uncanny Causality* (New York: Routledge, 1987), Mark Thornton Burnett, *Constructing 'Monsters' in Shakespearean Drama and Early Modern Culture* (Basingstoke and New York: Palgrave Macmillan, 2002).

7   William Carroll ' "The Form of Law': Ritual and Succession in *Richard III*,' in *True Rites and Maimed Rites*: Ritual and Anti-Ritual in Shakespeare and His Age, Linda Woodbridge and Edward Berry (eds), (Urbana: University of Illinois Press, 1992), 203–19, illuminates the rituals disturbed by this usurping king, including the rituals of marriage, baptism and burial. This essay builds on his study of Richard and disrupted ritual.

8   Michael Torrey, ' "The plain devil and dissembling looks": Ambivalent Physiognomy and Shakespeare's *Richard III*', ELR 30 (2000): 123–53, 126.

9   Katherine Schaap Williams, 'Enabling Richard: The Rhetoric of Disability in *Richard III*, *Disability Studies Quarterly* 29.4 (2009). Online: http://www.dsq-sds.org/article/view/997/1181, also explores the interpretive flexibility surrounding Richard. The play, she argues, 'remains ambiguous' about his body, 'staging instead a frenzy of interpretive fervor about what Richard's body really means'.

10   Richard even deforms the theatre space itself, pulling back the actor's mask to establish a transgressive intimacy with his audience.

11   '1 Murderer: "What, art thou afraid?" / 2 Murderer: "Not to kill him – having a warrant – but to be damned for killing him, from the which no warrant can defend me" ' (1.4.107–9).

12   Theodor Meron, 'Crimes and Accountability', *The American Journal of International Law* (Jan 1998): 1–40.

13   Carroll, 205. As if aware of the powerlessness of secular law, Clarence changes register, moving from English to divine law: 'I charge you … / By Christ's dear blood' (1.4.188–9) and 'the great King of kings / Hath in the table of His Law commanded / That thou shalt do no murder' (194–6). Clarence pleads that God's law should nonetheless be honored when it comes to his own punishment.

14   Meron, 97.

15   Andrew W. Neil, *Exceptionalism and the Politics of Counter-Terrorism: Liberty, Security, and the War on Terror* (New York: Routledge, 2010), 96.

16   Carl Schmitt, *Political Theology: Four Chapters on the Concept of Sovereignty*, trans. George Schwab (Chicago: University of Chicago Press, 1985), 5, 9.

17   Giorgio Agamben, *Homo Sacer: Sovereign Power and Bare Life*. trans. Daniel Heller-Roasen (Stanford: Stanford University Press, 1998), 32. While Agamben posits the permanent existence of a state of exception, and thus a transhistorical truth to this condition of sovereign power, Shakespeare instead helps us to see the way in which exceptional politics

might appear under certain historical conditions, as a result of a particularly charismatic leader taking advantage of a power vacuum in the aftermath of war, or as a result of a weak monarch. For a helpful discussion of Schmitt and Agamben, see Dani Filc and Hadas Ziv, 'Exception as the Norm and the Fiction of Sovereignty: The Lack of the Right to Health Care in the Occupied Territories' in *Evil, Law and the State: Perspectives on State Power and Violence*, John T. Parry (ed.), (Amsterdam: Rodopi, 2006), 71–86. See also Subrata Roy Chowdhury, *Rule of Law in a State of Emergency* (London: Pinter Publishers, 1989); George Schwab, *The Challenge of the Exception: An Introduction to the Political Ideas of Carl Schmitt Between 1921 and 1936* (NY: Greenwood Press, 1970, 1989); Bonnie Honig, *Emergency Politics: Paradox, Law, Democracy* (Princeton University Press, 2009).

18 Agamben, 20, 87.

19 Agamben, 31.

20 Agamben, *State of Exception*, trans. Kevin Attell (Chicago: University of Chicago Press, 2005), 53.

21 Walter Benjamin, 'Critique of Violence', trans. Edward Jephcott, in *Selected Writings*, vol. 1, *1913–26*, Marcus Bullock and Michael W. Jennings (eds), Cambridge: Belknap Press, 1996, 252. Agamben cites and analyses this passage in *State of Exception*, 53.

22 Meron, 38.

23 Charnes, 68.

New Directions: 'Some tardy cripple': Timing Disability in *Richard III*

1 William Shakespeare, *Richard III* 2.1.90. All Shakespeare citations for this play are drawn from *King Richard III*, James R. Siemon (ed.) (London: Arden Shakespeare, 2009). Special thanks to Stephen Greenblatt and Lalita Pandit for offering feedback on an earlier draft of this essay, which was circulated at Professor Greenblatt's seminar, entitled 'Early Modern Lives', held in Seattle, WA, at the 2011 Shakespeare Association of America (SAA) meeting. Thanks as well to Allison Hobgood and Lindsey Row-Heyveld for their feedback on various sections of this essay. And, finally, I would like to praise the Tyler Rigg Foundation, which, through the 'Tyler Rigg Foundation Award', supports disability scholarship via the journal *Disability Studies Quarterly*.

2 See David Mitchell and Sharon Snyder, *Narrative Prosthesis: Disability and the Dependencies of Discourse* (Ann Arbor: University of Michigan Press, 2001), 20.

3 This is Richard's textual introduction to the world, in 'The Persons

of the Play', for the drama entitled *The First Part of the Contention of the Two Famous Houses of York and Lancaster (2 Henry VI)* in *The Norton Shakespeare*, Stephen Greenblatt, Walter Cohen, Jean Howard, and Katharine Eisaman Maus (eds) (New York: W. W. Norton, 1997). Excepting those in *Richard III*, all Shakespeare quotations in this essay are drawn from The *Norton Shakespeare*.

4   In addition to such conventional uses of eyesight and blindness in *Lear*, for example, or to sanity and 'madness' in *Hamlet,* the sonnets incorporate, perhaps less familiarly, a narrator who is of 'strength by limping sway disabled' (66.8), one who urges his auditor to 'Speak of my lameness, and I straight will halt [limp]' (89.3) in *The Norton Shakespeare*.

5   For more on medieval disability studies, see Tory Vandeventer Pearman, *Women and Disability in Medieval Literature* (New York: Palgrave Macmillan, 2010); Irina Metztler, *Disability in Medieval Europe: Thinking About Physical Impairment in the High Middle Ages, C. 1100–1400* (London; New York: Routledge, 2006); *Disability in the Middles Ages: Rehabilitations, Reconsiderations, Reverberations*, Joshua Eyler (ed.) (Farnham, England; Burlington, Vermont: Ashgate, 2010); Edward Wheatley, *Stumbling Blocks Before the Blind: Medieval Constructions of Disability* (Ann Arbor: University of Michigan Press, 2010); and Lois Bragg, *Oedipus Borealis: The Aberrant Body in Old Icelandic Myth and Saga* (Madison, New Jersey: Fairleigh Dickinson University Press, 2004). For more on early modern disability studies, see the essays published under the title *Disabled Shakespeares*, in the journal *Disability Studies Quarterly* 29.4 (2009), Allison Hobgood and David Houston Wood (eds), and the introduction, entitled 'Ethical Staring', to our forthcoming volume, *Recovering Disability in Early Modern England*, Hobgood and Wood (eds), (Columbus, Ohio: Ohio State University Press, 2013).

6   See Bragg, *Oedipus Borealis*, 167. Note that Lois Bragg also publishes under the name Edna Edith Sayers.

7   Drawing on Erving Goffman and Lerita Coleman's work on stigma, Shakespearean disability scholarship tends to push beyond figurative readings of disability, attending to the politico-historical realities that undergird and produce such disability representations. See Goffman, *The Disability Studies Reader*, Lennard Davis (ed.) 1st edn, (New York: Routledge, 1997), 203–15, and *Stigma: Notes on the Management of Spoiled Identity* ([1963] Harmondsworth, 1968); and Coleman, 'Stigma: An Enigma Demystified', *The Disability Studies Reader* Lennard Davis (ed.) 1st edn, (New York: Routledge, 1997), 216–31.

8   See Rosemarie Garland-Thomson, 'The Beauty and the Freak', *Points of Contact: Disability, Art, and Culture*, Susan Crutchfield and Marcy Epstein (eds), (Ann Arbor: University of Michigan Press, 2000), 181.

9   See David Mitchell and Sharon Snyder, *Narrative Prosthesis: Disability and the Dependencies of Discourse* 20; see also Mitchell and Snyder, 'Narrative Prosthesis and the Materiality of Metaphor', *The Disability Studies Reader*, 205–16. Unless otherwise specified, all references to Mitchell and Snyder in this essay refer to *Narrative Prosthesis: Disability and the Dependencies of Discourse*.

10   Ibid., 22.

11   Ibid., 23.

12   For more on revenge tragedy and disability issues, such as narrative prosthesis, see Lindsey Row-Heyveld, 'Antic Dispositions: Mental and Intellectual Disabilities in Early Modern Revenge,' *Recovering Disability in Early Modern England*, Hobgood and Wood (eds), (Columbus, Ohio: The Ohio State University Press, forthcoming 2013).

13   See Linton, *Claiming Disability: Knowledge and Identity* (New York: New York University Press, 1998), 2.

14   See Pearman, *Women and Disability in Medieval Literature*, 3.

15   See Mitchell and Snyder, *Narrative Prosthesis*, 25.

16   See Eyler, *Disability in the Middle Ages*, 4. Also note *Vital Signs: Crip Cultural Talks Back*, dir. David T. Mitchell and Sharon Snyder (Brace Yourselves Productions, 1997), an extraordinary documentary which details the stigmatizing effects inflicted by the medical model upon the very individuals such a model seeks to aid.

17   See Garland-Thomson, 'The Beauty and the Freak', 181.

18   See Eyler, *Disability in the Middles Ages*, 4. As Lennard Davis observes: 'Impairment is the physical fact of lacking an arm or a leg. Disability is the social process that turns an impairment into a negative by creating barriers to access', in *Bending over Backwards: Disability, Dismodernism, and Other Difficult Positions* (New York: New York University Press, 2002), 12.

19   See Metzler, *Disability in Medieval Europe*, 190. Metzler's reasoning follows the logic of the social model regarding disability: 'disability', as a concept, is socio-culturally constructed; 'impairment', as a fact, on the other hand, is transhistorical (33).

20   See Comber, 'A Medieval King "Disabled" by an Early Modern Construct', in Eyler, *Disability in the Middle Ages*, 191. Comber subsequently makes the distinction that while the *textual* Richard is not disabled, the *performed* Richard, in fact, is: 'performatively, his *disability* is never lost. He remains, in perpetuity, a product of the religious, dramatic, social and political constructs which created him' (195). I engage the efficacy of this approach to Richard's disability below.

21   See David Mitchell and Susan Snyder, *Cultural Locations of Disability* (Chicago and London: University of Chicago Press, 2006), 6.

22   See Eyler, *Disability in the Middles Ages*, 6.

23   See the forthcoming essay, 'Ethical Staring', in *Recovering Disability in Early Modern England*, Hobgood and Wood (eds), (Columbus, Ohio: Ohio State University Press, 2013).

24   See Eyler, *Disability in the Middle Ages*, 6.

25   See Wheatley, *Stumbling Blocks Before the Blind*, who observes of the religious model: 'Repeatedly in medieval literature, art, and religious teaching, impairment ... functioned in ways largely structured by Jesus's miracles ... Indeed, proof that a potential saint had performed miracles while alive was integral to the canonization process, and paramount among those was the cure of impairments' (11). For more on disability and the Reformation, see Lindsey Row-Heyveld, ' "The lying'st knave in Christendom": The Development of Disability in the False Miracle of St Alban's', *Disability Studies Quarterly* 29.4 (2009).

26   Ibid., 11.

27   See Eyler, *Disability in the Middle Ages*, 7.

28   Eyler, *Disability in the Middle Ages*, 6.

29   See *Looking for Richard*, dir. Al Pacino (Fox Searchlight Pictures, 1996).

30   See Linda Charnes, *Notorious Identity: Materializing the Subject in Shakespeare* (Cambridge, MA: Harvard University Press, 1993), 28.

31   Charnes, *Notorious Identity: Materializing the Subject in Shakespeare*, 30.

32   See Stephen Greenblatt, *Shakespearean Negotiations: The Circulation of Social Energy in* Renaissance England (Oxford: Clarendon Press, 1988), 66–93.

33   For more on early modern medical differentiation between humoral forms identified as 'natural/ kindly' and 'unnatural/unkindly', see any of the following primary sources: Robert Burton, *Anatomy of Melancholy* (Oxford, 1621); Timothy Bright, *A Treatise on Melancholie* (London, 1586); Helkiah Crooke, *Mikrokosmographia* (London, 1618); Thomas Wright, *The Passions of the Minde in Generall* (London, 1605); and Stephen Batman, *Batman upon Bartholome* (London, 1582). For secondary works on this differentiation between humoral forms, see those studies in note 36 below.

34   See Charnes, *Notorious Identity*, 23. For more on the correlation between ugliness and morality, see Joel Elliot Slotkin, 'Sinister Aesthetics', 8–11, 18–22.

35   Montaigne and Bacon's interests in the reality of disabled lives centres to a marked degree upon their fascination with their alleged sexual proclivities (see Ian Moulton, ' "A Monster Great Deformed": The Unruly Masculinity of Richard III', *Shakespeare Quarterly* 47.3 [Autumn 1996], esp. 262–8). Moulton observes that while the 'birth of a deformed child was inevitably seen as portentous' (262), dispassionate views of such non-normativity were also gaining currency. As Montaigne suggests: 'Those that we call monsters are not so to God, who sees in the immensity

of His work the infinite forms that He has comprehended therein; and it is to be believed that this figure which astonishes us has relation to some other figure of the same kind unknown to man' ('Of a Monstrous Child'). Montaigne concludes his essay: 'Whatever falls out contrary to custom we say is contrary to nature, but nothing, whatever it be, is contrary to her. Let, therefore, this universal and natural reason expel the error and astonishment that novelty brings along with it'. See Slotkin, 'Sinister Aesthetics', for discussion of morality and ugliness (8–11, 18–22); and Charnes, *Notorious Identity*, for discussion on the relationship between moral probity and posture (24–5).

36   For more on early modern embodiment, see Gail Kern Paster, *The Body Embarrassed: Drama and the Disciplines of Shame* (Ithaca: Cornell University Press, 1993) and *Humoring the Body: Emotions and the Shakespearean Stage* (Chicago: University of Chicago Press, 2004); *Reading the Early Modern Passions*, Gail Kern Paster, Mary Floyd-Wilson and Katherine Rowe (eds), (Philadelphia: University of Pennsylvania Press, 2004); Mark Breitenberg, *Anxious Masculinity in Early Modern England* (Cambridge: Cambridge University Press, 1996); Michael Schoenfeldt, *Bodies and Selves in Early Modern England Physiology and Inwardness in Spenser, Shakespeare, Herbert, and Milton* (New York: Cambridge University Press, 1999); Mary Floyd-Wilson, *English Ethnicity and Race in Early Modern Drama* (Cambridge University Press, 2006); Garrett Sullivan, *Memory and Forgetting in English Renaissance Drama: Shakespeare, Marlowe, Webster* (Cambridge: Cambridge University Press, 2005); *Environment and Embodiment in Early Modern England*, Garrett Sullivan and Mary Floyd-Wilson (eds), (Houndmills, Basingstoke: Palgrave Macmillan, 2007); *Renaissance Drama 35*, Mary Floyd-Wilson and Garrett Sullivan (eds), (Evanston, IL: Northwestern University Press, 2006); Tanya Pollard, *Drugs and Theatre in Early Modern England* (Oxford: Oxford University Press, 2005); and David Houston Wood, *Time, Narrative, and Emotion in Early Modern England* (Farnham, England; Burlington, VT: Ashgate, 2009).

37   See the collection of essays entitled *Disabled Shakespeares*, in *Disability Studies Quarterly* 29.4 (2009), especially my essay on humoural adustion and Michael Cassio's drunkenness in *Othello*, entitled '"Flustered with flowing cups": Humoralism, Alcoholism, and the Prosthetic Narrative in *Othello*'.

38   Paster's assessment of the 'semi-permeable irrigated container' of the humoural self thus changed into the Cartesian self Sutton describes as 'a static, solid container, only barely breached, in principle autonomous from culture and environment, tampered with only by diseases and experts'. Writing on the verge of this tectonic shift from humoural to Enlightenment philosophies of mind, Shakespeare portrays stigmatized

illness, disease, and deformity – in a word, disability – by conceiving of it in ways that explore this tension (see Paster, *The Body Embarrassed*, 8; and John Sutton, *Philosophy and Memory Traces: Descartes to Connectionism* (Cambridge [England]; New York: Cambridge University Press, 1998), 39–41.

39 See Moulton, ' "A Monster Great Deformed" ', 261.

40 Moulton, ' "A Monster Great Deformed" ', 262.

41 See Charnes: *Notorious Identity*, 'whatever "inwardness" Shakespeare achieves with Richard depends precisely upon his construction as stock villain' (29).

42 See Wheatley, *Stumbling Blocks Before the Blind*, 25.

43 This figurative representation of time confirms in some measure Rosalind's assertion in *As You Like It*, as well, that time really does travel 'at divers paces with divers persons' (3.2.282–3).

44 See Timothy Hampton, 'Strange Alteration', *Reading the Early Modern Passions*, Paster, Rowe, and Floyd-Wilson (eds) (Philadelphia: University of Pennsylvania Press, 2004); and Wood, *Time, Narrative, and Emotion*.

45 See Cathy Yandell, *Carpe Corpus* (Newark: University of New Jersey Press, 2000), 25.

46 See Elihu Pearlman, 'The Invention of Richard Gloucester', *Shakespeare Quarterly*, 43.4 (1992), 410–29.

47 See Ian Moulton, ' "A Monster Great Deformed" ', 251–68.

48 See Wood, *Time, Narrative, and Emotion*, 15–43. Note also Patricia Parker, 'Shakespeare and Rhetoric: "Dilation" and "Delation" ', *Shakespeare and the Question of Theory*, Patricia Parker and Geoffrey Hartman (eds), (New York: Methuen, 1985) on the rhetorical and generic traditions associated with delay and with action.

49 I cite these moments with permission from a remarkable, unpublished paper entitled 'The Performance of Disability and the Disabling of Performance in *Richard III*', written by Lindsey Row-Heyveld. The paper was presented at the 2009 SAA seminar entitled 'Disabled Shakespeare', in Washington, DC, which I co-chaired with Allison Hobgood.

50 See John Julian Norwich, *Shakespeare's Kings: The Great Plays and the History of England in the Middle Ages: 1337–1485* (Scribner, 2001), 360. For more on Lennard Davis's concept of 'Dismodernism' and the rhetoric of time in *Richard III*, see Katherine Schaap Williams, 'Enabling Richard: The Rhetoric of Disability in *Richard III*', *Disability Studies Quarterly* 29.4 (Fall 2009) http://dsq_sds.org/article/view/997/1181.

51 See Charnes, *Notorious Identity*, 52–3.

52 One might think of the 'magic' materialization of Hermione's wrinkles upon the statue in Act 5 of *The Winter's Tale*.

53 See Mitchell and Snyder, *Narrative Prosthesis*, 20.

54   See Wheatley, *Stumbling Blocks Before the Blind*, 26.

55   See Harry Berger, 'Conscience and Complicity in *Richard III*', *Richard III: Norton Critical Edition*. Thomas Cartelli (ed.), (New York, Norton, 2009): 414. Also note Hamlet's similarly ambiguous self-assertion as God's 'scourge and minister' (3.4.159), and Grendel's entrance into Heorot, in *Beowulf*, in which the poet informs us that: 'godes yrre bær [he bore God's anger]' (*Beowulf: A New Verse Translation [Bilingual Edition]*, trans. Seamus Heaney [New York: W. W. Norton, 2001] line 711).

56   See Wheatley, *Stumbling Blocks Before the Blind*, 11.

57   Wheatley, *Stumbling Blocks Before the Blind*, 26.

58   See Comber, 'A Medieval King "Disabled" by an Early Modern Construct', 191.

59   See Eyler, *Disability in the Middle Ages*, 6.

60   Such a reading of *Richard III* would maintain a certain complexity given Richmond's assertion that, in sleeping late on the day of battle, he has proven to be a 'tardy sluggard' (5.3.225). While the ostensible light-heartedness of the confession might generate empathy or even laughter, it also links the imminent King Henry VII with his predecessor, Richard III, the 'tardy cripple', in an essential (and haunting) way.

New Directions: 'Put[ing] on Some *Other* Shape': *Richard III* as an Arab V.I.P.

1   William Shakespeare, *3 Henry VI The Arden Shakespeare Complete Works* Ann Thompson, Richard Proudfoot and David Scott Kastan (eds), (London: The Arden Shakespeare, 2001).

2   Saskia Kossak, *'Frame My Face to All Occasions': Shakespeare's Richard III on Screen* (Vienna: Braumüller, 2005), ix.

3   William Shakespeare, *King Richard III: The Arden Shakespeare*, James R. Siemon (ed.), (London: Methuen Drama, 2009), 1.1.21. All further references will be taken from this edition and cited in the text.

4   John W. Blanpied, *Time and the Artist in Shakespeare's English Histories* (Newark and London: University of Delaware Press, 1983), 85.

5   Special thanks to the directors Tim Langford and Shakir Abal for allowing me to include images from the film in this essay.

6   It is somewhat ironic that Olivier's *Richard III* should be hailed as the 'definitive' Shakespeare film given its conspicuous 'staginess'.

7   James N. Loehlin, ' "Top of the World, Ma": *Richard III* and Cinematic Convention', in Lynda E. Boose and Richard Burt (eds), *Shakespeare the Movie: Popularising the Plays on Film, TV and Video* (London and New York: Routledge, 1997), 75.

8   Michael Anderegg, *Cinematic Shakespeare* (Lanham, MD and Oxford: Rowman and Littlefield, 2004), 103.

9   Douglas Brode, *Shakespeare in the Movies: From the Silent Era to Shakespeare in Love* (Oxford University Press, 2000), 35. Stephen M. Buhler goes one step further and brands McKellen's Richard downright 'camp' in his essay in Mark Thornton Burnett and Ramona Wray (eds) *Shakespeare, Film, Fin de Siècle* (New York and Basingstoke: Palgrave, 2000), pp. 40–57.

10   Also according to Brode, Al Pacino gets the balance between creepy and sexy just right and, as a combo of 'Burbage and Kean', is the 'perfect Richard' (38).

11   Barbara Hodgdon, 'Spectacular Bodies: Acting + Cinema + Shakespeare', in Diana Henderson (ed.), *A Concise Companion to Shakespeare on Screen* (Oxford: Blackwell, 2006), 106.

12   For more on the influence of Shakespeare's *Richard III* on *Scarface* (and *vice versa*), see James Loehlin, '"Top of the World, Ma", in Boose and Burt, 1997; 67–9 and Linda Bradley Salamon, 'Postmodern Villainy in *Richard III* and *Scarface*', *Journal of Popular Film and Television*, 28.2 (2000), 54–63.

13   Richard Corliss quoted in Kathy M. Howlett, *Framing Shakespeare on Film* (Ohio University Press, 2000), 136. See Thomas Cartelli, 'Shakespeare and the Street: Pacino's *Looking for Richard*, Bedford's *Street King*, and the Common Understanding', in Richard Burt and Lynda E. Boose (eds), *Shakespeare the Movie II: Popularising the Plays on Film, TV, Video and DVD* (London and New York: Routledge, 2003), 186–99.

14   See Denise Albanese, 'The Shakespeare film and the Americanization of culture' in Jean Howard (ed.), *Marxist Shakespeares* (London: Routledge, 2001), 206–26. Quotation taken from Margo Jefferson, 'Welcoming Shakespeare into the Caliban Family', *New York Times* (12 November 1996).

15   Given that it is more with the audience whom Richard seems to identify rather than the 'royal' cast, from whom he is disconnected and critical of throughout, it makes sense that he be regarded as a 'street' figure in recent filmic versions of the play. Given, too, the democratizing nature of film, it is not surprising that Richard should be transformed onscreen into a less regal and a more common, everyman figure.

16   Thomas Cartelli and Katherine Rowe, *New Wave Shakespeare on Screen* (Cambridge and Malden, MA: Polity, 2007), 103.

17   Kossak, 167.

18   Mark Thornton Burnett, *Filming Shakespeare in the Global Marketplace* (New York and Basingstoke: Palgrave Macmillan, 2007), 145.

19   Ibid.

performance on both sides of the 1990 Kuwait war was mediocre' (*Middle East Quarterly*, 6.4 [1999], 17–27)

44   Muḥammad Mursī Abd Allāh, *The United Arab Emirates: A Modern History* (London: Croom Helm, 1978), 209.

45   Sukanta Chaudhuri and Chee Seng Lim, 'Introduction', in Chaudhuri and Lim (eds), *Shakespeare Without English: The Reception of Shakespeare in Non-Anglophone Countries* (New Delhi: Dorling Kindersley, 2006), xii–xiii.

46   The most vocal sceptics of foreign Shakespeare include Rustom Bharucha and Patrice Pavis.

47   See Janne Louise Andersen, 'Sulayman Al Bassam's Progress: How the Arab Spring Revitalized the Kuwaiti Playwright's Passion', *Rolling Stone* (1 November 2011).

48   Noel Carroll, *Theorizing the Moving Image* (Cambridge University Press, 1996), 84.

49   See Paul Wells' chapter on the documentary form in Jill Nelmes (ed.), *An Introduction to Film Studies* (London and New York: Routledge, 2003), 187–211.

50   Bill Nichols, *Representing Reality: Issues and Concepts in Documentary* (Indiana University Press, 1991), 42.

51   For more on Richard's porcine qualities see Kevin De Ornellas, '"Thou Eluish Markt Abortiue Rooting Hog": Images of the Boar in Filmed *Richard III*s', in Sarah Hatchuel and Nathalie Vienne-Guerrin (eds), *Shakespeare on Screen: 'Richard III'* (Rouen: Publications de l'Université de Rouen, 2005),139–60.

52   See, for instance, Roy Strong, *Splendor at Court: Renaissance Spectacle and the Theater of Power* (Houghton Mifflin, 1973) and Stephen Orgel, *The Illusion of Power: Political Theater in the English Renaissance* (University of California Press, 1975) – two seminal studies on this subject.

53   Sebastian Lefait, 'The Hybridisation of Film Form in *Richard III*', in Hatchuel and Guerrin, 2005; 44.

54   See Graham Holderness, 'Introduction' to Sulayman Al-Bassam, *The Al-Hamlet Summit: A Political Arabesque* (University of Hertfordshire Press, 2006), 16.

55   Ibid.

56   Homi Bhabha quoted in Ankie Hoogvelt, *Globalisation and the Post-Colonial World: The New Politic Economy of Development* (Johns Hopkins University Press, 2001), 158.

57   Bill Ashcroft, Gareth Griffiths, Helen Tiffin, 'Introduction', in Ashcroft *et al.* (eds), *The Post-Colonial Studies Reader* (London and New York: Routledge, 1995), 8.

58   H. R. Coursen, 'Filming Shakespeare's History: Three Films of *Richard III*', in Russell Jackson (ed.), *The Cambridge Companion to Shakespeare on Film* (Cambridge University Press, 2000), 103.

59   *The New York Times* (11 June 2009) – emphasis mine. It is Olivier who
      should be credited with turning the play into a psychological study.

60   Ibid.

61   Visit the film's website: http://www.richard3anarabV.I.P.com/images/
      Press%20Kit_English.pdf

62   The Sykes–Picot Agreement (1916) was a secret agreement between the
      governments of the UK and France, drawing up their proposed spheres
      of influence and control in Middle East should the Triple Entente
      succeed in defeating the Ottoman Empire duringWorld War I. Its mention
      here suggests Richard does not distinguish between Westerners – all, in
      his opinion, are responsible for violence and oppression in the region
      throughout the last century.

63   See Graham Holderness, *The Shakespeare Myth* (Manchester University
      Press, 1988), 168. Nixon, in turn, is also frequently likened to Scarface.

64   In 1974, David Edgar produced a musical about Nixon based on
      Shakespeare's *Richard III* comically entitled, *Dick Deterred*.

65   Vassilis Fouskas and Bülent Gökay, *The New American Imperialism: Bush's
      War on Terror and Blood for Oil* (Greenwood Publishing Group, 2005),
      195. Nafeez Mosaddeq Ahmed, *Behind the War on Terror: Western Secret
      Strategy and the Struggle for Iraq* (Clairview, 2003), 63.

66   Jonathan Bate and Eric Rasmussen, 'Introduction' in Bate and Rasmussen
      (eds), *Richard III* (The Royal Shakespeare Company, 2008), 8.

Resources for Teaching and Studying *Richard III*

1   See, for example Guy Spielmann, 'Teaching Early Modern Spectacle
     through Film: Exploring Possibilities, Challenges and Pitfalls through a
     French Corpus', in Derval Conroy and Danielle Clarke (eds), *Teaching the
     Early Modern Period* (Houndmills: Palgrave Macmillan, 2011): 231–50 and
     Miriam Gilbert, 'Teaching Shakespeare Through Performance', *Shakespeare
     Quarterly* 35.5 (1984): 601–8.

2   Matthew C. Hansen, 'Learning to Read Shakespeare: Using Read-Throughs
     as a Teaching and Learning Strategy', *Working Papers on the Web* 4
     (2002) Online: http://extra.shu.ac.uk/wpw/renaissance/hansen.htm#fn2.
     A similar strategy is discussed in Henry Phillips, 'Teaching French
     Seventeenth-Century Theatre: Saying is Believing' in Conroy and Clarke,
     227–30.

3   See, for example, Michael Hattaway (ed.), *The Cambridge Companion to
     Shakespeare's History Plays* (Cambridge: Cambridge University Press, 2002)
     and Warren L. Chernaik, *The Cambridge Introduction to Shakespeare's
     History Play* (Cambridge: Cambridge University Press, 2007).

4   Patricia A. Cahill, *Unto the Breach: Martial Formations, Historical Trauma,*

    and the Early Modern Stage (Oxford: Oxford University Press, 2008),
    especially 166–208 and 209–20.

5   Van Elk, Martine. ' "Determined to Prove a Villain": Criticism, Pedagogy,
    and *Richard III*', *College Literature*, 34.4 (2007): 1–21.

6   Jane Donawerth, 'Teaching Shakespeare in the Context of Renaissance
    Women's Culture', *Shakespeare Quarterly*, 47.4 (1996): 476–89, 479.

7   Donawerth, 'Teaching Shakespeare in the Context of Renaissance Women's
    Culture', 488.

BIBLIOGRAPHY

A Mirour for Magistrates (London: F. Kyngston, 1610).

Agamben, Giorgio, *State of Exception*, trans. Kevin Attell (Chicago: University of Chicago Press, 2005).

—*Homo Sacer: Sovereign Power and Bare Life*, trans. Daniel Heller-Roasen (Stanford: Stanford University Press, 1998).

Ahmed, N. M., *Behind the War on Terror: Western Secret Strategy and the Struggle for Iraq* (East Sussex: Clairview, 2003).

Albanese, D., 'The Shakespeare Film and the Americanisation of Culture', in *Marxist Shakespeares*, Jean Howard (ed.), (London: Routledge, 2001), 206–26.

Allāh, M. M. A., *The United Arab Emirates: A Modern History* (London: Croom Helm, 1978).

Anderegg, M., *Cinematic Shakespeare* (Lanham, MD and Oxford: Rowman and Littlefield, 2004).

Andersen, J. L., 'Sulayman Al Bassam's Progress: How the Arab Spring Revitalized the Kuwaiti Playwright's Passion', *Rolling Stone* (1 November 2011).

Ashcroft, B., G. Griffiths and H. Tiffin, 'Introduction', in *The Post-Colonial Studies Reader*, Ashcroft *et al.* (eds), (London and New York: Routledge, 1995), 7–17.

Aune, M. G., 'The Uses of *Richard III*: From Robert Cecil to Richard Nixon', *Shakespeare Bulletin* 24 (2006): 23–47.

Bacon, Francis, *The Essays*, John Pitcher (ed.), (New York: Penguin, 1985).

Badawi, M. M., 'Perennial Themes in Modern Arabic Literature', *British Journal of Middle Eastern Studies* 20 (1993): 3–19.

Baker, Susan, 'Shakespearean Authority in the Classic Detective Story', *Shakespeare Quarterly* 14 (1995): 424–48.

Baldwin, David, 'King Richard's Grave in Leicester', Transactions of the Leicestershire Archaeological & Historical Society 60 (1986): 21–4.

Bate, Jonathan, 'Introduction' in *Richard III*, Jonathan Bate and Eric Rasmussen (eds.), (New York: The Royal Shakespeare Company, 2008), vii–xiv.

—(ed.) *The Romantics on Shakespeare* (London: Penguin, 1992)

Batman, Stephen, *Batman upon Bartholome.* (London, 1582).

Bernard Beckerman, 'Scene Patterns in *Doctor Faustus* and *Richard III*', in *Shakespeare and his Contemporaries: Essays in Comparison*, E. A. J. Honigmann (ed.), (Manchester: Manchester University Press,1986), 31–41.

Belsey, Catherine, 'Little princes: Shakespeare's royal children', in *Shakespeare and Childhood*, Kate Chedgzoy, Susanne Greenhalgh and Robert Shaughnessy (eds), (Cambridge: Cambridge University Press, 2007), 32–48.

Benjamin, Walter, 'Critique of Violence', trans. Edward Jephcott, in *Selected Writings,* Vol 1, *1913–26*, Marcus Bullock and Michael W. Jennings (eds), (Cambridge: Belknap Press, 1996).

—'Theses on the Philosophy of History', trans. Harry Zohn, in *Illuminations*, Hannah Arendt (ed.), (New York: Schocken Books, 1968).

Beowulf: A New Verse Translation (Bilingual Edition), trans. Seamus Heaney (New York: W. W. Norton, 2001).

Berger, Harry, Jr, 'Conscience and Complicity in *Richard III*', in *Richard III: A Norton Critical Edition*, Thomas Cartelli (ed.), (New York: W. W. Norton, 2009), 400–17.

Besnault, Marie-Hélène and Michel Bitot, 'Historical Legacy and Fiction: The Poetical Reinvention of King Richard III', in *The Cambridge Companion to Shakespeare's History Plays*, Michael Hattaway (ed.), (Cambridge: Cambridge University Press, 2002), 106–125.

Blake, Ann, 'Shakespeare and the Medieval Theatre of Cruelty', in *Renaissance Poetry and Drama in Context: Essays for Christopher Wortham*, Andrew Lynch and Anne M. Scott (eds), (Newcastle: Cambridge Scholars, 2008), 7–22.

Blanpied, John W., *Time and the Artist in Shakespeare's English Histories* (Newark and London: University of Delaware Press, 1983).

Bloom, Gina, *Voice in Motion: Staging Gender, Shaping Sound in Early Modern England* (Philadelphia: University of Pennsylvania Press, 2007).

Bodin, Jean, *The Six Bookes of a Commonweale*, trans. Richard Knolles, (London, 1606).

—*On Sovereignty: Four Chapters from The Six Books of the Commonwealth*, trans. Julian H. Franklin (ed.), (Cambridge: Cambridge University Press, 1992).

Bonetto, Sandra, 'Coward Conscience and Bad Conscience in Shakespeare and Nietzsche', *Philosophy and Literature* 30 (2006): 512–27.

Bragg, Lois, *Oedipus Borealis: The Aberrant Body in Old Icelandic Myth and Saga* (Madison, NJ: Fairleigh Dickinson University Press, 2004).

Brantley, B., 'Review of *Richard III: An Arab Tragedy*', *New York Times* (11 June 2009).

Breitenberg, Mark, *Anxious Masculinity in Early Modern England*, Cambridge Studies in Renaissance Literature and Culture (Cambridge and New York: Cambridge University Press, 1996).

Bright, Timothy, *A Treatise on Melancholie*, (London, 1586).

Brode, D., *Shakespeare in the Movies: From the Silent Era to Shakespeare in Love* (Oxford: Oxford University Press, 2000).

Brooks, H. F., '*Richard III*: Unhistorical Amplifications. The Women's Scenes and Seneca', *Modern Language Review*, 75 (1980), 721–37.

Brown, Kate E. and Howard I. Kushner, 'Eruptive Voices: Coprolalia, Malediction, and the Poetics of Cursing', *New Literary History* 32 (2001): 537–62.

Buhler, Stephen M., 'Camp *Richard III* and the Burdens of (Stage/Film) History', in *Shakespeare, Film, Fin de Siècle*, Mark Thornton Burnett and Ramona Wray (eds), (New York: St Martin's Press, 2000), 40–57.

Burden, Dennis H., 'Shakespeare's History Plays: 1952–1983', *Shakespeare Survey* 38 (1985), 1–18.

Burnett, Mark Thornton, *Filming Shakespeare in the Global Marketplace* (New York and Basingstoke: Palgrave Macmillan, 2007).

—*Constructing 'Monsters' in Shakespearean Drama and Early Modern Culture* (Basingstoke: Palgrave Macmillan, 2002).

Burton, Hal, *Great Acting* (London: British Broadcasting Corporation, 1967)

Cahill, Patricia A., *Unto the Breach: Martial Formations, Historical Trauma, and the Early Modern Stage* (Oxford: Oxford University Press, 2008).

Campana, Joseph, 'Killing Shakespeare's Children: The Cases of *Richard III* and *King John*', *Shakespeare* 3 (2007): 18–39.

Campbell, Gordon and Thomas Corns, *John Milton, Life, Work and Thought* (Oxford: Oxford University Press, 2008)

Canino, Catherine Grace, *Shakespeare and the Nobility: The Negotiation of Lineage* (Cambridge: Cambridge University Press, 2007).

Carroll, N., *Theorizing the Moving Image* (Cambridge: Cambridge University Press, 1996).

Carroll, William, ' "The Form of Law": Ritual and Succession in *Richard III*', in *True Rites and Maimed Rites: Ritual and Anti-Ritual in Shakespeare and His Age*, Linda Woodbridge and Edward Berry (eds), (Urbana: University of Illinois Press, 1992), 203–19.

Cartelli, Thomas, 'Shakespeare and the Street: Pacino's *Looking for Richard*, Bedford's *Street King*, and the Common Understanding', in *Shakespeare, the Movie, II: Popularizing the Plays on Film, TV, Video, and DVD*, Richard Burt and Lynda E. Boose (eds), (London: Routledge, 2003), 186–99.

Cartelli, Thomas and K. Rowe, *New Wave Shakespeare on Screen* (Cambridge and Malden, MA: Polity, 2007).

Cerasano, S. P. 'Churls Just Wanna Have Fun: Reviewing *Richard III*', *Shakespeare Quarterly* 36 (1985): 618–29.

Charnes, Linda, *Notorious Identity: Materializing the Subject in Shakespeare* (Cambridge: Harvard University Press, 1993).

Chaudhuri, S. and C. S. Lim, 'Introduction', in *Shakespeare Without English: The Reception of Shakespeare in Non-Anglophone Countries*, S. Chaudhuri and C. S. Lim (eds), (New Delhi: Dorling Kindersley, 2006), vii–xvi.

Chernaik, Warren, *The Cambridge Introduction to Shakespeare's History Plays* (Cambridge: Cambridge University Press, 2007).

Chillington Rutter, Carol. 'Rough Magic: Northern Broadsides at Work at Play', *Shakespeare Survey* 56 (2004), 236–45.

Chowdhury, Subrata Roy, *Rule of Law in a State of Emergency* (London: Pinter Publishers, 1989).

Cibber, Colley, *An Apology for the Life of Mr Colley Cibber Written by Himself*, Robert W. Lowe (ed.), (London: John C. Nimmo, 1889), 2 vols.

Clark, Sandra, *Shakespeare Made Fit: Restoration Adaptations of Shakespeare* (London: Dent, 1997).

Coleman, Lerita, 'Stigma: An Enigma Demystified', in *The Disability Studies Reader*, Lennard Davis (ed.), 1st edn (New York: Routledge, 1997) 216–31.

Colley, Scott. *Richard's Himself Again: A Stage History of Richard III* (New York and London: Greenwood Press, 1992).

Comber, Abigail Elizabeth, 'A Medieval King "Disabled" by an Early Modern Construct: A Contextual Examination of *Richard III*', in *Disability in the Middle Ages: Reconsiderations and Reverberations*, Joshua R. Eyler (ed.), (Farnham: Ashgate, 2010), 183–96.

Cook, Ann Jennalie, *The Privileged Playgoers of Shakespeare's London* (Princeton: Princeton University Press, 1981).

Corbett, Richard, *The Poems of Richard Corbett*, J. A. W. Bennett and H. R. Trevor-Roper (eds), (Oxford: Clarendon Press, 1955), 43.

Coursen, H. R., 'Filming Shakespeare's history: three films of *Richard III*', in *The Cambridge Companion to Shakespeare on Film* Russell Jackson (ed.), (Cambridge: Cambridge University Press, 2000), 99–116.

Crooke, Helkiah, *Mikrokosmographia*, 2nd edn (London: W. Iaggard, 1618).

Danson, Lawrence, *Shakespeare's Dramatic Genres* (Oxford: Oxford University Press, 2000).

Davis, Lennard J., *Bending over Backwards: Disability, Dismodernism, and Other Difficult Positions* (New York: New York University Press, 2002).

—(ed.), *The Disability Studies Reader*, 1st edn (New York: Routledge, 1997).

De Atkine, N. B., 'Why Arabs Lose Wars', *Middle East Quarterly* 6.4 (1999): 17–27.

De Ornellas, K., '"Thou Eluish Markt Abortiue Rooting Hog": Images of the Boar in Filmed *Richard III*s', in *Shakespeare on Screen: Richard III*, Sarah Hatchuel and Nathalie Vienne-Guerrin (eds), (Rouen: Publications de l'Université de Rouen, 2005), 139–60.

Dobson, Michael, *The Making of the National Poet* (Oxford: Clarendon Press, 1992)

—'Shakespeare Performances in England', *Shakespeare Survey* 56 (2003): 256–86.

—'Shakespeare Performances in England', *Shakespeare Survey* 57 (2004): 258–89.

Dollimore, Jonathan, *Radical Tragedy: Religion, Ideology and Power in the Drama of Shakespeare and his Contemporaries* (Hemel Hempstead: Harvester, 1989).

Dollimore, Jonathan and Alan Sinfield (eds), *Political Shakespeare: New Essays in Cultural Materialism* (Manchester: Manchester University Press, 1985).

Donaldson, Peter, 'Cinema and the Kingdom of Death: Loncraine's *Richard III*', *Shakespeare Quarterly* 53 (2002): 241–59.

Downer, Alan (ed.), *Oxberry's 1822 Edition King Richard III With the Descriptive Notes Recording Edmund Kean's Performance Made by James H. Hackett* (facsimile edition), (Society for Theatre Research, 1959).

Dubrow, Heather, ' "I fear there will a worse come in his place": Surrogate Parents and Shakespeare's *Richard III*', in *Maternal Measures: Figuring Caregiving in the Early Modern Period*, Naomi J. Miller and Naomi Yavneh (eds), (Aldershot: Ashgate, 2000), 348–62.

Ellinghausen, Laurie, ' "Shame and Eternal Shame": The Dynamics of Historical Trauma in Shakespeare's First Tetralogy', *Exemplaria* 20 (2008): 264–82.

Erne, Lukas, *Shakespeare as Literary Dramatist* (Cambridge: Cambridge University Press, 2003).

Eyler, Joshua (ed.), *Disability in the Middle Ages: Rehabilitations, Reconsiderations, Reverberations* (Farnham, Burlington and VT: Ashgate, 2010).

Filc, Dani and Hadas Ziv, 'Exception as the Norm and the Fiction of Sovereignty: The Lack of the Right to Health Care in the Occupied Territories', in *Evil, Law and the State: Perspectives on State Power and Violence*, John T. Parry (ed.), (Amsterdam: Rodopi, 2006), 71–86.

Floyd-Wilson, Mary and Garrett Sullivan (eds), *Renaissance Drama* 35 (Evanston, IL: Northwestern University Press, 2006)

—*English Ethnicity and Race in Early Modern England* (Cambridge: Cambridge University Press, 2003.)

Folkerth, Wes, *The Sound of Shakespeare* (London: Routledge, 2002).

Ford, John, *Perkin Warbeck* in *'Tis Pity She's a Whore and Other Plays* Marion Lomax (ed.), (Oxford: Oxford University Press, 1995).

Fouskas, V. and B. Gökay, *The New American Imperialism: Bush's War on Terror And Blood for Oil* (Westport, CT: Greenwood Publishing Group, 2005).

Freedman, Barbara, 'Critical Junctures in Shakespeare Screen History: The Case of *Richard III*', in *The Cambridge Companion to Shakespeare on Film*, Russell Jackson (ed.), (Cambridge: Cambridge University Press, 2000), 47–71.

Freud, Sigmund, 'Some Character-Types Met with in Psycho-Analytic Work', in *Character and Culture*, Philip Rieff (ed.), (New York: Collier Books, 1963), 157–81.

Friedman, Michael D., 'Horror, Homosexuality, and Homiciphilia in McKellen's *Richard III* and Jarman's *Edward II*', *Shakespeare Bulletin* 27 (2009): 567–88.

Garber, Marjorie, *Shakespeare's Ghost Writers: Literature as Uncanny Causality* (London: Methuen, 1987).

—*Shakespeare and Modern Culture* (New York: Pantheon Books, 2008).

Garland-Thomson, Rosemarie, *Extraordinary Bodies: Figuring Physical Disability in American Literature and Culture*, (New York: Columbia University Press, 1997).

—'The Beauty and the Freak', in *Points of Contact: Disability, Art, and Culture*, Susan Crutchfield and Marcy Epstein (eds), (Ann Arbor: University of Michigan Press, 2000) 181–96.

Goffman, Erving, *Stigma*: *Notes on the Management of Spoiled Identity* ([1963] Harmondsworth, 1968).

—*Stigma* (excerpts), in *The Disability Studies* Reader, Lennard Davis (ed.), (New York: Routledge, 1997) 203–15.

Goodland, Katharine, *Female Mourning in Medieval and Renaissance English Drama: From the Raising of Lazarus to King Lear* (Aldershot: Ashgate, 2005).

—'"Obsequious Laments": Mourning and Communal Memory in Shakespeare's *Richard III*', in *Shakespeare and the Culture of Christianity in Early Modern England*, David Beauregard and Dennis Taylor (eds), (New York: Fordham University Press, 2003), 44–79.

Goodman, Christopher, *How a Superior Power Ought to be Obeyed* (1558).

Goy-Blanquet, Dominique, *Shakespeare's Early History Plays: From Chronicle to Stage* (Oxford: Oxford University Press, 2003).

Greenblatt, Stephen, *Renaissance Self-Fashioning*: *From More to Shakespeare* (Chicago and London: University of Chicago Press, 1980).

—*Shakespearean Negotiations*: *The Circulation of Social Energy in Renaissance England* (Oxford: Clarendon Press, 1988).

—'Preface to the Japanese Translation of *Renaissance Self-Fashioning*', in *Shakespeare and the Japanese Stage*, T. Sasayama, J. R. Mulryne and M. Shewring (eds), (Cambridge: Cambridge University Press, 1998), 141–4.

—*Hamlet in Purgatory* (Princeton: Princeton University Press, 2001).

Greenblatt, Stephen. *et al.* (eds), *The Norton Shakespeare* (London: W. W. Norton, 1997).

Grene, Nicolas, *Shakespeare's Serial History Plays* (Cambridge: Cambridge University Press, 2002).

Guneratne, Anthony R., *Shakespeare, Film Studies, and the Visual Cultures of Modernity* (New York: Palgrave Macmillan, 2008).

Gurr, Andrew. *The Shakespearean Stage* (Cambridge: Cambridge University Press, 1992).

Hall, Peter and John Barton (eds), *The Wars of the Roses: Adapted for the Royal Shakespeare Company from William Shakespeare's Henry VI, Parts I, II, II, and Richard III.* (London: BBC, 1970).

—*Playgoing in Shakespeare's London*, 3rd edn (Cambridge: Cambridge University Press, 2004).

Hampton, Timothy, 'Strange Alteration', in *Reading the Early Modern Passions* Gail Kern Paster, Katherine Rowe and Mary Floyd-Wilson (eds), (Philadelphia: University of Pennsylvania Press, 2004) 272–93.

Hampton-Reeves, Stuart and Carol Chillington Rutter, *Shakespeare in Performance*: *The Henry VI Plays*, (Manchester: Manchester University Press, 2007).

Hankey, Julie (ed.) *Richard III*, Plays in Performance series, (London: Junction Books, 1982).

Harbage, Alfred *Shakespeare's Audience* (New York: Columbia University Press, 1941).

Harris, Amanda. 'Adopt and Actor Globe blog' http://www.globe-education. org/discovery- space/plays/richard-iii-2003 [accessed 5 March 2010].

Hassel, Chris, 'Context and Charisma: The Sher-Alexander *Richard III* and its Reviewers', *Shakespeare Quarterly* 36 (1985): 630–43.

Hatchuel, Sarah, ' "But did'st thou see them dead?": Performing Death in Screen Adaptations of *Richard III*', in *Shakespeare on Screen*: *Richard III*, Sarah Hatchuel and Nathalie Vienne-Guerrin (eds), (Rouen: Publications de l'Université de Rouen, 2005), 263–80.

Hazlitt, William, *The Round Table and Characters of Shakespeare's Plays*, Catherine Macdonald Maclean (ed.), (London: Everyman, 1936),

Heller, Agnes, *The Time Is Out of Joint*: *Shakespeare as Philosopher of History* (Lanham: Rowman and Littlefield, 2002).

Hobgood, Allison P., and David Houston Wood, 'Introduction', in *Disabled Shakespeares*, *Disability Studies Quarterly* 29:4 (Fall 2009): n.p. http:// dsq-sds.org/article/view/991/1183

—'Ethical Staring', in *Recovering Disability in Early Modern England*, Allison P. Hobgood and David Houston Wood (eds), (Columbus, Ohio: Ohio State University Press, 2013).

—(eds), *Recovering Disability in Early Modern England* (Columbus, Ohio: Ohio State University Press, 2013).

Hodgdon, Barbara, 'Spectacular Bodies: Acting + Cinema + Shakespeare', in *A Concise Companion to Shakespeare on Screen*, Diana Henderson (ed.), (Oxford: Blackwell, 2006), 96–111.

—'Replicating Richard: Body Doubles, Body Politics', *Theatre Journal* 50 (1998): 207–25.

Höfele, Andreas, 'Making History Memorable: More, Shakespeare and Richard III', *The Yearbook of Research in English and American Literature (REAL)* 21 (2005): 188–203.

—*Stage, Stake, and Scaffold*: *Humans and Animals in Shakespeare's Theatre* (Oxford: Oxford University Press, 2011).

Holderness, Graham, *Shakespeare Recycled*: *The Making of Historical Drama* (Hemel Hempstead: Harvester, 1992).

—*Shakespeare*: *The Histories* (New York: St Martin's Press, 2000).

—'Introduction', to S. Al-Bassam, *The Al-Hamlet Summit*: *A Political Arabesque* (Hatfield: University of Hertfordshire Press, 2006), 9–21.

—*The Shakespeare Myth* (Manchester: Manchester University Press, 1988).

Holland, Peter, 'Shakespeare Performances in England', *Shakespeare Survey* 43 (1991).

—*English Shakespeares: Shakespeare on the English Stage in the 1990s* (Cambridge: Cambridge University Press, 1997).

Holinshed, Raphael, *The Chronicles of England, Scotland and Ireland* (London, 1587).

Hollinger, K., *Feminist Film Studies* (New York: Routledge, 2012).

Holst-Warhaft, G., *Dangerous Voices: Women's Laments and Greek Literature* (London and New York: Routledge, 1992).

Honig, Bonnie, *Emergency Politics: Paradox, Law, Democracy* (Princeton: Princeton University Press, 2009).

Hoogvelt, A., *Globalisation and the Post-Colonial World: The New Politic Economy of Development* (Baltimore: Johns Hopkins University Press, 2001).

Hopkins, Lisa, *John Ford's Political Theatre* (Manchester: Manchester University Press, 1994).

—'Strange truths: The Stanleys of Derby on the English Renaissance Stage', in *Shakespeare's Histories and Counter-Histories*, Dermot Cavanagh, Stuart Hampton-Reeves and Stephen Longstaffe (eds), (Manchester: Manchester University Press, 2006), 85–100.

Hortmann, Wilhelm, *Shakespeare on the German Stage: The Twentieth Century* (Cambridge: Cambridge University Press, 1998).

Howard, Jean E. and Phyllis Rackin, *Engendering a Nation: A Feminist Account of Shakespeare's English Histories* (London and New York: Routledge, 1997).

Howlett, Kathy M., *Framing Shakespeare on Film* (Athens: Ohio University Press, 2000).

Hunt, Maurice, 'Ordering Disorder in *Richard III*', *South Central Review* 6.4 (Winter 1989): 11–29.

Jackson, Ken, '"All the World to Nothing": Badiou, Žižek and Pauline Subjectivity in *Richard III*', *Shakespeare* 1 (2005): 29–52.

Jefferson, M., 'Welcoming Shakespeare into the Caliban Family', *New York Times* (12 November 1996).

Jenkins, Harold. 'Shakespeare's History Plays: 1900–1951', *Shakespeare Survey* 6 (1953): 1–15.

Jowett, John (ed.), *The Tragedy of King Richard III* (Oxford: Oxford University Press, 2000).

Kastan, David Scott, *Shakespeare and the Shapes of Time* (Hanover, NH: University Press of New England, 1982).

—'Proud Majesty Made a Subject: Shakespeare and the Spectacle of Rule', *Shakespeare Quarterly* 37 (1986): 459–75.

Klett, Elizabeth. 'Re-dressing the Balance: All-female Shakespeare at the Globe

Theatre', in James C. Bulman (ed.), *Shakespeare Re-Dressed: Cross-Gender Casting in Contemporary Performance* (New Jersey: Farleigh Dickinson University Press, 2008), 166–88.

Knight, G. Wilson, *Collected Works* (London and New York: Routledge, 2002), 12 vols.

Knight, Joseph, *Theatrical Notes* (London: Lawrence and Bullen, 1893).

Kossak, Saskia, ' "*Frame My Face to All Occasions*': *Shakespeare's Richard III on Screen* (Vienna: Braumüller, 2005).

Kott, Jan, *Shakespeare Our Contemporary*, trans. Boleslaw Taborski (London: Routledge, 1991).

Lefait, Sébastien, 'The Hybridisation of Film Form in *Richard III*', in *Shakespeare on Screen*: *'Richard III*', Sarah Hatchuel and Nathalie Vienne-Guerrin (eds), (Rouen: Publications de l'Université de Rouen, 2005), 41–64.

Lezra, Jacques, '*Phares,* or Divisible Sovereignty', *Religion and Literature* 38 (2006): 13–39.

Linton, Simi, *Claiming Disability: Knowledge and Identity* (New York: New York University Press, 1998).

Litvin, M., *Hamlet's Arab Journey: Shakespeare's Ghost and Nasser's Ghost* (Princeton: Princeton University Press, 2011).

Loehlin, James N., ' "Top of the World, Ma": *Richard III* and Cinematic Convention', in *Shakespeare, the Movie: Popularizing the Plays on Film, TV, and Video*, Lynda E. Boose and Richard Burt (eds), (London: Routledge, 1997), 67–79.

Logan, Robert A., *The Influence of Christopher Marlowe on Shakespeare's Artistry*, (Aldershot: Ashgate, 2007).

Lopez, Jeremy, *Theatrical Convention and Audience Response in Early Modern Drama* (Cambridge: Cambridge University Press, 2003).

—'Time and Talk in *Richard III* I.iv', *SEL* 45 (2005), 299–314.

Low, Jennifer A. and Nova Myhill (eds), *Imagining the Audience in Early Modern Drama, 1558–1642* (New York: Palgrave, 2011).

Lull, Janis (ed.), *King Richard III*: *The New Cambridge Shakespeare* (Cambridge: Cambridge University Press, 1999).

McMillin, Scott and Sally-Beth MacLean, *The Queen's Men and their Plays* (Cambridge: Cambridge University Press, 2006).

Manningham, John, *The Diary of John Manningham of the Middle Temple*, Robert Parker Sorlien (ed.), (New Hampshire: University Press of New England, 1976)

Marche, Stephen, 'Mocking Dead Bones: Historical Memory and the Theater of the Dead in *Richard III*', *Comparative Literature* 37 (2003): 37–57.

Marlowe, Christopher, *Doctor Faustus*, John D. Jump (ed.), (Manchester: Manchester University Press, 1982).

Marriott, J. A. R. *English History in Shakespeare* (London: Chapman & Hall, 1918).

Maus, Katharine Eisaman, *Inwardness and Theater in the English Renaissance* (Chicago and London: University of Chicago Press, 1995).

McRuer, Robert, 'Fuck the Disabled: The Prequel', in *Shakesqueer: A Queer Companion to the Complete Works of Shakespeare*, Madhavi Menon (ed.), (Durham: Duke University Press, 2011), 294–301.

Meron, Theodor, 'Crimes and Accountability', *The American Journal of International Law* (Jan 1998): 1–40.

Metzler, Irina, *Disability in Medieval Europe: Thinking About Physical Impairment in the High Middle Ages, c. 1100–1400* (London and New York: Routledge, 2006).

Milton, John, *Eikonoklastes. John Milton: Complete Poems and Major Prose*, Merritt Y. Hughes (ed.), (Indianapolis: Indiana, Hackett, 2003)

Mitchell, David T., and Sharon L. Snyder, (dir.) *Vital Signs: Crip Culture Talks Back* (Brace Yourselves Productions, 1997).

—*Narrative Prosthesis: Disability and the Dependencies of Discourse* (Ann Arbor: University of Michigan Press, 2000).

—*Cultural Locations of Disability* (Chicago and London: University of Chicago Press, 2006).

Mitchell, Deborah, '*Richard III*: Tonypandy in the Twentieth Century', *Literature/Film Quarterly* 25 (1997): 133–45.

Montaigne, Michel de, 'Of a Monstrous Child,' *The Essays of Michel de Montaigne*, http://www.gutenberg.org/files/3600/3600-h/3600-h.htm#link2HCH0086

Mornay, Philippe Duplessis [Stephanus Junius Brutus, the Celt; also attributed to Languet, Hubert], *Vindiciae, contra tyrannos: Or, Concerning the Legitimate Power of a Prince Over the People, and of the People Over a Prince* (1579), trans. George Garnett (ed.), (Cambridge: Cambridge University Press, 1994).

Moulton, Ian Frederick, ' "A Monster Great Deformed": The Unruly Masculinity of Richard III', *Shakespeare Quarterly* 47 (1996): 251–68.

Mullaney, Steven, 'Affective Technologies: Toward an Emotional Logic of the Elizabethan Stage', in *Environment and Embodiment in Early Modern England*, Mary Floyd-Wilson and Garrett A. Sullivan, Jr (eds), (Basingstoke: Palgrave, 2007), 71–89.

Munro, Lucy, ' "Little apes and tender babes": Children in Three Film Versions of *Richard III*', in *Shakespeare on Screen: Richard III*, Sarah Hatchuel and Nathalie Vienne-Guerrin (eds), (Rouen: Publications de l'Université de Rouen, 2005), 161–77.

Neely, Carol Thomas, *Distracted Subjects: Madness and Gender in Shakespeare and Early Modern Culture* (New York: Cornell University Press, 2004).

Neil, Andrew W., *Exceptionalism and the Politics of Counter-Terrorism: Liberty, Security, and the War on Terror* (New York: Routledge, 2010).

Nichols, Bill, *Representing Reality: Issues and Concepts in Documentary* (Bloomington, IN: Indiana University Press, 1991).

Norwich, John Julius, *Shakespeare's Kings: The Great Plays and the History of England in the Middle Ages: 1337–1485* (Scribner, 2001).

Odell, George C. D., *Shakespeare From Betterton to Irving* (New York: Charles Scribner's Sons, 1920), 2 vols.

Olsen, Greta, 'Richard III's animalistic criminal body', *Philological Quarterly* 82.3 (2005): 301–24.

Orgel, Stephen, *The Illusion of Power: Political Theater in the English Renaissance* (Los Angeles and London: University of California Press, 1975).

Pacino, Al, (dir.) *Looking for Richard* (Fox Searchlight Pictures, 1996).

Parker, Patricia, 'Shakespeare and Rhetoric: "Dilation" and "Delation"', in *Shakespeare and the Question of Theory*, Patricia Parker and Geoffrey Hartman (eds), (New York: Methuen, 1985) 54–74.

Paster, Gail Kern, *The Body Embarrassed: Drama and the Disciplines of Shame in Early Modern England* (Cornell, New York: Cornell University Press, 1993)

—*Humoring the Body: Emotions and the Shakespearean Stage* (Chicago: Chicago University Press, 2004).

Paster, Gail Kern, Katherine Rowe and May Floyd-Wilson (eds) *Reading the Early Modern Passions: Essays in the Cultural History of Emotion* (Philadelphia: University of Pennsylvania Press, 2004).

Pearlman, Elihu, 'The Invention of Richard Gloucester', *Shakespeare Quarterly* 43.4 (1992): 410–29.

Pearman, Tory Vandeventer, *Women and Disability in Medieval Literature (The New Middle Ages)* (New York: Palgrave Macmillan, 2010).

Phillippy, Patricia, *Women, Death and Literature in Post-Reformation England* (Cambridge: Cambridge University Press, 2002).

Pollard, Tanya, 'Audience Reception', in *The Oxford Handbook of Shakespeare*, Arthur Kinney (ed.), (Oxford University Press, 2012), 458–73.

—*Drugs and Theater in Early Modern England* (Oxford: Oxford University Press, 2005).

Ponet, John, *A Short Treatise of Politic Power* (1556).

Pownall, David, *Richard III Part Two* in *Plays One* (London: Oberon Books, 2000).

Prescott, Paul, *Richard III: A Guide to the Text and its Theatrical Life*, The Shakespeare Handbook Series (New York: Palgrave Macmillan, 2006).

Pronko, L., 'Approaching Shakespeare through Kabuki', in *Shakespeare East and West*, M. Fujita and L. Pronko (eds), (Tokyo: Japan Library, 1996), 23–40.

Rackin, Phyllis, *Stages of History: Shakespeare's English Chronicles* (Ithaca: Cornell University Press, 1990).

—'History into Tragedy: The Case of *Richard III*', in *Shakespearean Tragedy and Gender,* Shirley Nelson Garner and Madelon Sprengnether (eds), (Bloomington and Indianapolis: Indiana University Press, 1996), 31–53.

Rasmussen, Eric, *The Shakespeare Thefts: In Search of the First Folios* (Houndmills and New York: Palgrave Macmillan, 2011).

Reeder, Robert, ' "You are Now Out of Your Text": The Performance of Precocity on the Early Modern Stage', *Renaissance Papers* (2001): 35–44.

Richmond, Hugh M., *Shakespeare in Performance: King Richard III* (Manchester: Manchester University Press, 1989).

Robson, Mark, 'Shakespeare's Words of the Future: Promising *Richard III*', *Textual Practice* 19 (2005): 13–30.

Rossiter, A. P., *Angel with Horns and other Shakespeare Lectures* (New York: Theatre Arts Books, 1961).

Row-Heyveld, Lindsey, 'The Performance of Disability and the Disabling of Performance in Richard III', unpublished paper, presented at 'Disabled Shakespeares', a seminar held at the 2009 Shakespeare Association of America meeting, Washington, DC, co-chairs, Allison P. Hobgood and David Houston Wood.

—' "The lying'st knave in Christendom": The Development of Disability in the False Miracle of St Alban's' in *Disability Studies Quarterly* 29.4 (2009): n.p.http://www.dsq-sds.org/article/view/994/1178.Web. [accessed 3 June 2010].

—'Antic Dispositions: Mental and Intellectual Disabilities in Early Modern Revenge', in *Recovering Disability in Early Modern England*, Allison P. Hobgood and David Houston Wood (eds), (Columbus, Ohio: The Ohio State University Press, 2013).

Salamon, L. B., 'Postmodern Villainy in *Richard III* and *Scarface*', *Journal of Popular Film and Television* 28.2 (2000), 54–63.

Salgādo, Gāmini (ed.), *Eyewitnesses of Shakespeare: First Hand Accounts of Performances, 1590–1890* (London: Sussex University Press, 1975)

Schalkwyk, David, 'Text and Performance, Reiterated: A Reproof Valiant or Lie Direct?' *Shakespeare International Yearbook* 10 (2010): 47–75.

Schmitt, Carl, *Political Theology: Four Chapters on the Concept of Sovereignty*, trans. George Schwab (Chicago: University of Chicago Press, 1985).

Schoenfeldt, Michael Carl, *Bodies and Selves in Early Modern England: Physiology and Inwardness in Spenser, Shakespeare, Herbert, and Milton*, Cambridge Studies in Renaissance Literature and Culture 34 (New York: Cambridge University Press, 1999).

Schwab, George, *The Challenge of the Exception: An Introduction to the Political Ideas of Carl Schmitt Between 1921 and 1936* (New York: Greenwood Press, 1970, 1989).

Schwyzer, Philip, 'Lees and Moonshine: Remembering Richard III, 1485–1635', *Renaissance Quarterly* 63 (2010): 850–83.

Shakespeare, William, *King Henry VI, Part 3* edn, John D. Cox and Eric Rasmussen. Arden Edition of the Works of William Shakespeare (London and New York: Methuen, 2001).

Shakespeare on Screen: Richard III, Sarah Hatchuel and Nathalie Vienne-Guerrin (eds), (Rouen: Publications de l'Université de Rouen, 2005).

Shaughnessy, Robert, 'Introduction', in *Shakespeare on Film: Contemporary Critical Essays*, R. Shaughnessy (ed.), (New York and Basingstoke: Palgrave, 1998), 1–17.

—*Representing Shakespeare: England, History, and the RSC* (New York and London: Harvester Wheatsheaf, 1994).

Shaw, George Bernard. *Our Theatres in the Nineties* (London: Constable and Company 1932), 3 vols.

Sher, Antony, *The Year of the King* (London: Nick Hern Books, 2004).

Siemon, James R., 'Reconstructing the Past: History, Historicism, Histories', in *A Companion to English Renaissance Literature and Culture*, Michael Hattaway (ed.), (Oxford: Blackwell, 2000), 662–73.

—'Sounding Silences: Stubbs, More, and Shakespeare's Richard Plays', in *Renaissance Refractions: Essays in Honour of Alexander Shurbanov*, Boika Sokolova and Evgenia Pancheva (eds), (Sofia: St Kliment Ohridski University Press, 2001), 127–41.

—' "The power of hope?" An Early Modern Reader of *Richard III*', in *A Companion to Shakespeare's Works: The Histories*, Richard Dutton and Jean E. Howard (eds), (Oxford: Blackwell, 2003), 361–78.

—'Halting Modernity: Richard III's Preposterous Body and History', in *Shakespeare in Europe: History and Memory*, Marta Gibińska and Agnieszka Romanowska (eds), (Kraków: Jagiellonian University Press, 2008), 113–25.

—(ed.), *King Richard III: The Arden Shakespeare, Third Series* (London: Methuen Drama, 2009).

Slotkin, Joel Elliot, 'Honeyed Toads: Sinister Aesthetics in Shakespeare's *Richard III*', *The Journal for Early Modern Cultural Studies* 7 (2007): 5–32.

Smith, Peter J., *Social Shakespeare* (Houndmills: Palgrave, 1995).

Spivack, Bernard, *Shakespeare and the Allegory of Evil* (New York: Columbia University Press, 1958).

Stern, Tiffany, *Making Shakespeare: From Stage to Page* (London: Routledge, 2004).

—*Documents of Performance in Early Modern England* (Cambridge: Cambridge University Press, 2009).

Stoll, Abraham, 'Macbeth's Equivocal Conscience', in *Macbeth: New Critical Essays*, Nick Moschovakis (ed.), (London: Routledge: 2008), 132–0.

Strier, Richard, *The Unrepentant Renaissance: From Petrarch to Shakespeare to Milton* (Chicago: University of Chicago Press, 2011).

Strohm, Paul, *Politique: Languages of Statecraft Between Chaucer and Shakespeare* (Notre Dame: Notre Dame University Press, 2005).

Sullivan, Garrett and Mary Floyd-Wilson (eds), *Environment and Embodiment in Early Modern England* (Houndmills, Basingstoke: Palgrave Macmillan, 2007).

Sutton, John, *Philosophy and Memory Traces: Descartes to Connectionism* (Cambridge; New York: Cambridge University Press, 1998).

Targoff, Ramie, '"Dirty" Amens: Devotion, Applause, and Consent in *Richard III*', *Renaissance Drama*, n.s. 31 (2002): 61–84.

Tey, Josephine, *The Daughter of Time* (Harmondsworth: Penguin, 1975).

The Three Parnassus Plays (ed.) J. B. Leishman (London: Ivor Nicholson & Watson, 1949).

Thorne, Alison, '"O, lawful let it be / That I have room ... to curse awhile": Voicing the Nation's Conscience in Female Complaint in *Richard III, King John,* and *Henry VIII*', in *This England, That Shakespeare: New Angles on Englishness and the Bard*, Willy Maley and Margaret Tudeau-Clayton (eds), (Farnham: Ashgate, 2010), 105–24.

Tillyard, E. M. W., *Shakespeare's History Plays* (London: Chatto and Windus, 1974).

Torrey, Michael, '"The plain devil and dissembling looks": Ambivalent Physiognomy and Shakespeare's *Richard III*', *English Literary Renaissance* 30 (2000): 123–53.

Totaro, Rebecca, '"Revolving This Will Teach Thee How to Curse": A Lesson in Sublunary Exhalation', in *Rhetorics of Bodily Disease and Health in Medieval and Early Modern England*, Jennifer C. Vaught (ed.), (Farnham: Ashgate, 2010), 135–51.

Tynan, Kenneth, *Theatre Writings*, Dominic Shellard (ed.), (London: Nick Hern Books, 2007).

Van Elk, Martine, '"Determined to prove a villain": Criticism, Pedagogy, and *Richard III*', *College Literature* 34.4 (Fall 2007): 1–2.

Vanhoutte, J., *Strange Communion: Motherland and Masculinity in Tudor Plays, Pamphlets, and Politics* (London: Associated University Presses, 2003).

Vickers, Brian (ed.) *Shakespeare: The Critical Heritage* (London: Routledge, 1981), 6 vols.

Vienne-Guerrin, N., 'Evil Tongues in *Richard III* on Screen', in *Shakespeare on Screen: 'Richard III'*, Sarah Hatchuel and Nathalie Vienne-Guerrin (eds), (Rouen: Publications de l'Université de Rouen, 2005), 24.

Walsh, Brian, *Shakespeare, The Queen's Men, and the Elizabethan Performance of History* (Cambridge: Cambridge University Press, 2009).

Watson, Robert N. *Shakespeare and the Hazards of Ambition* (Cambridge: Harvard University Press, 1984).

Weimann, Robert, *Author's Pen and Actor's Voice: Playing and Writing in Shakespeare's Theatre* (Cambridge: Cambridge University Press, 2000).

Wells, Paul, 'The Documentary Form: Personal and Social Realities', in *An Introduction to Film Studies*, J. Nelmes (ed.), (London and New York: Routledge, 2003), 187–211.

Wells, Stanley (ed.), *Shakespeare in the Theatre: An Anthology of Criticism* (Oxford: Oxford University Press, 2000).

Wheatley, Edward, *Stumbling Blocks Before the Blind: Medieval Constructions of Disability* (Ann Arbor: University of Michigan Press, 2010).

Wilks, John S., *The Idea of Conscience in Renaissance Tragedy* (London: Routledge, 1990).

William Shakespeare Richard III: Nouvelles Perspectives Critiques, Francis Guinle and Jacques Ramel (eds), (Montpellier: Centre d'Études et de Recherches sur la Renaissance Anglaise, 2000).

Williams, Katherine Schaap, 'Enabling Richard: The Rhetoric of Disability in *Richard III*', *Disability Studies Quarterly* 29 (Fall 2009), n.p. http://dsq_sds.org/article/view/997/1181.

Williamson, Elizabeth, 'The Uses and Abuses of Prayer Book Properties in *Hamlet, Richard III,* and *Arden of Faversham*', *English Literary Renaissance* 39 (2009): 371–95.

Williamson, Sandra L. and James E. Person Jr (eds), *Shakespearean Criticism Volume 14* (Detroit: Gale Research, 1991).

Wilson, Richard, 'A sea of troubles: the thought of the outside in Shakespeare's histories', in *Shakespeare's Histories and Counter-Histories*, Dermot Cavanagh, Stuart Hampton-Reeves and Stephen Longstaffe (eds), (Manchester: Manchester University Press, 2006), 101–34.

Wood, David Houston, ' "Fluster'd with flowing cups": Alcoholism, Humoralism, and the Prosthetic Narrative in *Othello*', *Disability Studies Quarterly* 29.4 (2009): n.p. http://dsq-sds.org/article/view/998/1182

—*Time, Narrative, and Emotion in Early Modern England*, *Literary and Scientific Cultures of Early Modernity* (Farnham and Burlington, VT: Ashgate, 2009).

Wright, Thomas, *The Passions of the Minde in Generall* (London, 1605).

Yandell, Cathy, *Carpe Corpus* (Newark: Delaware, 2000).

Zamir, Tzachi, *Double Vision: Moral Philosophy and Shakespearean Drama* (Princeton: Princeton University Press, 2007).

INDEX